Hunting for Empire

The Nature | History | Society series is devoted to the publication of high-quality scholarship in environmental history and allied fields. Its broad compass is signalled by its title: nature because it takes the natural world seriously; history because it aims to foster work that has temporal depth; and society because its essential concern is with the interface between nature and society, broadly conceived. The series is avowedly interdisciplinary and is open to the work of anthropologists, ecologists, historians, geographers, literary scholars, political scientists, sociologists, and others whose interests resonate with its mandate. It offers a timely outlet for lively, innovative, and well-written work on the interaction of people and nature through time in North America.

General Editor: Graeme Wynn, University of British Columbia

Claire Elizabeth Campbell, *Shaped by the West Wind: Nature and History in Georgian Bay*

Tina Loo, *States of Nature: Conserving Canada's Wildlife in the Twentieth Century*

Jamie Benidickson, *The Culture of Flushing: A Social and Legal History of Sewage*

William J. Turkel, *The Archive of Place: Unearthing the Pasts of the Chilcotin Plateau*

John Sandlos, *Hunters at the Margin: Native People and Wildlife Conservation in the Northwest Territories*

James Murton, *Creating a Modern Countryside: Liberalism and Land Resettlement in British Columbia*

NATURE | HISTORY | SOCIETY

Hunting for Empire

Narratives of Sport
in Rupert's Land, 1840-70

GREG GILLESPIE

FOREWORD BY GRAEME WYNN

UBC Press • Vancouver • Toronto

© UBC Press 2007

16 15 14 13 12 11 10 09 08 07   5 4 3 2 1

Printed in Canada on ancient-forest-free paper (100% post-consumer recycled) that is processed chlorine- and acid-free, with vegetable-based inks.

Library and Archives Canada Cataloguing in Publication Data

Gillespie, Greg, 1973-
   Hunting for empire : narrative of sport in Rupert's Land, 1840-70 /
Greg Gillespie.

(Nature, history, society, ISSN 1713-6687)
Includes bibliographical references and index.
ISBN 978-0-7748-1354-9 (bound); 978-0-7748-1355-6 (pbk)

   1. Big game hunting – Prairie Provinces – History – 19th century. 2. British – Canada – History – 19th century. 3. Travelers' writings, British – 19th century – History and criticism. 4. Imperialism – History – 19th century. 5. Great Britain – Colonies – America – History – 19th century. 6. Rupert's Land – Description and travel. 7. Rupert's Land – History – 19th century. I. Title. II. Series.

SK151.G54 2007   799.2'6097109034   C2007-903460-8

Canadä

UBC Press gratefully acknowledges the financial support for our publishing program of the Government of Canada through the Book Publishing Industry Development Program (BPIDP), and of the Canada Council for the Arts, and the British Columbia Arts Council.

This book has been published with the help of a grant from the Canadian Federation for the Humanities and Social Sciences, through the Aid to Scholarly Publications Programme, using funds provided by the Social Sciences and Humanities Research Council of Canada.

Printed and bound in Canada by Friesens
Copy editor: Andy Carroll
Proofreader: Gail Copeland
Indexer: Noeline Bridge

UBC Press
The University of British Columbia
2029 West Mall
Vancouver, BC V6T 1Z2
604-822-5959 / Fax: 604-822-6083
www.ubcpress.ca

In memory of my grandmother, Ada Evelyn Buick, 1909-2007

It has a stark beauty all its own. It's like much of the high desert of the United States.

– Mission Commander Neil Armstrong after planting the American flag on the surface of the moon, 21 July 1969

Contents

Contents

Figures

Domesticating the Exotic

by Graeme Wynn

R EFLECTING ON GREG GILLESPIE'S manuscript and thinking about writing this foreword, I am haunted by a parade of bumper stickers: "What is the definition of a workaholic? Someone who doesn't hunt"; "Deer hunters will do anything for a buck"; "Hunters get more buck for their bang"; "Hunting is done to death." Too long at my desk, and feeling neither the lure of the chase nor need for greater excitement or another dollar, I am particularly struck by the last of these aphorisms. Is there anything more to be said about hunting from a scholarly perspective?[1]

Any good library holds dozens, even hundreds, of books and even more articles and essays on the topic. They range from claims that hunting is a sacred art to meditations upon hunting as an integral part of human nature; from reflections on the characteristics of hunters and those opposed to hunting to treatises on the ethos behind killing animals for sport; from discussions of hunting by indigenes to analyses of the roles that hunters and fishers played in furthering the conservation movement; from the politics of the Black Act of 1723, intended to protect game for the English aristocracy, to the dispossession and exclusion of Native peoples through the establishment of game parks and sanctuaries in the "new worlds"; and from thrilling fictional adventure stories for young boys, through romantic tales of "great white hunters," to first-person accounts of their escapades by scores of those who set out in quest of game from Argentina to Zimbabwe between the eighteenth and twentieth centuries.[2]

In the last twenty years, there have been dozens of studies of hunting in different parts of the globe, and many have taken their cue from John MacKenzie's declaration that more attention should be given to the place of hunting in the establishment and extension of British imperialism since the nineteenth century.[3] This is a vast and intricate subject because the contributions of hunting to the imperial enterprise were many and complex – although few scholars would go quite so far as the Scot Denis Lyell, who hunted in India and Africa just over a century ago and attributed the imperial edifice that spanned the globe, the Pax Britannica, to the attraction of its constituent countries as "the home of wild game."[4]

More often than not, to be sure, wild animals were abundant when Europeans first came to new world territories, and many of the indigenous beasts that the newcomers encountered were immensely intimidating in size and/or ferocity. In these circumstances hunting, long the indulgent perquisite of the British upper classes, assumed new and useful meanings. Imperial hunters were easily seen as harbingers of civilization. They opened the way to settlement and saved unfortunate locals from people-eating beasts.

Hunters on remote frontiers also exhibited and epitomized the bravery and composure required of distant representatives of the crown. When "muscular Christianity" – the conviction that sport fostered Christian morality, physical fitness, and "manly" character – held sway in English private schools, it was easy to extend to the hunting grounds of empire the claim made by influential novelist Charles Kingsley and others, that the playing fields of England imparted "virtues which no books can give ... not merely daring and endurance, but, better still temper, self-restraint, fairness, honor, unenvious approbation of another's success, and all that 'give and take' of life which stand a man in good stead when he goes forth into the world, and without which, indeed, his success is always maimed and partial."[5]

Hunting abroad was indubitably more dangerous, exciting, invigorating, and affirming than it was "at home." By one account, written by an East India Company official who regarded work as an unfortunate interruption of his favourite pastime, "the Gentlemen of England" hardly knew what sport was. "Knocking over" partridges and hares "in a little bit of a plantation, or an unromantic grain field" stood no comparison with shooting in the subcontinent: "The one is confined ... the other boundless, the one dull and tame, the other exciting to a degree."[6]

With time, and increased hunting pressure attributable to the fashionable desire to display stuffed animals, trophy heads, and skins in natural history museums and private homes, as well as to lucrative markets for tusks and robes, hunters decimated local animal populations. (Some of these were also afflicted by newly introduced and devastating diseases such as rinderpest, which swept through east and southern Africa in the 1890s. As celebrated elements of the indigenous fauna grew scarcer, attitudes toward them changed: no longer the threats to "progress" they had once been, they now seemed to warrant protection. Various groups agitated for legislation to establish game reserves, and others chartered societies to conserve certain species of animals. Access to game was restricted, regulations established new property rights over "wild animals," and wardens and rangers exercised authority over extensive territories and the people and fauna within them. Then reserves were turned into parks, and tourists and cameras replaced hunters and guns within their bounds. Thus, big-game hunting "the most atavistic and antagonistic connection between humans and animals," became, in historian Harriet Ritvo's words, "the fitting emblem of the new style in which the British empire attempted to govern both the human and the natural worlds. The need to conquer through force had almost disappeared." In its place was "a new need to exploit through management. Hunting and protection had become opposite sides of the same coin."[7]

In Canada, scholarly interest in hunting and its corollary, wildlife protection, has been reinvigorated with the emergence of environmental history as a significant field of study. The years since the turn of the millennium have seen a relative outpouring of work elaborating on and extending themes broached in Janet Foster's landmark 1978 study, *Working for Wildlife*, republished in 1998. For example, the Nature/History/Society series in which *Hunting for Empire* appears includes Tina Loo's *States of Nature*, and John Sandlos' *Hunters at the Margins* among its first half-dozen titles. Loo traces the development of Canadian wildlife conservation from its social, political, and historical roots, and Sandlos argues that the introduction of game regulations, national parks, and game sanctuaries was central to the assertion of state authority over the traditional hunting cultures of the Dene and Inuit. Two slightly earlier books from UBC Press also contribute to understanding of these topics. George Colpitts' *Game in the Garden* explores the ways in changing attitudes toward wild animals shaped social relations among western Canadians before the Second World War, and J. Alexander Burnett's *A Passion for Wildlife* chronicles both the history of the Canadian Wildlife Service and the evolution of Canadian wildlife policy in the second half of the twentieth century.[8]

To these focused monographs, the same press has recently added *The Culture of Hunting in Canada,* a diverse set of historical, contemporary, reflective, descriptive and analytical essays edited by Jean Manore and Dale

Miner.[9] Several of these UBC Press authors and essayists have also contributed to the journal literature, in which they have argued, for example, that "big game hunting in British Columbia constituted its practitioners as masculine and bourgeois, while simultaneously racializing and sexualizing them" and that indigenous traditions were misrepresented with significantly deleterious consequences for Native peoples.[10] Others have contended that real men hunted buffalo, elaborated on the economic and moral lessons offered by hunting, asked who controlled the hunt, and traced the decline of game with the spread of settlement and the rise of sport hunters.[11] When the scope is extended to include the equally rapidly expanding body of work examining the role of sport fishers in excluding Native peoples from traditional resources and monopolizing access to streams, it is clear that much has been learned about fish and game and about those who preyed upon or sought to preserve wild and aquatic life in Canada.[12]

Amid this burgeoning literature, Greg Gillespie has found room to offer new and thought-provoking perspectives on the history of gun sport and British encounters with overseas nature in *Hunting for Empire.* He does this by carefully circumscribing his topic and by adopting a particular (and in the context of Canadian historical writing, relatively unfamiliar) approach to the past. First, Gillespie trains the spotlight of his attention on three decades or so in the middle of the nineteenth century and centres his analysis on some fourteen or fifteen published accounts of expeditions through the western interior of Rupert's Land by people who engaged in hunting for sport. None of this makes him oblivious to earlier or later developments or provides him with licence to ignore other writing on this period and general topic. It does, however, place his work firmly and nicely in the interstices between studies that deal with hunting by Natives and newcomers during the period in which fur trading dominated the western interior and those that address sport hunting and attitudes toward wildlife in the years after Canadian confederation.[13] Second, Gillespie views this topic from the perspective of postmodern cultural studies and cultural history. Briefly put (and thus inherently inadequately), his account rests on textual analysis, or the identification of discourses and meanings in the documents of the past. Sometimes known as deconstructionist history and influenced by the so-called linguistic turn in humanities scholarship, work of this sort is not yet commonplace in historical scholarship, although it has gained considerable purchase in several of the social sciences. In general terms, inquiries that start from this position are more relativist and presentist than is traditional historical scholarship, especially in their denial, at the extreme, of all claims to fact, truth, and objectivity.[14]

Gillespie is explicit about his commitment to the epistemological foundations of cultural analysis, and there is no doubt that they inflect the story he tells in *Hunting for Empire*. This is, at base, a study of imperial ideas rather than a portrait of Canadian space. Gillespie focuses quite closely on the narratives produced by British travellers who hunted for sport in Rupert's Land. He reads these accounts as part of a broader literary tradition, and pays particular attention to the linguistic codes, systems of meaning, and forms of representation that shape and structure their messages. Thus *Hunting for Empire* is an exercise in the interpretation of texts and a commentary on what they reveal of their creators rather than an account of the western interior of northern North America. It aims to understand the cultural experience of a small number of upper-class Britons who travelled into this territory, and is therefore more concerned with their attitudes, expectations, suppositions, and reflections than in when and where they went, the material circumstances they encountered, or how their presence affected the indigenous peoples and biophysical environments of the locales through which they passed.

This emphasis shifts the usual focus of historical engagement with the western interior of northern North America, but there is nothing untoward in that. Fresh approaches and the novel questions and creative interpretations they produce are only to be welcomed. Moreover, variants of the lens through which Gillespie views sport hunters in Rupert's Land have been deployed by others. Although recent work in cultural studies is often explicit about its "a-disciplinary" character – proponents describe their field as a "simmering stew of the ideas, voices and lives of people all over the world" concerned to challenge established knowledge hierarchies and devoted to explicating the depth and breadth of "the ordinary" in everyday life – there is a long and venerable tradition of scholarship turned to these broad ends.[15] Think, for example, of anthropologist Clifford Geertz's influential argument, in 1973, for "thick description" as the route to rich ethnographic understanding of the symbolic meaning of cultural practices.[16] Famously and controversially realized in his vivid account of cock fighting in Bali, and built on a view of "man as an animal suspended in webs of significance he himself has spun," Geertz's analytical technique drew insight both from Max Weber, one of the founders of sociology, and from Gilbert Ryle, one of the leading analytical philosophers of the early twentieth century, to insist that even the simplest act can mean different things depending on the cultural codes at work. To borrow the example that Geertz takes from Ryle, resting content with a "thin" account of the rapid closing and opening of a human eye will produce misunderstanding when a blink is not a blink but a twitch, a conspiratorial wink, a parody of a wink, or someone "practicing burlesque of a friend faking a wink to deceive an innocent into thinking a conspiracy is in motion." Only a "thick description" sensitive to cultural contexts, behavioural norms, and individual characteristics allows one to distinguish blinks from twitches and to understand the implications of different types of deliberate movements of the eyelid. In Geertz's semiotic approach to cultural understanding, interpretation depends on making the leap from parts to the whole, on relating local detail to global structures, and on recognizing that "small facts speak to large issues, winks to epistemology and sheep raids to revolution, because they are made to."[17]

Despite the considerable body of accomplished historical scholarship inspired by Geertz's musings and the large, recent outpouring of new cultural histories on a wide range of topics, some readers may find *Hunting for Empire* unorthodox because of its claims for the large significance of small things and its commitment to finding meaning in the association of big ideas with particular turns of phrase or fragments of detail.[18] Traditionally minded historians might regard some of these links as too easy and incline to mutter "show, don't tell" when Gillespie finds his hunters using the language of scientific positivism to establish their authority, sees early- and mid-nineteenth-century British school teachers drawing on "Social Darwinism" to inculcate a belief in the eminence of imperial Britain, and gives the code of gentlemanly hunting a significant place in his analysis of sport hunters' behaviour in the western interior of North America. The strict chronological sticklers among them might even wonder about anachronism, on the grounds that scientific positivism, *sensu strictu*, implies reference at the earliest to the work of Auguste Comte, whose writings were unlikely to have influenced this particular generation of hunters, or that the term Social Darwinism was first used in print in 1879.[19]

Similar challenges are levelled at almost every piece of innovative scholarship: standards of scholarly practice evolve, and if students in the humanities and social sciences have learned anything in the last few decades it is that meanings of words and ideas are forever shifting and contested. Rather than engage in hair-splitting critique and grow vexed over this or that perceived imprecision, it surely serves reader and author better to acknowledge that Gillespie's basic claims are not without point. The doctrine of empiricism, emphasizing the role of experience in the development of knowledge, formulated by John Locke in the seventeenth century and elaborated by members of the Scottish Enlightenment, helped to shape Comte's ideas and held considerable influence in nineteenth-century Britain. It is clearly reflected in the sayings and doings of Gillespie's hunters. The ideas of Thomas Hobbes ("nature red in tooth and claw") and Thomas Malthus (in essence "starvation of the weakest," or inverted as Herbert Spencer had it, "survival of the fittest") adumbrated many of the arguments of so-called Social Darwinists. And if the sportsman's code reached its gentlemanly apogee late in the nineteenth century, or perhaps even in the early twentieth, in the codification produced by William Hornaday of New York, as some suggest, its foundations surely lie, as Gillespie points out, in Izaak Walton's *The Compleat Angler,* published in 1653.[20]

Mutterings aside, Gillespie's commitment to a broad interdisciplinary perspective is as salutary as it is unusual. Recall that the hunters' narratives at the heart of this book have been read and written about before. Years ago, they were "mined" for what they could contribute to then fashionable narratives about heroic explorers. For all his scholarly interest in the study of hunting, Gillespie avoids a similarly blinkered interpretation of these books simply as sporting accounts. Instead, he reads them in the round, as cultural texts. This carries him into thoroughly interdisciplinary territory limned in the very structure of his book. His central chapters demonstrate this range in their focus on "authorship," "sport," "science," and "nature." As an interrogation of the ways in which authors sought to establish the veracity or "author-ity" of their accounts, the first of these is rooted in literary criticism and explores issues of concern to contemporary anthropologists who have come to question the ways in which classic ethnographies claim weight through their authors' assertions about "being there" among the observed.[21] The second places Rupert's Land hunters in their historical-imperial context. A direct response to MacKenzie's suggestion that hunting and imperialism were intricately connected, it examines the class and cultural underpinnings of British hunting and the ways in which these shaped the attitudes and actions of its agents who came to the interior of North America for sport. Chapter 4 focuses on the hunters' cultural appropriations of the northwest territory, demonstrating that they used instruments of science – the Linnean system, cartography, and so on – at least as effectively as they did their guns (and with longer lasting impact). Finally, Chapter 5 reveals how these writing hunters deployed ideas of the picturesque and the sublime to tame and order the wild landscapes of America as they sought to describe and render them intelligible to readers "at home." So the compass of this inquiry is extended into yet other realms as it engages with ideas and literatures nominally associated with fields such as the history of science, art history, and aesthetics.

Gillespie's efforts to find significance in small things often forgotten also produce some remarkable results. At best, his critical reading of the narratives of big-game hunting and the alternative interpretations of both the activity and the motivations of those who engaged in it shares with the work of other practitioners of the new cultural history a capacity to yield insights that force readers to think anew about particular facets of the past. Gillespie, like most scholars influenced by the postmodern, postcolonial impetus of recent decades, adopts a revisionist agenda. Specifically, he demonstrates that the truth claims made by the authors of hunting narratives were highly suspect, and that despite the patina of authority with which their books were burnished, they can in no way be characterized as "accurate reflections of historical realities" (p. 116). More generally, he seeks to provide a critical analysis of imperialism and to change our understanding of the ways in which British hunter-explorers engaged with the interior of northern North America. But he is a judicious revisionist. He weighs competing interpretations of British imperialism, most explicitly those offered by Edward Said and David Cannadine, and elects in the end to follow the latter in the conviction that this project turned at least as much upon the "replication of sameness and similarities originating from home," as it did (in Said's view, favoured by most postcolonialists) on the "insistence on difference and dissimilarities originating from overseas."[22]

There is a phrase in Cannadine's extended essay, *Ornamentalism: How the British Saw Their Empire* that Gillespie uses only once in passing (p. 13) but that I take as something of a leitmotif for the story told in *Hunting for Empire*. Elaborating on the different perspectives he and Said offer on the process of imperialism, Cannadine insists that from his perspective the British empire "was about the familiar and the domestic, as well as the different and the exotic: indeed it was in large part about *the domestication of the exotic*" (emphasis added). By this, Cannadine means to suggest that imperial agents – and by extension therefore we can include Gillespie's hunters – were engaged in the long and often challenging task of "comprehending and ... reordering ... the foreign in parallel, analogous, equivalent [and] resemblant terms."[23]

Indeed. Remember this phrase and its corollaries through the pages that follow. Events, emotions, and ideas are complex, evanescent, and often insubstantial things and even highly accomplished writers have difficulty capturing them on the page. Actions and sentiments, and descriptions of them, are frequently heavy with meaning and subject to various interpretations. Although he rightly emphasizes his account in different ways to reflect the diverse content of his sport hunters' narratives and to draw out the intricacies of their many facets, much of the story that

Gillespie gives us turns on the complex, contingent, ever-shifting process of reducing the strangeness of the new (or rendering the unfamiliar familiar) to which travellers past, present, and everywhere almost invariably contribute. When hunter-explorers gazed upon and "thereby appropriated" landscapes hitherto seen by few (if any) other Europeans, they sought to communicate their form and character to those who had not visited them in terms that they might understand. If, as Mary Louise Pratt and others would argue, comparing the South Saskatchewan River to the River Thames privileged English terms and concepts over indigenous knowledge of, and local names for, that North American feature and imposed European forms of power on the landscape and its inhabitants, it is worth acknowledging that some of those who conjured this comparison probably did so with no greater motive than the hope of providing their readers with a meaningful way to measure what they could not look upon directly.[24] Similarly, it is worth remembering that there was borrowing as well as appropriation: the indigenous Cree people knew the "swift-flowing river" of their traditional territory as "Kisiskatchewan."

By the same token, when James Carnegie, discomfited by the wilderness of Rupert's Land and a lack of suitably/similarly educated companions, read Shakespeare by the light of his campfire, he blanketed himself against an alien setting with the bard's recognizable prose. When he showered footnotes upon his pages he was, often as not, endeavouring to bring to order the cacophony of information about new things produced by his own observations and those of others. Similarly, the "rational restraint" expected of gentlemanly hunters implied their capacity to tame the urge to savagery in themselves (associated with the "primitive" and the "exotic"), even as they were unable to bring under full and actual control the frontier and its many violent, aggressive, threatening characteristics. Displaying the heads and hides of unfamiliar beasts from distant locales in the heart of one's household and creating museum dioramas of colonial landscapes featuring their fiercest animal inhabitants, shot, stuffed, and sterilized (and thus rendered impotent) spoke to the same domesticating impulse.[25] And so too, of course, the making of maps, the development of careful descriptions and inventories of natural history, and the deployment of ideas about the picturesque and sublime in describing landscapes were part of the process of ordering the world, aligning its features with established precepts and bringing its remote and unfamiliar parts into concordance with the known.

None of this is to deny the other, often multiple, meanings attributable to what Gillespie effectively reveals as the far from innocent acts entailed in hunting across the farther reaches of the empire and in writing about the experience. By illuminating these, this book makes a distinct contribution to a growing body of work interrogating the origins, character, and functioning of imperial knowledge systems in colonial spaces. In the large pond constituted by these inquiries and entered from many angles by scholars with widely different interests, the intellectual ripples produced by *Hunting for Empire* parallel the arguments put forward by some researchers and cross or challenge the conclusions of others. This is how it should be. Both the substance of Gillespie's understanding of the fascinating point at which hunting, empire, and travel writings coalesced in the western interior of Rupert's Land and the cultural studies perspective that he brings to this topic enter the broader marketplace of ideas for discussion, evaluation, and emulation.[26] Here, as Geertz has said of interpretive anthropology, "progress is marked less by a perfection of consensus than by a refinement of debate."[27] In substance, students of imperialism, the early Canadian west, environmental history, Canadian studies, hunting, and sport history will find much in this book that is fresh and thought provoking. In approach, it also offers much to consider and reflect upon. Neither unreflexively "traditional" nor unabashedly deconstructionist in its approach, *Hunting for Empire* helps point the way toward a vigorous and vital history for the twenty-first century, a history that must, in my view, be "stimulated and enriched by the insights of post-modernism, rather than overwhelmed and undermined by them."[28]

Acknowledgments

TWO DECADES AGO, historian John MacKenzie called for scholars to develop a body of critical historical research dealing with hunting and imperialism. In *The Empire of Nature: Hunting, Conservation, and British Imperialism* (1988) MacKenzie wrote, "the significance of hunting in the imperialism of the nineteenth and twentieth centuries has never been fully recognized." Indeed, an examination of leading journals from the last decade reveals that research on hunting remains at the scholarly periphery. No single research monograph offers a starting point, a base through which to advance and conceptualize the study of hunting as a cultural practice. I hope this book begins to address this issue.

I happened on big-game hunting narratives as I sifted through innumerable volumes of nineteenth-century British travel literature for a course with Roger Hall as a graduate student at the University of Western Ontario. Through my research I developed a fascination with the topics of hunting, travel writing, and empire. This fascination carried me into other fields I might otherwise have passed by, such as environmental history, cultural geography, literary criticism, and English literature. I am a better scholar for having read within these broad and fascinating disciplines.

I owe a debt of gratitude to Nancy Bouchier for her collegiality and helping me with my writer's craft. I also want to thank John Bale, Doug Booth, Don Hair, Roger Hall, Colin Howell, Fred Mason, Don Morrow, Kevin Wamsley, and Graeme Wynn, who provided their professional criticism of the manuscript at different points along the road to publication.

I would like to thank the Missouri Historical Society as well as John Lutman, Librarian, at the J.J. Talman Regional Collection, D.B. Weldon Library. Finally, I also want to thank Randy Schmidt, Camilla Blakeley, and everyone at UBC Press for their efforts.

I am grateful to the Social Sciences and Humanities Research Council of Canada, which funded this project through a Doctoral Fellowship. Some of the material for Chapters 2 and 5 have been reprinted in revised form, with permission, from Greg Gillespie, "'I Was Well Pleased with Our Sport among the Buffalo': Big Game Hunting, Travel Writing, and Cultural Imperialism in the British North American West, 1847-1873," *Canadian Historical Review* 83, 4 (2002): 555-84.

Introduction

As a contributor to the study of popular culture in Canada, I seek to write sport, leisure, and recreation into our shared understanding of the past. I use the lens of cultural history, with a specific theoretical focus on textualism and meaning, to examine the themes of hunting, travel writing, and empire.[1] I also draw on the approaches of cultural studies, literary criticism, cultural anthropology, poststructuralism, and social and postcolonial theory. I bring these perspectives to bear in my analysis of race, class, and gender construction, landscape formation, exploration, and sport hunting – all situated within the context of dispossession and appropriation. This interdisciplinary approach informs my understanding and provides depth to my engagement of matters variously and traditionally considered within the broad disciplines of sport, environmental, and imperialism history, as well as English literature, and Canadian studies.

I hope the varied nature of my analysis brings these wide-ranging topics into closer conversation. This is perhaps a lofty goal, given the narrowness of academic research today, yet it is one I believe in. I hope too that each discipline will find insight and evidence of my debt to their work. I will be most gratified if students in these fields come to recognize, in the pages and arguments of this book, both the ground we share and the complementary nature of our perspectives on the past.

To provide a framework for analysis, I divide *Hunting for Empire* into theme-based sections focused on authorship, sport, science, and nature, with Chapters 1 and 6 serving as introductory and concluding bookends.

Chapter 1 sets the stage by discussing the geographical and historical context of the study, specifically, the western interior of Rupert's Land and the British hunters' primary attraction to the region. This chapter further informs those that follow by outlining the theoretical approach used in the analysis of hunting and exploration narratives.

Chapter 2 discusses "authorship" by providing an analysis of the remarks in the prefaces of hunting books and considers the ways through which the hunters sought to establish their literary authority. Authors conditioned the interpretation of sport, science, and nature, and thus the interpretation of their imperial narratives, with specific literary strategies at the opening of their books. Big-game hunters used their prefatory remarks to establish a positivist tone and plant the seed of commonsense acceptance of their narratives as "truth" and "fact." These sorts of comments influenced how readers interpreted and understood forthcoming landscape and map constructions: as factual depictions of the frontier, rather than as subjective constructions based on a set of British-specific cultural codes and ways of seeing. Despite conscious and sustained efforts to establish their literary authority and the authority of their pictorial representations, British hunters ultimately undermined their own assertions of positivism, resulting in what I refer to as the prefatory paradox. Through statements of self-deprecation, pandering to reviewers and readers, highlighting errata, and admitting to narrative omissions, as well as through changes in diction or grammar, authors ultimately undermined their own positivist assertions.

Chapter 3 considers "sport" by analyzing big-game hunters situated in their class-based imperial hunting culture. This broad chapter considers the educational background and imperial ideologies expressed by hunters in their travel narratives. It outlines how the sporting preconditions and cultural biases of the hunters influenced the ways in which they participated in and drew meaning from colonial big-game hunting. I employ the term "hunting" in the elite British sense. Big-game hunters and sportsmen based their understanding of sport on class, enjoying hunting for the sake of the sport and not for pecuniary profit – at least none that they admitted to directly. Some hunted purely for sport, others for trophies to fill out their collections, and others desired specimens for personal or museum collections of natural history. I endeavour throughout this chapter to contextualize this group of big-game hunters within the larger nineteenth-century British imperial hunting cult.

Chapter 4 examines the varied forms of "science" used by the hunters to construct an anticipatory geography of imperialism. These men constructed an image of the interior in a two-pronged manner that included a circum-scription and systematization of the landscape. Through the Linnaean system of Latin nomenclature, British men identified flora and fauna, christened them with new names, and catalogued them into the European system of nature. They also advocated the introduction, or acclimatization, of colonial game back to Great Britain. On the other hand, they introduced wildlife into colonial frontiers that made the landscape appear British. British big-game hunters also constructed numerous maps in their construction of the frontier. Like Adam walking through the Garden of Eden, hunters renamed animals and landscape features after themselves and their upper-class peers. In doing so, they constructed landmarks: cultural constructs that etched themselves into the history of Rupert's Land. Many of these landmarks remain today, the legacy of the British big-game hunters' cultural appropriation of the western interior.

Chapter 5 discusses "nature" by focusing on the cultural construction and appropriation of the wilderness landscape. Like the first book in the Nature/History/Society series at UBC Press, by Claire Campbell, this chapter brings an interdisciplinary perspective to the study of cultural landscape.[2] The big-game hunters' landscapes centred on two forms of aesthetic description: the picturesque and the sublime. Describing the appearance of their wilderness frontier to readerships at home required an understanding of these two nineteenth-century aesthetics. I argue that British hunters invoked the principles of the picturesque and the sublime to construct a British-looking image of the territory, an image referenced in ways their readers understood.[3] Travel readers took pleasure in such aesthetic digressions, enjoying descriptions of foreign landscapes in territories never before traversed or hunted by white men. Although the picturesque and sublime varied considerably, they both held an underlying proprietary ideology. Any discussion of landscape formation and landscape theory must also include references to temporality. As an ongoing cultural process, landscapes result from imbuing places with layers of meaning over time.[4] In this way, landscape formation is both an outlet for, and the outcome of, human agency: landscape is at once both constituted and constitutive.[5] Analysis of conceptual metaphors and symbolism provides opportunities to examine the ways in which human agents, in this case big-game hunters, asserted proprietorship through the construction of cultural landscapes while, at the same time, creating a stage through which to produce and celebrate imperial masculinities. In this chapter, I use the terms "scientific gaze" and "aesthetic gaze" to refer to the British class-based positivist perspective that space could be fixed and described objectively by a central viewer, resulting in the ordering and controlling of that space.[6] This mediated cultural perspective reaffirmed the construction of the land from the dominant position of the colonizer. I also employ the term "aesthetic code," or in specific cases "picturesque code" or "sublime code."[7] A code is a class-based, constructed set of cultural components that, in this case, guided the application and interpretation of the picturesque and the sublime. These components developed through aesthetic debates between leading British landscape designers during the eighteenth and early nineteenth centuries and are defined and discussed in Chapter 5.

In the final chapter, I conclude by extending the landscape discussion from the previous chapter into the final two decades of the nineteenth century. I argue that the CPR appropriated the colonial and imperial landscapes constructed by British hunters and explorers from the 1840s to 1870s as their own corporate and consumer landscapes in the last quarter of the nineteenth century. I suggest that the CPR co-opted the imperial hunting landscapes created by the hunters, and the literary conventions and strategies used to construct them, to target a new generation of elite British sportsmen, mountaineers, and other high-end tourist traffic to the Canadian West in the 1880s and 1890s.

My emphasis on big-game hunting, and specifically imperialism, during the third quarter of the nineteenth century, steers this book in directions different from those defined in the work of historians Elizabeth Vibert, George Colpitts, and Tina Loo. According to Vibert, fur traders hunted avidly across the western interior in the early nineteenth century. They took part in sport hunting and discussed the practice in their fur-trade narratives. More than this, these middle-class men imagined themselves in aristocratic ways through their engagement in the socially exclusive practice of big-game hunting. Both Colpitts and Loo orient their work outside of an imperial model and steer around the specific period under examination in this book, the 1840s to the 1870s. Like Loo's, Colpitts' fine study of wildlife and sport tourism in western Canada concentrates primarily on the period following Confederation and the transfer of the western interior from the Hudson's Bay Company. The big-game hunters and explorers who are the focus of this book were a small but distinctive group who conducted their explorations and imperial sport in a unique context – between the subsistence and sport hunting fur traders well documented by Vibert and those who contributed to the rise of the middle-class sport tourism industry whom Colpitts and Loo examine in the later nineteenth century.

In the area of cultural landscape, a theme that includes research in both environmental history and Canadian studies, my work leans closer to those more explicitly imperial in tone and analysis. In this respect, my analytical approach mirrors those of Colin Coates and Ian MacLaren. Coates situates his research within a larger imperial process and his work reveals the capacity of British imperialists to use aesthetic landscape principles and maps to construct distinctly British visions of Lower Canada. Although our geographical contexts are different, our research shares this fundamental starting point. MacLaren's work emphasizes aesthetic explanation and discusses the need for explorers to see British landscapes in a land that rarely resembled Britain. Despite a section in his dissertation, MacLaren's many publications avoid discussion of sport hunting narratives in favour of those written by fur traders, missionaries, artists, and frontiersmen. His depth of approach, particularly in the aesthetic examination of pictures and textual images, remains the standard in the analysis of British travel writing.

The secondary literature on imperialism represents one of the largest bodies of historical and cultural research in existence; historians approach the field from innumerable perspectives. In recent years, excellent scholarly volumes have emerged from university presses emphasizing the marginalized voices of Native peoples, Métis, and French Canadians in the history of imperialism and colonialism – and rightly so.[8] I have a different orientation in mind for this book. I seek to write the British empire, and in this specific case, big-game hunters, back into the history of British imperialism in Canada.[9] Rather than emphasizing the colonial/periphery over the imperial/metropole, like much research on imperialism in Canada, or vice versa, I write about the metropole within, indeed saturated by, the periphery. Those reading from either vantage point will find like-minded perspectives dotted through the chapters that follow. The extent to which one considers the perspective, role, and agency of the colonized typically distinguishes the first orientation of imperial research from the second.[10] Although I discuss Native and Métis peoples and demonstrate their historical agency within the hunter-guide relationship, my focus rests with British hunters as my primary historical actors. This book endeavours to look at the western interior through their imperial eyes.

I

An Imperial Interior Imagined

WHEN I WAS A BOY, MY SCOTTISH FATHER took my older brother and me to the Sportsman's Barbershop in the small town of Grimsby, Ontario, to get our hair cut. Unlike the unisex hairstylists of the 1990s, the Sportsman's Barbershop served an exclusively male clientele during the late 1970s. The barber who owned the place wanted to make men feel comfortable and themed his shop to construct a decidedly masculine space. He decorated the interior to reflect Canada's outdoor sporting heritage and included pictures of bear, moose, and other big game. A set of mounted deer antlers hung above the mirror for each chair. Framed images of Queen Elizabeth II and the Union Jack looked down upon the patrons from the centre of the barbershop. The magazine rack held titles relating to the outdoors, fish, and buck hunting. The proprietor even had a small stack of boys' books dealing with stories of hunting and adventure. I recall, as a shy, freckled, blonde-haired blue-eyed lad, sitting on a chair, feet dangling off the floor, reading stories, daydreaming, or listening to lively hunting discussions while quietly waiting my turn. Amid the high-pitched hum of the barber's clippers, I listened with fascination to the shared sporting experiences of the barbershop patrons. Within the masculine confines of the Sportsman's Barbershop, men constructed and reaffirmed themselves through the culture of hunting and stories of the Canadian wilderness – all under the watchful eye of the Queen.

This book provides a cultural history of hunting, travel writing, and empire – themes that still resonate from my experiences as a young lad in that wee barbershop nestled at the corner of Main Street and Christie.

I examine the cultural interconnectedness of these three themes through a specific form of historical evidence: published narratives of big-game hunting and exploration from the western interior of Rupert's Land during the third quarter of the nineteenth century. The genre of colonial sporting adventure books developed during the 1800s and forms a subgroup of the seemingly infinite body of published narratives known generically as British travel literature. These books reveal a fascinating history of cultural experience along British North America's western frontier. Through their narratives, British big-game hunters constructed the region from a proprietary perspective, identified material resources, and hinted at the capacity of the land to support future British colonization, all on the cusp of a vanishing frontier.

Hunting for Empire analyzes cultural imperialism as revealed through the narratives of upper-class British men who travelled across the western interior of Rupert's Land for sport and exploration between the 1840s and the early 1870s. As a cultural history, this book scrutinizes big-game hunting narratives by situating them as cultural texts – as a series of literary and pictorial representations invested with a broad array of meanings, inferences, rituals, and symbols.[1] Within these texts, I focus on four themes central to the genre of hunting narratives – authorship, sport, science, and nature – that also serve to structure the chapters of this book. These themes provide focus to the analysis of hunting texts and collectively express the lived discourse of imperial big-game hunting. I should also say that I approach this study as a cultural scholar interested broadly in sport and imperialism, rather than as a historian of the Canadian West specifically. From this perspective, I focus on the hunters' cultural presuppositions regarding their proprietary view of land, and on the meanings associated with participation in their imperial sport, rather than emphasizing specific localities in the western interior or providing a chronicle of expeditions made or buffalo killed.[2] Of specific interest in this study are the cultural strategies employed in hunting narratives to construct and appropriate space, as well as the meanings imbued in and drawn from acts such as hunting, collecting trophies, and landscape formation.

Two of the first British big-game hunters to journey to the western interior travelled with fur trader George Simpson on his annual canoe voyage from Lachine in 1841.[3] The Earls of Caledon and Mulgrave, British Army officers stationed in Lower Canada in the late 1830s and early 1840s, accompanied Simpson to the Red River Settlement. From there the two men struck west to hunt the buffalo. In his famous travel book, *Narrative of a Journey Round the World During the Years 1841 and 1842,*

Simpson extolled the courage and hunting prowess of the two upper-class sportsmen.[4] The subsequent reports of "good sport" had by Caledon and Mulgrave, alongside news of a hunting excursion the year before to Missouri and Kansas by British officers also stationed in the Canadas, initiated a "prairie fever" of sorts among wealthy British elites eager to add buffalo to their list of bagged game.[5] A small but increasing flow of imperial-minded big-game hunters began travelling to the plains of British North America for sport. By the late 1850s, enough sporting gentlemen visited the region that the Hudson's Bay Company charged a fee of ten shillings a day (five for servants) for food and lodging while staying at company posts.[6]

A number of elite British sportsmen followed Caledon and Mulgrave in the 1840s and 1850s. Sir Frederick Ulric Graham, the Baronet of Netherby, travelled to hunt the buffalo and regain his health in the colonial wilderness in 1847. In the 1850s, Lords Robert Grosvenor, a relative of the Duke of Westminster, and Frederick Cavendish, the son of the Duke of Devonshire, followed Graham's expedition. Two young sporting gentlemen, Viscount Henry "Teddie" Chaplin and Sir Frederick Johnstone, arrived in the western interior in 1861 with arctic explorer Dr. John Rae, who served as the boys' chaperone. Chaplin organized the big-game hunting expedition at the age of twenty and invited his school chum Johnstone to take part in the hunt. Both were from wealthy English families, and Chaplin was a close friend of the Prince of Wales while at the University of Oxford. Alongside their quest for buffalo, cabri (antelope), and wapiti (red deer/elk), Rae conducted astrological observations with equipment purchased by the Royal Geographical Society and entered unmapped regions of the interior.[7] During their expedition, Rae renamed Native landmarks with new British names, such as Lake Chaplin and Lake Johnstone.[8] The town of Chaplin, Saskatchewan, still bears Henry's name today and immortalizes his imperial hunting expedition to the western interior of Rupert's Land. Sadly, few travel narratives exist today of these early big-game hunting expeditions.

The trickle of big-game hunters who travelled to the region between the early 1840s and mid-1850s gave way in the following decade to an increasing number of scientists, explorers, and surveyors on "official" missions for the British and Canadian governments. However, to label these men so narrowly fails to address their cultural propensity for the imperial sport of big-game hunting – particularly when "official" missions were often carried out under the guise of buffalo hunting expeditions.[9] We need to recognize that socially elite British men during the mid-nineteenth century viewed the activities of

1.1 "My Last Buffalo Hunt." Although Palliser never wrote a narrative of his buffalo-hunting experiences in the western interior, his narrative of hunting on the plains of the United States included several images depicting the sport. John Palliser, *Solitary Rambles and Adventures of a Hunter in the Prairies* (London: J. Murray, 1853), 268.

exploration *and* hunting as equally important aspects of a colonial adventure; an idea sometimes lost in the historiography of Rupert's Land prior to the 1870s. Described by historian Irene M. Spry as "the Irish sportsman who became an explorer," British officer John Palliser travelled to the West under the auspices of a British scientific expedition, yet he always took the opportunity to run with the buffalo for sport and sustenance.[10] Indeed, one might better characterize Palliser's trip as a Royal Geographical Society-sanctioned big-game hunting expedition than a mission of exploration. In slight contrast to Palliser, James Carnegie, the Earl of Southesk, constructed maps and named landmarks on his trip, but he travelled explicitly for the sport provided by big game and expressed an anti-modern sentiment for a rest-cure in the invigorating colonial wilderness. The varying motivations of imperial-minded men like Palliser and Carnegie, along with an early context for expeditions of a sporting and scientific nature, requires a malleable application of the term "hunter" during the period under discussion. The narratives I examine in this book reflect a group of *men who hunted for sport* while in the western interior, rather than a group of *sport hunters* strictly defined. Regardless of whether they travelled for the purpose of exploration, leisure, science, or art, these men fell into the category of hunters when they gazed at vast herds of buffalo and charged headlong into the British big-game hunting impulse (Figure 1.1).

Social class plays an important role in the analysis of these men and
their imperial hunting culture. Many of these sporting gentlemen came
from England's nobility and minor nobility and held titles such as
baronet, viscount, and earl. They trained in England's elite universities
and possessed capital and leisure, like Graham and Carnegie. These elites
lived on private estates, owned land, and possessed military experience
as well as the personal wealth for year-long sporting tours. However, not
all British men who travelled to the western interior possessed such elite
social status. Men like William Francis Butler (Figure 1.2) came from the
lesser ranks of the upper class and held little beyond their commission as
military officers.[11] Like Butler, these men hunted big game in addition
to performing their official duties, or as soldiers while on leave from
garrisons in eastern British North America. Regardless of their social
position within the lower or middle ranks of the upper class, these men
viewed England's aristocracy as a "reference group" for their own leisure
activities.[12] Participation in the sport of big-game hunting reaffirmed their
own class status and distinguished them from the lower orders. In this
way, hunting and, most importantly, the class-based culture celebrated
through the sport, confirmed their place in the new colonial socio-
economic hierarchy.

An elite public (private) school and university education during
the nineteenth century included exposure to the culture of English
athleticism. Through participation in the British sporting ethic, an ethic
that applied equally to rugby and cricket as well as hunting and angling,
these men desired more than mere athletic participation. They sought
moral and physical improvement through sport, and, when in colonial
destinations, to display their racial and technological superiority (Figure
1.3).[13] In this way the cultural act of big-game hunting connected to an
array of other imperatives. British big-game hunting interwove the tenets
of Muscular Christianity, modern science, and imperial duty. Activities
like big-game hunting provided men with the opportunity to display the
characteristics and qualities of imperial manhood. Through the culture
of athleticism, British men believed that sporting activities like hunting
offered opportunities for character formation and mental instruction.
Most of all, as early as the mid-nineteenth century, but particularly in
the final decades of the 1800s, men came to view big-game hunting
in two interconnected ways: as an antidote to the effeminacy of urban
civilization, and as an anti-modern escape from industrial British society.[14]
Through the socially exclusive sport of big-game hunting, British men
reaffirmed their patriotism and their right to the manly exercise reserved

1.2 "W.F. Butler." British sportsman and explorer William Francis Butler mapped and hunted in the western interior of Rupert's Land in 1872. William Francis Butler, *The Wild North Land* (London: Low, Marston, Low, and Searle, 1873), frontispiece.

1.3 "The Vanquished Foe." Berkeley's hunting expeditions led him along the 49th parallel, and his views of imperial sporting culture are typical of the mid-nineteenth century. Grantley Fitzhardinge Berkeley, *The English Sportsman in the Western Prairies* (London: Hurst and Blackett, 1861), frontispiece.

exclusively for the social elite.[15] They presented these moral imperatives to rationalize their participation in the gore and butchery of the hunt.

Formal British education intertwined the concepts of sport, geography, and empire. In some instances, hunters provided the first recorded geographical explorations, or clarified points of geographical interest mentioned in the narratives of previous explorers, hunters, or fur traders. They revelled in filling their travel narratives with maps using latitude and longitude relative to Greenwich, England, to indicate their position, and the position of the territory, relative to the rest of the British empire. Empire builders at home in England celebrated the exploits of famous big-game hunters as much for their additions to geographical knowledge as for their hunting prowess.[16] The upper-class big-game hunter represented the harbinger of empire, and his departure to regions unknown harkened the introduction of civilization to the uncivilized corners of the world.[17] As part of a broader imperial culture, the act of big-game hunting reflected back to the imperial centre desirous images of domination, control, and authority in distant colonies. The depiction of big-game hunters engaging in their upper-class privilege signified the imperial might of Great Britain.[18]

Although no unassailable label exists, I use the term "western interior of Rupert's Land" to bring geographical focus to a district and sub-districts that held shifting official titles during the 1800s. The majority of the hunting expeditions took place in the prairie, grassland, and park country of the western interior prior to Confederation (in what is now southern Alberta, Saskatchewan, and Manitoba). Some explored into the region of New Caledonia, however, or what is now British Columbia.[19] King Charles II of England originally ceded the vast region known as Rupert's Land to the Hudson's Bay Company in 1670, and it remained a British territory until its purchase by the Dominion of Canada in 1870.[20] This region included the area from Lake Superior to Hudson's Bay, and across to the Rocky Mountains. After 1870 the area west of Manitoba became known as the North-West Territories and led to the creation of the North-West Mounted Police to govern the region in 1873.[21] Protected from large-scale settlement until after the introduction of the railroad in the 1880s, the western interior consisted of bands of Native peoples and Métis, as well as fur traders at Hudson's Bay Company posts, scattered missionary settlements, and select big-game hunters, adventurers, prospectors, scientists, and explorers.[22] British hunters travelled to the interior via the Red River Settlement by canoe along old fur trade routes or they journeyed overland via Saint Paul, Minnesota.

The prevailing British view of the western interior by this period explains, in part, why some big-game hunters travelled to this far-flung frontier. As late as the 1850s, the image of the West constructed in England by fur traders, explorers, and missionaries – as a dangerous, remote, and primeval wilderness – remained largely unchanged.[23] Stories of roaming bands of hostile Blackfoot and Cree further encouraged this view. Farther north, John Franklin and other British explorers presented the North-West as a desolate arctic waste in the minds of the British reading public in the late 1700s and early 1800s. With the exception of the Red River Settlement, the western interior of Rupert's Land appeared too remote and too hostile as a potential area for British colonization by the mid-nineteenth century: dangerous Indian country to the south and a frozen tundra to the north.[24] To stay-at-home imperialists in England, the western frontier of British North America remained an obscure corner of the British empire.

Although popular perception turned travellers away, dreams of romantic frontiers increased the sense of danger and adventure for a small group of men – particularly for those interested in hunting big game. Some looked beyond the big cats offered in Africa and India and began searching for a new sporting paradise. These men undertook the arduous journey and travelled for exploration and to shoot the plains buffalo. The western interior of Rupert's Land provided everything a red-blooded big-game hunter hoped for in a colonial expedition: unknown wilderness territories, noble savages, and unique big game. Indeed, the idea that the colonial wilderness gave rise to a sense of adventure and a spirit of freedom epitomized the big-game hunter's view of the territory by the mid-nineteenth century.[25] Although the image of the wilderness turned most away, the romantic primitivism of the western interior only heightened its attractiveness as a destination for sporting adventure during the mid-nineteenth century.

The hunters' perception, and primary attraction to the region, changed soon afterwards. By the 1850s and 1860s, the image of Rupert's Land, both in England and the new Dominion of Canada, evolved from a desolate primeval expanse to a potentially fertile region for settlement. The expeditions made by Palliser and Henry Hind in the late 1850s – big-game hunters in their own right – confirmed the resource potential of the area prior to Confederation.[26] Albeit slowly, change followed this reconsideration. The Canadian Pacific Railroad arrived at Winnipeg and Calgary in the early 1880s, and European immigrants followed slowly. Most important, the seemingly inexhaustible buffalo, so integral to the British hunter's primary attraction to the area, were effectively destroyed by the 1870s.[27] Following this decade, the western interior, no longer an evocative frontier on the edge of empire, and without the unique sport provided by the buffalo, possessed little draw as a destination for imperial adventure until after the introduction of the railroad. Along with the frontier, the initial sporting appeal of this distant corner of the empire passed into history. As we shall see in the chapters that follow, the hunters' literary and cultural legacy remained.

Between the 1840s and the early 1870s, perceptions of the western interior were changing.[28] This unique period offered a fascinating cultural milieu: the pre-modern and modern, the last vestiges of the fur trade, and the beginning of the Dominion Land Survey.[29] Just decades later, the West stood on the cusp of a dramatic transformation brought by the railroad and settlement. This rough quarter-century represents an intriguing between-time in the history of the western interior. The narratives written by big-game hunters and explorers during this period *followed* a series of fur-trade narratives that had already constructed the interior in the late 1700s and early 1800s as resource-laden but remote and primeval.[30] Fur traders and fur-trade companies promoted this image in part to deter exploration and settlement of their main wildlife fur preserve. These same hunting books *preceded* the rise of Canadian Pacific Railway (CPR) corporate advertising that co-opted the colonial wilderness landscapes in British fur-trade and big-game hunting narratives to promote the Canadian West to a new generation of elite British sportsmen and tourists in the final decades of the nineteenth century.[31] During this period, the CPR marketed imperial discourse and specific sporting landscapes of consumption back to Great Britain.

The brief time span during which the western interior presented an attraction for British big-game hunters explains why few published narratives exist of their experiences. Individuals such as Graham required the permission of the Hudson's Bay Company to hunt and explore in Rupert's Land, and men like him only travelled to the region between the 1840s and the extinction of the buffalo. Compared to the published narratives of the British fur traders that preceded them, or the promotional sporting pamphlets published by the CPR that followed them, the narratives of big-game hunters and explorer-hunters are few. Rather than simply ignoring these unique narratives and their fascinating time period, I focus on providing critical cultural commentary to explain their story and place in the history of the western interior. Viewing this set of primary sources as a limitation only heightens their intellectual and historical interest and, to my mind, presents a compelling rationale for their analysis. Although limited in number, the voices in these books cry out for historical scrutiny, and I endeavour to provide a close and nuanced reading of their narratives.

Like all genres of travel writing, hunting and exploration texts present a challenging set of concerns regarding their use as historical source documents. British hunters followed a set of literary conventions and made distinctions about what to include and exclude in their narratives. None of their descriptions provides a prolonged, detailed account of everything that happened in a given historical situation or regarding a specific individual. The internalization of cultural experience typically precludes such accounts. Their books are aimed directly at their elite brethren across the British empire and convey the experience of the British North American frontier. One cannot mistake the imperial tone and character of these books. Some may consider the cultural myopia of nineteenth-century British imperialists to be an inherent drawback, and as a source for the history of marginalized groups this may be, but I view the cultural selectivity of travel narratives as a strength of this form of evidence, particularly when examining British imperial discourse.

Like most publications, hunting narratives underwent an editorial process. Authors wrote field notes around the campfire, or brief logbook entries while on horseback, and rewrote their observations either on their trip back to England or years afterwards. The preliminary drafts received edits between the author and the publisher prior to publication.[32] The publisher's artist created engravings from the author's sketches, and these also underwent a process of revision. These procedures resulted in a diverse structural range within the genre. Some authors divided their journals into chapters, some listed dates and places frequently, and still others provided maps and engravings, where others did not.[33] Although most published their narratives within a few years of their return, some waited over a decade, and one family, that of the aforementioned Graham, published his narrative posthumously in the form of his journal notes almost fifty years after his expedition in 1847. Despite their diversity of construction, hunting narratives comment on a broad array of subjects consistent with a new cultural encounter, and they offer insight into landscape aesthetics, the elite code of hunting sportsmanship, natural history, and frontier exploration.

Given these important issues related to hunting narratives as primary sources, one might ask the question: how would a study that focuses on the editorial process alter our interpretation of the pictorial and literary images constructed by British hunters? As mentioned, all travel narratives underwent some sort of editorial procedure for publication, and I recognize that an examination of the personal papers of either the authors or their publishers might produce insight into this process. However, we must also acknowledge that the British imperial public came to know distant frontiers like the western interior through the *published* word, and not by the scraps left on the editorial room floor. This means that hunting accounts represent a negotiation between the hunters' journal notes and the revisions designed to meet the literary expectations of their British readership. Although I discuss editorial procedures in Chapter 2, I reiterate that the focus of this book remains with the published narratives, as these texts provided the popular images of the western interior as the British and Canadian public came to know them.

Many of the popular images in hunting narratives took the form of cultural landscapes. The inclusion of class-based aesthetic landscape descriptions broadened the appeal of travel narratives within the nineteenth-century book trade in England.[34] The depiction of the imperial practice of big-game hunting situated *within* picturesque and sublime landscape imagery further contributed to the popularity of narratives. So much so that some non-sporting nineteenth-century journals in Great Britain, such as *Nineteenth-Century* and *Blackwood's Magazine*, published material from hunting narratives.[35] Big-game hunters and their publishers also produced multiple editions and printed extracts in sporting journals such as *Field* and *Sporting Magazine*. As well, the British men who travelled to the western interior published narratives from other British colonies, where they combined hunting, natural history, and exploration.[36]

The varied nature of the themes I discuss in this book requires a broad definition of the term "imperialism." By imperialism I refer to the cultural processes, practices, and discourses through which the British constructed, produced, extended, and celebrated their empire.[37] By emphasizing the cultural constructedness of imperialism, I endeavour to examine the cultural attitudes and practices of the British empire alongside the traditional topics of land acquisition, political declarations of ownership, and resource exploitation. This provides the opportunity to examine British imperialism informed by militarism, social class, racial prejudice, and the belief in the civilizing mission.[38] During the nineteenth century, these attitudes and beliefs pervaded British cultural texts such as maps, paintings, sketches, music, and all forms of literature including travel writing. The process of cultural appropriation, as exhibited in these texts, includes one underlying assumption: that claims of ownership made by distant imperial powers did not presuppose the cultural possession of colonial frontiers.[39] This reminds us that political, economic, or martial declarations of ownership made in far-off European metropoles did not necessarily include a cultural embrace of the land. Whether colonists, explorers, fur traders, or big-game hunters, the empire's agents needed to assert cultural proprietorship of colonial space – and they did so in ways both clever and complex.

The appropriative representations of the western interior of Rupert's Land constructed by imperial big-game hunters suggest a distinct cultural discourse. They reveal a negotiation of sameness and otherness – or what British historian David Cannadine calls Ornamentalism.[40] Cannadine brings this theory forward in his book *Ornamentalism: How the British Saw Their Empire* in response to the overapplication of Edward Said's concept of Orientalism in colonial and imperial scholarship.[41] Rather than an undigested application of Orientalism that overemphasizes othering and the exotic, Ornamentalism calls for balance in interpretation. I am aware that Cannadine intended his theory to speak directly to issues of social class and hierarchy in British colonies during the nineteenth century. However, I broaden the application of his theory in my own work, as his argument speaks equally well when considered against the beliefs, attitudes, and representations of cultural imperialism. The British empire, he argues, constructed colonial lands and foreign cultures based as much on resemblance as difference. Cannadine presents a compelling case in his effort to, as he says, reorient Orientalism. He writes that

British imperialists envisaged their colonies through extension, or in some cases, through outright idealization of England.[42] They imagined their colonies and appropriated the frontiers of empire through a specific set of imperial eyes that hunted for signs of home. This process included "comprehending and reordering the foreign in parallel, analogous, equivalent, [and] resemblant terms" in addition to othering strategies.[43] From this understanding, Ornamentalist constructions of dissimilar cultures and colonial geographies teetered precariously along an axis of similarity and difference.

Rather than suggesting that the cultural constructions and representations within hunting and exploration narratives reveal a strict form of othering or Orientalism, I prefer to examine the relationship and interplay of the Ornamental, which is inclusive of the similar and the different. Like Cannadine, I believe a case for common ground is long overdue. The narratives and pictorial constructions of imperialists such as big-game hunters reveal an emphasis on difference, dissimilarities, otherness, and the exotic, as well as sameness, similarities, the familiar, and the domestic. British hunters brought their cultural baggage and projected specific visions from the imperial metropole onto the colonial periphery. At the same time, they imported and analogized colonial visions back to the empire. Viewing imperialism as Ornamentalism presents an opportunity to examine not only the exotic but also the domestication of the exotic. Put differently, we can examine the cultural representation of otherness as well as the sameness of the otherness – a key distinction in the examination of cultural landscapes in Chapter 5. The hunters' picturing and visualizing of the British empire in these ways included a well-choreographed and adaptable cult of geopolitical associationism, not unlike that shown in American astronaut Neil Armstrong's quote in the epigraph of this book a hundred years later.

The anti-conquest is a style of representation that connects to the Ornamentalist model. British imperialists such as big-game hunters used the anti-conquest strategy of representation to draw attention to the seeming innocence of the imperial process while simultaneously underscoring their appropriation and control of the interior.[44] Through hunting and exploration narratives, British hunters naturalized their appropriation of colonial territories; by constructing British-looking images of the western interior, these men validated and legitimized their cultural appropriation of colonial space.

The processes of imperialism and the cultural practice of big-game hunting are best understood from a postmodern, postcolonial understanding

– not as monolithic processes or rigid cultural practices but rather as complex, dynamic, and, at times, tantalizingly subtle processes with their own inherent incongruities and contradictions. From this perspective, I examine the act of big-game hunting as a ritualized expression of class, gender, and social privilege. Understanding the culture of the hunt includes the analysis of the sport in both literary and pictorial form in hunting narratives – in brief, I look at hunting as a point of cultural articulation, as a nexus, of imperial culture. With so many points of interconnection, cultural ambiguities saturate the practice of big-game hunting.[45] British hunters applied their imperial culture in different and uneven ways, and, at times, the act of big-game hunting seemed itself an exercise in social and cultural contradiction. Throughout the pages that follow, I detail the many and varied paradoxes of British hunters and their hunting cult. All cultures contain inherent flaws and contradict themselves in one way or another. These contradictions or incongruities include any number of beliefs, values, ideals, representations, symbols, or cultural practices that claimed to do one thing and then either explicitly, but usually implicitly, did the opposite. This makes the scholarly examination of culture a messy and complex business: it's like a figurative old ball of dirty string tightly wound, rather than a neatly gift-wrapped package. If you look closely, the ball of string has overlapping threads aligned in innumerable directions. I envision these as the inconsistencies and contradictions of culture. As we shall see, cultural contradictions worked in two ways: they served to both privilege and undermine the authority and culture of big-game hunters. By drawing attention to and analyzing these incongruities, I situate imperialism as a negotiated process, and big-game hunting as a shifting cultural practice.

The discourses of authorship, sport, science, and nature rest at the centre of imperial big-game hunting narratives. Through these important aspects of imperial appropriation, this book attempts to discern the cultural processes through which British big-game hunters appropriated and represented the land, its resources, and its peoples. Emerging from the forms, codes, and conventions of the leisured elite, British big-game hunting narratives tell of specific cultural attitudes, historical circumstances, and ways of seeing. They viewed the landscape from the perspective of the world's foremost imperial power and presented images of similarity and difference to position the western interior of Rupert's Land as part of the broader empire. Due to their construction for imperial audiences, they reveal more about the imagined, culturally constructed images of the British empire than about colonial physical geography. The hunters considered the land from the standpoint of its exploitable resources and assessed the capacity of the region for future British colonization. Within their hunting and exploration narratives, British hunters described, measured, sketched, canoed, portaged, stalked, dated, and mapped their way across vast distances, all the while hunting for empire.

2

The Prefatory Paradox: Positivism and Authority in Hunting Narratives

B RITISH BIG-GAME HUNTERS USED THE PREFACE of their narratives to establish their narrative authority. The preface of a hunting narrative provided an introduction to the book and preceded the main body of text. Unlike a book's foreword, hunters wrote their own prefatory remarks. At first glance, the preface of a hunting and exploration text appears benign and includes information about the book's origin, scope, purpose, plan, intended audience, and the author's acknowledgments. Within this seemingly straightforward commentary, authors revealed intimate details concerning the construction and revision of their narratives as well as their ontological assumptions about knowledge and the world in which they lived. They also used the prefaces of their books to reinforce the authenticity and truthfulness of their accounts of big-game hunting, scientific descriptions, and picturesque sporting landscapes.[1] Through these claims of objectivity, usually presented in the first sentence, authors established the tone of their narratives and incorporated the totality of their written experiences under the positivistic umbrella of truth and facts.[2] The hunters employed numerous literary strategies to this end. They used explicit truth statements, commented on the length of time from experience to documentation in their journals, and referenced relevant texts with footnote citations. British hunters used these important strategies to ensure that their narratives spoke with authority and emphasized imperial order and control. Despite their repeated and sustained efforts to adhere to a pre-existent cultural expectation designed to produce acceptance of their narrative as truth, however, the hunters contradicted their own positivism. By including statements of self-deprecation, pandering to reviewers and readers, highlighting errata, admitting to narrative omissions, authors ultimately undermined their own positivist assertions of truth.

In order to speak convincingly and with accuracy, authors first sought to establish themselves as the sole purveyors of truth. Narrators remained the authoritative figure to ensure their voice remained uncontested. The primacy and legitimacy of their voice came from two perspectives: the construction of the author as both narrator and protagonist. This split construction provided a unified authorial voice through the form and structure of the text.[3] By definition, however, it also created an inescapable duality of voice. Instead of authors as univocal truth producers, hunting narratives reveal an inescapable authorial duplicity between the author-as-narrator and the author-as-protagonist. This worked against the univocality sought by authors.

An analysis of narrative authority draws attention to the ways through which British hunters established themselves as the central authorial voice, both as narrator and as protagonist. It also highlights the specific strategies and codes used in the construction of the narrative text. Authors tried desperately to present the narrator/protagonist as unified and commonsensical. Nonetheless, the author-as-narrator and author-as-protagonist duality remains a key feature of imperial big-game hunting narratives. The prefaces of hunting texts offer a unique opportunity to examine this construction; the preface is one of a select number of places where the author-as-narrator spoke solely and directly to the reader. In prefatory remarks, the hunter-as-narrator subordinated the hunter-as-protagonist. The use of the first person pronoun within prefatory remarks provided the foundation for the false unification of the author-as-narrator/protagonist throughout the breadth of the narrative.[4] This strategy, in addition to others, constructed the single authoritative author and his authority as truth producer at the outset and situated the consumption of his narrative as a set of facts observed first-hand.

In their prefatory remarks, British hunters employed the discourse of positivism to establish their literary authority. The preface of a hunting narrative, like all travel and exploration books, reveals a particular ontology. Big-game hunters privileged the language of scientific positivism and thereby couched their experiences and descriptions, indeed, the totality of the forthcoming text, within this positivist discourse. Through positivism, British hunters repeatedly and dogmatically asserted the absolute truthfulness of their narratives. The use of positivist vocabulary distanced

exploration narratives from mere travel guidebooks and presented the
expectation of professionally written exploration literature. Its authors used
their prefaces to reaffirm the readers' expectation of serious literature and
to distinguish their work from the less serious reportage-style travel genre.[5]
In this way, authors of mid-nineteenth-century narratives constructed the
verisimilitude of their texts.

The positivism espoused by British big-game hunters emphasized
knowledge creation through sensory observation and description.
This view of knowledge privileged these two processes with a specific
epistemological status. Personal observation and experience, as expressed
through empirical positivist discourse, established the basis of truth
construction. The verification theory, central to positivism, reaffirmed
the creation of positive knowledge through the retesting of phenomena
based on observation: first-hand observation and description provided
the foundation of their epistemology. In conjunction with their claim of
first-hand accounts, British hunters used positivist language to construct
their authority. Their lexis included words such as real, reality, truth,
truthfulness, actual, actually, actuality, absolute, definitive, fact, complete,
and certain. This logocentric imperial vocabulary denied the relative and
inherently subjective nature of language and experience. The discourse
of positivism, also the discourse of science and the upper class, invoked a
reverence for the commonsense reliability and forthrightness of hunting
and exploration narratives. Through this language, prefatory remarks cast
a shadow of innocence over the obvious subjective nature of their colonial
experiences. As positivists, and as individuals educated in scientific method,
big-game hunters trusted in their own objectivity. They believed that the
facts and truth relayed in their narratives corresponded to a universal
positivist reality regardless of individual perspective or experience. They
viewed themselves as observers who could describe and record truth in
an objective fashion. Like most nineteenth-century British travellers,
British big-game hunters viewed knowledge that corresponded to their
positivist ontology and world view as factual and meaningful. They
viewed knowledge that they could not encode as facts, or experiences
beyond their cultural comprehension, as meaningless.

Authors of hunting and exploration narratives linked the establishment
of truth to the immediacy of transposition from observation to
documentation in their journals. Hunters relied on their first-hand
observance of individuals and events as their basis for their positivist
ontology. With observation so integral to positivist logic, the hunters
reassured their readers of the short time span between lived experience and

capturing lived experience in their travel narratives. British hunters used this strategy to speak to the accuracy and veracity of their accounts. The connection between personal observation and positivist documentation obligated the hunters to comment on this important time interval. Big-game hunter Charles Alston Messiter wrote, "I can only say that I have related them [his experiences] exactly as they occurred, exaggerating nothing and taking them from my journals written on the spot."[6] James Carnegie offered a similar statement in his prefatory remarks. He transcribed his journal over nightly campfires with "none of it written, save a sentence or two, at intervals of more than a few days after the occurrences it relates." He also recorded his descriptions of "newly explored valleys" he traversed in 1860 "while the memory of the localities was still fresh in my mind."[7]

Establishing the authority of a hunting and exploration narrative rested on a staunch and definitive declaration of truth. Truth declarations functioned in specific ways. Statements of truth formed part of a code or cannon of exploration literature structured to produce acceptance of what the narrative reported.[8] These declarations reassured the reader that the author personally observed the individual, event, or landscape he described, and they formed the foundation of the central voice crucial to the construction of his authority. Declarations of truth privileged the vocabulary outlined earlier, as well as other positivist phrases such as relied on, guarantee of perfect accuracy, exact truthfulness, complete confirmation of the fidelity of the narrative, general simplicity and truthfulness, exactly as they occurred, as it was, and personal and accurate observations. This sort of language situated the forthcoming text firmly within positivist discourse – as a set of impartial facts detached from the subjectivities of the central author. In this way, authors of hunting and exploration narratives used their prefatory remarks to cast a shroud over, and thereby distance themselves from, their role in the creation of their own narratives.

A brief survey of examples taken from the prefatory remarks of hunting narratives reveals the obligatory nature of truth statements and the positivist ontology of the hunters. Carnegie believed his narrative had "at least the merit of being a true reflex of the thoughts and feelings of the time, as well as a faithful narrative of incident, conversation, and adventure." He encouraged his reader to rely on the truth of his narrative as the information consisted of "actual extracts from the journal." Carnegie even offered a "guarantee of perfect accuracy" and asserted that he preserved the "exact truthfulness" of his observations. In his view, he merely wished to report his experiences as they "actually" stood. In addition to the facts of his narrative, Carnegie spoke to the truth revealed in his illustrations and sketches. Each of his illustrations, he self-deprecated, represented "a truthful though imperfect portrayal of Nature."[9] William Butler spoke of narrating the "real occurrences" of his travels.[10] William Milton and Francis Cheadle addressed issues of truth as they related to the "objective existence" of the information in their *North-West Passage By Land*.[11] William Ross King emphasized the "personal and accurate observations" of natural history contained within his book.[12] John Palliser recorded a "mere matter-of-fact story."[13] Scotsman Robert Michael Ballantyne stated his observations of British North America emerged from "facts or [were] founded in facts."[14]

Despite the authors' attempts to secure the truthfulness of their accounts, some readers managed to look past the positivist language and criticized the information brought forward in hunting and exploration narratives. Milton and Cheadle used the prefatory remarks of their eighth edition to rebut accusations of inaccuracy years after the first publication of their book in 1865. Over that period, numerous other expeditions resulted in the publishing of narratives that spoke to the veracity of Milton and Cheadle's descriptions. They wrote, self-assuredly, "it is with legitimate satisfaction that we draw attention to the complete confirmation of the fidelity of the narrative which has been furnished by subsequent explorers."[15] They specifically cited the narrative entitled *Ocean to Ocean: Sandford Fleming's Expedition through Canada in 1872*, by Scotsman George Munro Grant, who accompanied chief engineer Sandford Fleming as secretary on a surveying expedition for the Canadian railroad.[16] Munro, wrote Milton and Cheadle, offered "testimony to the general simplicity and truthfulness of the narrative."[17] Truth declarations like these are legion in hunting and exploration narratives.

British hunters used parallel strategies, such as making declarations of plain language, writing in the third person, or making statements of non-prejudice, to further attest to the veracity of their narratives. They connected the truthfulness of their text with plain language and simple diction.[18] Authors who avoided elaborate language, typically found in picturesque and sublime landscape descriptions, distanced themselves from the genre of the travel guidebook and set themselves firmly within the field of serious hunting and exploration narratives. The use of positivism, in addition to making straightforward declarations of plain language, depersonalized the narrative and distanced the author from the text.[19] Statements of general simplicity or plain accounts invoked this sort of literary strategy. Beyond these attempts to remove themselves from their own narratives, at least one author even referred to himself as narrator in the third person when he gave a "guarantee of perfect accuracy so far as the writer could compass it."[20]

Hints of new discoveries in prefatory remarks, particularly of "virgin land" untouched by Europeans, further attested to the truth of a narrative. Hunters teased their readers with statements like these in their prefaces. Discovery claims represented an act of imperial penetration, on one hand, and an anti-modern romantic fascination with images of a primeval world untouched by the ravages of industrial civilization, on the other. One author wrote, "I am personally accountable, not only for its arrangement; but for the details of a certain portion of the country, never before (nor probably since) visited by any European."[21] "The forests of the North Thompson" observed Milton and Cheadle, "had not seemingly been trodden by human foot since our visit nine years before."[22] These prefatory statements of untouched or virgin land parallel the Monarch-of-All-I-Survey genre of landscape description popular throughout the nineteenth century. These grandiose and dramatic narrations described for imperial audiences the moment at which the author-as-protagonist gazed upon (and thereby appropriated) new colonial landscapes.[23] The essence of these descriptions, alongside an explicit declaration of virgin land, immortalized the moment of capture for British readers. The preface of hunting narratives provided little opportunity for such extravagant literary constructions, but British hunters made sure they hooked readers with abbreviated Monarch-of-All-I-Survey statements in their prefatory remarks.

The Monarch-of-All-I-Survey style of landscape description connects to a larger discovery myth. In order to discover new untouched land, hunter-explorers first denied prior knowledge of colonial space. The construction of the author as hunter-explorer rested on the understanding that during his travels he eventually discovered something, or gazed upon new land for the first time.[24] Historian Mary Louise Pratt writes, "as a rule the 'discovery' of sites involved making one's way to the region and asking the local inhabitants if they knew of any big lakes, etc. in the area, then hiring them to take you there, whereupon with their guidance and support, you proceeded to discover what they already knew."[25] Rather than identifying others as inhabitants, this perspective viewed residents as occupiers of the land imperialists discovered and reserved the authority of discovery to imperialists.[26] This provided a key element of their sense of colonial entitlement and licensed their forms of meaning and appropriation. The discovery myth remained the central contradiction of exploration and an essential element of the canon of the hunter-explorer.

Despite the many and varied strategies through which they constructed their narrative authority, British hunters routinely contradicted their claims of objectivity and truth. Within their prefatory remarks, the hunters made statements of self-deprecation that served to undermine their truth assertions. The hunters questioned their own use of diction, the circumstances in which they recorded their experiences, their writing style and literary skill, the deficiencies of their composition, or the meticulousness of the journal entries from which they wrote their published narratives. Carnegie used his prefatory remarks to state, "I do not, of course, attach value to the mere diction of my journal, as possessing any merit or importance in itself." He also regretted "that circumstances should have prevented me from forming a better record of my explorations than a mere approximate sketch" and that "whatever the extent of its imperfections, it may still be found to possess some degree of interest, and to afford some new information in regard to a country not yet superfluously depicted and described."[27] Butler hoped his readers might forgive the "faults and failings" of his narrative of sport, exploration, and adventure in Rupert's Land.[28] Messiter ensured his readers understood his literary misgivings: "I must ask for some indulgence as regards my want of literary skill, as I am not used to writing."[29] Palliser's preface also cast a shadow over his writing abilities and "deficiencies of style and composition." He claimed his skills rested with the "use of the rifle and hunting-knife, [rather] than that of the pen."[30] Prefatory comments like these emphasized claims of false modesty or dismissals of personal literary ability.[31] They shifted the focus off the literary assessment of the narrative and worked as part of the process through which authors constructed their journals as commonsensical first-hand accounts of their colonial hunting experiences. By questioning their own use of language and literary skill, however, they cast doubt on the veracity of their own narrative descriptions. Through their uncertainty these deprecatory statements ultimately served to undermine the authors' assertions of truth and objectivity. In order to present an unbiased representation of the facts as observed and recorded in their texts, the hunters-as-narrators used these strategies to distance themselves from the writing of their own texts. This attempt by authors to remove themselves from their own narratives results in a paradox. Nonetheless, their repeated attempts convey the importance of these statements in constructing their narratives as positivistic representations of truth and facts.

British hunters followed their assertions of truth and paradoxical statements of deprecation with apologetic pandering to reviewers and readers.

Their pandering acknowledged that they wrote specifically and subjectively for reviewers and readerships. This contradicted the hunters' earlier claims of impartiality. Some, like Palliser, even apologized for the truthfulness of their narratives – the literary equivalent of damning oneself with faint praise. Palliser stated, "In this age of literature, when so many works of imagination are appearing every day, I should despair of such a mere matter -of-fact story finding any place in the attention or interests of the reading world, did I not firmly rely on your sympathies."[32] Others apologized for the mundane information they brought forward, fearing that readers and reviewers might find their narratives uninteresting. "I now submit my book to the courteous reader, in the hope that, whatever the extent of its imperfections, it may still be found to possess some degree of interest, and to afford some new information in regard to a country not yet super-fluously depicted and described."[33] Butler wrote that "a personal preface … [was] not my object, nor should these things find allusion here, save to account in some manner, if account be necessary, for peculiarities of language or opinion which may hereafter make themselves apparent to the reader."[34] In his other narrative dealing with sport, exploration, and adventure, he referred to the reviewers of his previous narrative and hoped to receive another favourable reading of his work. He even reminded reviewers that they previously "passed in gentle silence" regarding the mis-givings of his previous narrative of exploration and adventure.[35] By cater-ing to the desires of their readers and reviewers, the hunters highlighted the inherent bias, prejudices, and partialities of their text. Prefatory pan-dering like this eroded earlier claims of objectivity and their establishment of narrative authority.

In their prefaces, British hunters noted omissions and changes in grammar, diction, and format when revising their journals into narrative form. The acknowledgment of what they failed to include, or outright removed from their narratives, further undercut their truth claims. Messiter stated explicitly, "I have left out many incidents and experiences" in an effort "to avoid wearying the reader."[36] Carnegie's narrative of big-game hunting and adventure in 1859 provides specific insight into the construction, omission, and revision that travel narratives underwent during the mid-nineteenth century. Carnegie included in his preface a general overview of the current methods through which travel authors edited travel journals into book manuscript form. He stated that in preparing for publication, authors relied primarily on three editorial methods to revise their journals. The first, he suggested, was the publication of the journal "without omission or change." The second method preserved the day-to-day journal format but included a revision of the diction used in the daily passages. The third method involved a complete revision: "a recast of the whole and frame it into a continuous story." The first method, by Carnegie's reckoning, offered little to potential readers. Without revision for readability, he believed keeping the journal format resulted in a "formless and uneven" text. Publishing the entries unchanged produced "a mere assemblage of ill-balanced notes, abounding in rough disjointed sentences, dry repetitions, and frequent references to matters of a private nature." Carnegie characterized the second method as the "worst of all" as the process combined the "meagreness of the journal with the inexactness of an after-narrative, while presenting neither the freshness of the one, nor the smoothness and freedom of the other: to work in this system, though sometimes scarcely avoidable, is to invite trouble and run much risk of failure." The third method "which is now-a-days most in favour" offered authors additional options. However, he added, "the third system ... frequently leads to many small exaggerations amounting in the aggregate to a large untruthfulness, and almost certainly removes the freshness and individuality that characterize even the feeblest of daily records."[37] This method offered Carnegie room to employ his literary licence, but he referred to the method as "hazardous, owing after so long a lapse of time" between his travels in 1859 and his publication of the manuscript in 1875.

Rather than subscribing to any one of these editorial strategies, Carnegie outlined a combination of all three methods in his prefatory remarks. His comments provide fascinating insights into the editorial process authors undertook in rewriting their narratives. "I have employed sometimes one of them, sometimes another, varying the manner of my treatment according to the demands of each particular case."[38] Carnegie described his narrative in published form:

> My work, as it now stands, has been arranged on the following general system: In certain parts, and especially towards the beginning of the volume, I have, with large omissions, fused my journal into something of the narrative form, while preserving its order and partially retaining its diction; but where this has been done, I have endeavoured to make my intention clear, so that the reader may not be cheated into accepting the remarks of to-day as those of fifteen years ago. In other parts, I have followed my notes with some closeness, though not without more or less extensive alternation in the phraseology and construction. In most parts, however, and especially in the latter half of the volume, I have made a literal or almost literal, transcript from my diary, *marking such extracts, when they occur, by single inverted*

commas. Verbal changes, transposition of sentences and such-like trivial amendments, I have sometimes though sparingly, admitted, and in certain rare cases I have added a few words to explain or elucidate my meaning.[39]

Carnegie was so concerned with the format and the truth of his narrative that he parenthesized additional comments he included with the benefit of hindsight at the time of publication. Acknowledgments as explicit as Carnegie's are rare within travel narratives, yet they speak to the lengths authors went to ensure they maintained the truth value of their narratives.

Admissions of retrospective rewriting in prefatory remarks further undermined the hunters' authority. The revisions and additions to narratives after returning from their expeditions weakened their claims of objectivity regarding the unaltered recording of day-to-day experiences along the colonial frontier.[40] Big-game hunters admitted to retrospective rewriting in glancing fashion. Carnegie, for example, wrote the totality of his journal "save a sentence or two" during his journey.[41] His journal he wrote "for the most part" on a daily basis. He stated, "I have made a literal or almost literal, transcript from my diary." He acknowledged later in his prefatory remarks the existence of minor grammatical improvements and added explanation, but insisted that other than "these limitations the passages referred to may be relied on as actual extracts from the journal."[42] Ballantyne similarly fudged, "nearly all the incidents in this tale are either facts or founded in facts."[43] These retrospective rewrites and glancing, off-hand comments served to detract from the ability of the narrative to speak to the daily occurrences and incidents experienced in their narratives. Hedging statements like these clouded the truth status of the narrative and weakened the author's claims of accuracy and objectivity.

British hunters offered contradictory statements about the truth of the information they presented in their prefaces. They claimed their narratives steered clear of scientific information and yet they wanted their narratives, and the natural history or geographical knowledge contained therein, accepted by scientific or geographical organizations as valid, factual information. Here again, Carnegie's insightful narrative speaks to the ambiguity of knowledge denial and acceptance within the prefatory remarks of British big-game hunters:

> It was no definite purpose of mine to gather notes on subjects of a scientific nature, nor to closely record the geographical features of the country through which I travelled; where, however, details of that class do happen

to occur, I have thought it best to give them as they actually stand, without attempting to improve them by private collation with the valuable works on the same part of northern America ... Superior in various important respects as some of these works must undoubtedly be to mine – composed as they were by men of the British and Canadian Governments – I cannot but remember that my information, however cursorily noted, was wither gained by personal observation, or from sources so good, that, in the cases of difference (and a few such there may be), it is by no means impossible that I am in the right, and the more qualified author in the wrong.[44]

He asserted that he wished to add his narrative "as some small tribute to the treasury of geographical knowledge."[45]

By listing their academic degrees, military commissions, and political positions on the opening title page of their books, hunters used their class position to construct and legitimize their authority. By demarcating their education and social class, hunters spoke to the quality and character of the narrator/protagonist. Although implicit throughout the text, class-based designations at the opening of the narrative provided a vital foundation for the big-game hunters' authority claims. These explicit statements established a specific expectation for the veracity of the book prior to reading prefatory truth statements. Some, like Butler, further reinforced the point by including their military orders and reports at the end of their narratives. For readers, these class, educational, political, and martial associations established the quality, character, and patriotic Britishness of the author. They also reiterated that big-game hunters possessed desirable and noble qualities that other men failed to possess. The author-as-narrator reflected the qualities of the author-as-protagonist with an emphasis on the educated, heroic, respectable nature of his actions and character. The protagonist also displayed the social conservatism and social values of the narrator and his readers – the landed British elite. The acts of exploration and discovery hinged on the involvement of elite privileged men.[46] The participation of these men validated and endorsed the processes of appropriation and possession.

The discourse of social class, as employed to construct the hunters' authority, extended beyond the title page and prefatory remarks of hunting books and into the main narrative text. Class, as conveyed by the hunters, related to both economic status and to the social and cultural practices consistent with their socio-economic position.[47] Upper-class hunters distinguished themselves in their texts through socialization or the division of labour. They drew attention to their hierarchical position by identifying the type of day-to-day work required of an expedition isolated in a remote wilderness area. Most refused to exhaust themselves conducting labourer work, like setting up or breaking camp. The big-game hunters also used the issue of class as a strategy to marginalize other voices. This accomplished the narrative goal of moving the narrator/protagonist to the narrative fore, situating everyone else at the narrative periphery (or removing them altogether), and ensured the unified authoritative voice of the narrator remained absolute. Even in the midst of complete wilderness solitude, and with his servants and guides close by, Carnegie refused to socialize with his lower-class labourers. He sat alone reading Shakespeare's *Two Gentlemen of Verona* and lamented that he had "no companion of my own class."[48] Another strategy of class marginalization was to rarely refer to their individual servants or guides by their names, or naming them incorrectly. The hunters paid little notice to the individual personalities of their hired hands. Milton and Cheadle, for example, referred to their Native guide simply as the "Assiniboine," referring to his tribe rather than his given name, for over three hundred pages of text.[49] The class-based references used by the hunter-as-narrator and hunter-as-protagonist reveal an exercise in literary and cultural control, as they constructed silent expedition members.[50] British big-game hunters relegated everyone, including British attendants and guides, to the periphery within their narratives. Both implicitly and blatantly, big-game hunters constructed their authority through the demarcation of social class.

When expedition members raised a dissenting voice, British hunters referred to their superior class-based morality to reinforce their social status. They commented on the low moral fibre of their attendants, servants, gamekeepers, labourers, and guides.[51] These labourers possessed deplorable qualities such as untrustworthiness and acted without courage, resolve, or a sense of sporting etiquette. Rather than presenting a group of men dedicated to the success of the hunting expedition, the hunters constructed their labourers as a hindrance and noted their misgivings and irrational behaviour as an obstacle to the expedition. Graham wrote, "If I had little François Lucie, or Acaapoh, or any of the real thoroughbred 'Coureurs des Prairies' of the Saskatchewan here, we would have a shy at the Sioux country 'coute que coute,' but these fellows are no more equal to the above named, than a cockney is to a Highland deer-stalker."[52] The hunters possessed and displayed the snobbish and priggish attitudes consistent with the British officer class during the mid- to late nineteenth century. Hunting and exploration narratives from across the British empire reveal the cultural perspectives and social attitudes of this group of men. They viewed Native and Métis peoples as their racial inferiors and believed that they must appropriate colonial land for material gain. For the hunter-explorer the world consisted of objects to be described, appraised, and possessed.[53]

In addition to specific literary strategies and language designed to bolster (but which in most cases undermined) the veracity of their narratives from within, British hunters reinforced their books from without by aligning their texts with eminent British institutions. This strategy both strengthened the positivist approach of their books by reaffirming their content as accurate and, at the same time, broke the single, unified authoritarian voice they desperately sought. Imperial social and scientific institutions, formed largely by the landed elite of Great Britain, influenced the form of exploration discourse and aided the construction of authority in exploration narratives.[54] Some of these institutions held explicit associations with the government or the military and inexorably linked the process of new knowledge production to imperial expansion. These institutions had requirements specific to the application of science and beliefs regarding class conduct, colonization, and British imperialism. In this way, influential British organizations institutionalized the process of knowledge production and distribution. As they did with their claims of objectivity, British hunter-explorers used their affiliation with major imperial institutions to distance themselves from their narratives. What authors gave in accommodating institutional parameters they gained in authorial effacement.[55]

The Royal Geographical Society (RGS) stands at the forefront of institutions that promoted and aligned themselves with expeditions of exploration and natural history (and big-game hunting, albeit implicitly). Class-based institutions such as the RGS centralized and regulated knowledge gathering, and gave explorers and hunters a set of instructions for writing narratives of their expeditions.[56] The RGS, for example, only offered to fund Palliser's expedition (which he initially wanted to conduct strictly for big-game hunting and adventure) to British North America if he followed their guidelines, published his reports following their format in the *Journal of the RGS*, and included a botanist, geologist, naturalist, and astronomer on his trip.[57] "Under the façade of gentlemanly science, the RGS was an organization with a fundamentally instrumentalist agenda. And the agenda was the expansion of empire."[58] The RGS even married their interests with those of individual explorers through the creation of the Founder's and Patron's Medals.[59] The RGS honoured the well-known British big-game hunter and empire builder Frederick Selous with its prestigious Founder's

Medal in recognition of his lifetime contributions to the advancement of geography, science, and the British empire in 1892.[60] His connections to both the Natural History Museum as well as taxidermist Rowland Ward, considered by big-game hunters as the foremost taxidermist in England, situated Selous within the midst of the British imperial and sporting establishment. His affiliation with eminent and influential organizations contributed to the authority of his narratives and thrust him forward as a model of the imperialist hunter.

At least one big-game hunter revealed connections to the British Acclimatisation Society, an organization devoted to the importation, exportation, appropriation, and introduction of foreign animals and plants between England and the colonies. In some cases, shared membership by the British elite in these decidedly imperial institutions influenced the direction and tone of their operation. The British Acclimatisation Society acted as an ecological extension of imperialism largely for the hunting purposes of the upper classes in England. This organization contributed to the authority of hunting narratives, particularly in the case of William Ross King, whom I discuss at length in Chapter 4. Beyond his connection to the Acclimatisation Society, King aligned himself with key scientists and government officials. He stated in his prefatory remarks that he adopted the nomenclature of natural historian Spencer Fullerton Baird for birds and animals throughout his narrative.[61] He also used statistics obtained from Richard Nettle, the superintendent of the Fisheries of Lower Canada (Canada East) during the 1850s. This objective statistical government information, as well as Nettle's official and respectable position, enabled King to address the topic with "weight and authority."[62] Carnegie bolstered his information with the narrative and "facts" presented previously by Palliser. He wrote, "The outlines of the map in question – which are of my own framing – have been composed by adjustment from the principal maps in the Blue Books relating to Captain Palliser's Expedition."[63] Through direct connection to the authority of these eminent individuals and organizations, hunters validated their overt actions and expressions of imperialism. Affiliation with such prestigious institutions constructed and legitimized the authority of hunting narratives and their expeditions. Institutional approval endorsed the authoritative voice of the author-as-narrator and the imperial actions of the author-as-protagonist. Institutional affiliation certified the truth of the narrative. At the same time, the influence of institutions within these narratives contradicted their larger objective and broke the single, unified voice sought by the big-game hunters.[64]

In the preface and main narrative of their books, British hunters employed academic · citations and used supporting documentation to strengthen their authority. Their sources consisted of a wide range of literature but focused generally on hunting and exploration narratives, books dealing with the life and culture of North American Indians as observed by Europeans, and natural history volumes. Their sources reveal the hunters' discriminating intellectual eye and knowledge of books that related directly to the western interior of Rupert's Land and the American West. They used these sources to legitimize their interpretation and positivist construction of truth. Like explicit truth statements, the use of footnotes in the nineteenth century reveals a positivist view of knowledge. For the hunters, footnotes proved facts.[65] By citing key references dealing with the western interior, British hunters reinforced their own work intellectually, allied themselves with recognized authorities, and built upon the positivist storehouse of scientific knowledge.

Through citations, authors ensured the unequivocal and univocal interpretation of their positivist text. British hunters used footnotes to confer authority on themselves and their narratives. Footnotes spoke to the quality, intelligence, and education of the author; they identified an intellectual education and therefore membership in the social and landed elite. The author required specific intellectual training to encode footnotes, and the reader required parallel training to recognize and grasp the intellectual arguments, nuances, and information contained in cited references. In this way, social status influenced the acceptance and interpretation of travel narratives. Authors conducted a learned discourse with their readers and followed a normalized and widely accepted citation code for the organization of facts. The rhetoric of positivism, as expressed through annotations and references, revealed the precise location of facts down to the volume, issue, and page number.[66] By mustering and citing the facts of other hunters and explorers, authors presented their narratives as valid and employed a rigorous scholarly approach. The wider and more balanced the selection of sources, the stronger the author's positivist claim of objectivity. Footnotes acted as a buttress against potential scrutiny and criticism of the narrative in much the same way as Milton and Cheadle vindicated their narrative ten years after publication.

Of all the hunters, Carnegie's narrative reveals a particularly compelling set of references. Carnegie read and demonstrated knowledge of the narratives of other big-game hunters, most of which came from expeditions to Rupert's Land. A sampling of these reveals the diversity, popularity, and weight of his sources. They included John Palliser, *Solitary Rambles of a*

Hunter in the Prairies (1853), William Francis Butler, *The Great Lone Land* (1872), Robert Michael Ballantyne, *Hudson's Bay; or Everyday Life in the Wilds of North America* (1848), and the lesser known Llewellyn Lloyd, *Field Sports of the North of Europe* (1830). Another set of sources dealt with the culture and lifestyle of North American Indians as in Henry Rowe Schoolcraft, *History of the Indian Tribes of the United States: Their Present Condition and Prospects* (1857), Joseph Howse, *A Grammar of the Cree Language* (1865), and the popular classics of Paul Kane, *Wanderings of an Artist among the Indians of North America* (1859), and George Catlin, *North American Indians* (1841).[67] Carnegie included several books on natural history, including F.O. Morris, *History of British Butterflies* (1870), William Jardine, *The Naturalist's Library* (1833), Thomas Hooker, *Flora Boreali-Americana* (1840), and John Richardson's *Fauna Boreali-Americana* (1830) – a must-have for sportsmen and hunters. A final group of sources form the basis of early Canadiana, such as Samuel Hearne, *A Journey to the Northern Ocean* (1795), John Franklin, *Narrative of a Journey to the Shores of the Polar Sea in the Years 1819-1822* (1824), Henry Youle Hind, *Canadian Red River Exploring Expedition* (1860), and George Munro Grant, *Ocean to Ocean* (1873).

In total, Carnegie cited eighty-four sources in footnotes denoted by asterisks. He cited them repeatedly by volume and specified page numbers to verify his scholarship. The majority of his citations dealt with points of clarification, such as place names, geography, natural history observations, and the proper Linnaean Latin classifications for flora and fauna. Other citations discussed points of similarity or departure from the narratives of the other authors, some of which included delineating trophy size relative to the bags of other British big-game hunters. Carnegie used shortened citations and took the opportunity in his footnotes to elaborate upon the main body of text. The footnote on pages sixteen and seventeen, for example, is over 550 words alone. He even employed footnotes throughout his prefatory remarks. Carnegie used footnotes meticulously and reminded his readers that he acknowledged his references carefully.[68]

Milton and Cheadle included twenty-four citations in their narrative. They cited, and thereby allied themselves with, the authority of the *Journal of the Royal Geographical Society* (1860) specific to the report of Captain John Palliser and Dr. James Hector. New to their eighth edition, they included the Reports of the Government of Canada by engineer Fleming and the travel narrative written of that expedition, *Ocean to Ocean*, by Grant. Milton and Cheadle provided an addendum to the eighth edition that included numerous direct citations from Munro's travel book relative to points of similarity in their own narrative. They cited the exact page numbers for both texts to reiterate the veracity of their own narrative.

British army officer and big-game hunter William Ross King employed over seventy-seven footnotes in *The Sportsman and Naturalist in Canada*. His book discussed interpretations and schools of thought regarding current natural history and botany debates among the scientific community. He used direct citations and shortened citations, and he cited volumes, issues, and page numbers of important natural history books. These included, to name a few, William Yarrell, *A History of British Birds* (1842), the *Journal of the Academy of Natural Sciences, Report on Zoology of Pacific Routes* (1857), John Richardson's *Fauna Boreali-Americana* (1830), Richard Owen, *A History of British Fossil Mammals and Birds* (1846), Spencer Fullerton Baird, *Mammals of North America* (1859), Alexander Wilson, *American Ornithology* (1829), J.C. Louden, *Arboretum Britannicum* (1838), and William Scrope's *The Art of Deerstalking* (1838).

Despite their use of documentation and selection of references to speak to the authority and veracity of their narratives, British hunters created a footnote facade. Through the exactness of citations by volume and page number, they attempted to reassure readers of the objectivity of their recorded colonial experiences. Yet footnotes conveyed a false sense of objective, scholarly information to the narrative reader and further cultivated the dual narrative authority generated in hunting and exploration narratives. The amassing of citations, in any context, ultimately fails to "establish" anything in a given text.[69] Moreover, only the educated elite in the nineteenth century possessed the ability to decipher the encoded citations. Indeed, "appearances of uniformity are deceptive [within footnotes]. To the inexpert, footnotes look like deep root systems, solid and fixed."[70] What positivists conceived as the strength of the citation method ultimately served to undermine that which they hoped to establish. Through citations and references, authors positioned their narratives in their present: they fixed their construction of the truth to a specific time and place. Rather than reaffirming the universal applicability of their facts, the use of footnotes paradoxically spoke to the temporal, spatial, and cultural relativity of their subjective colonial experiences. The annotations and references in hunting narratives served to augment and yet simultaneously contradict the position and authority of the author.

The hunters included pictures and other narrative information illustrated or written by other authors, and this worked against their positivist unified voice. As discussed earlier, their statements of truth typically acknowledged the totality of the narrative, inclusive of pictures and maps, as their own. Authors then followed these statements with numerous exceptions. Carnegie stated, for example, that only two forms of evidence provided the foundation for his narrative: personal observation and other fact-based exploration narratives like his own. He then undermined the facts in other hunters' narratives by suggesting that his personal observations and facts might exceed those of other writers. In terms of illustrations, wrote Carnegie, "whether on separate pages or attached to the letterpress of the work, the greater number of these are derived from my own sketches and drawings; the exception entirely consisting in those which have been reproduced from photographs, or founded on them with some slight alteration."[71] Carnegie sketched his own images with the aid of an artist. Authors included images, engravings, and photographs they picked up during their expedition, or revised photographs into engravings for the purpose of publication. Carnegie wrote, "most of the smaller and less elaborate illustrations belong to the former of these classes, being facsimiles, or nearly so, of pen-and-ink memoranda hastily sketched into my journal; the exceptions are as follows: Buffalo-hide Line, Whisky [his dog], Snow-shoe and Skida – Sketches only recently prepared by me expressly for the present volume."[72]

The inclusion of errata within the narrative, following the author's positivistic prefatory remarks, provided damning contradictory statements. Errata referred to the list of authorial errors and/or publisher misprints in a book that were deemed of sufficient importance to be brought to the reader's attention. The errata within hunting narratives dealt with various sorts of minutiae, including names, Latin classifications, page number conflicts, or Native vocabulary. The acknowledgments of errata, twenty-nine in the case of Carnegie's narrative and six in King's book, undermined their assertions of truth and objective facts.[73] The inclusion of material acknowledged as someone else's, in addition to the acknowledgment of grievous errors within the text, further confused the authority of hunting narratives.

British big-game hunters worked feverishly in their prefatory remarks to ensure the commonsense acceptance of their depictions of sporting adventure and exploration. Through the discourse of scientific positivism, they sought to establish the absoluteness of their narrative voice, yet the nature and style of their prefatory remarks served to undermine their narrative authority. They invested meaning into their lived experiences of hunting and empire in Rupert's Land from which they later tried to dissociate themselves. Despite their best efforts, they failed to escape the fundamental dialectic they themselves created. The problem rested with the author-as-narrator's efforts to remove himself from his narrative while at the same time situating the author-as-protagonist within the newly constructed body of knowledge. Exploration epistemology depended on the transparency of the author-as-protagonist to the author-as-narrator.[74] The prefatory remarks of big-game hunters, designed to establish a single authoritative voice, reveal an exercise in cultural contradiction. The positivism espoused by hunters emphasized first-hand observance and description in the establishment of truth, yet the same positivist vocabulary used to establish truth ultimately distanced authors from the facts they presented in their narratives. Authors inverted the strategy of closeness-to-truth-as-evidence-of-truth for the author-as-protagonist with distance-from-truth-as-evidence-of-truth for the author-as-narrator in their prefatory remarks. To restate this complex dynamic differently, the big-game hunter-as-author attempted to divorce himself from the big-game hunter-as-protagonist in prefatory remarks. Authors used their prefatory remarks to delineate the positivistic truth and facts experienced by the big-game hunter-as-protagonist, yet sought to detach themselves from the narration of their own personal experiences and observations. By undercutting their own positivist ontology in this way, hunters routinely contradicted their own assertions of truth, resulting in the prefatory paradox.

3

Cry Havoc?
British Imperial Hunting Culture

Do not cry havoc, where you should but hunt with modest warrant.
Shakespeare, *Coriolanus,* III.1.274

IN THE MIDST OF *Coriolanus*, a play dealing with the Roman empire,
William Shakespeare invoked the language and culture of the hunt
to sound a note of caution. Even in the context of his own time,
Shakespeare understood the hunting rituals and practices of the English
upper class. He knew his reference resonated with English gentlemen who
conducted their sport in a manner consistent with their social station.
Unlike the lower classes, these men applied their intellect to hunting and
exercised rational restraint. Through their elite hunting culture, English
sportsmen learned to hunt with modest warrant and refrained, at all
times, from crying havoc and losing self-control – or so they claimed.

By the nineteenth century, sporting gentlemen learned the etiquette,
rituals, and codes of behaviour consistent with imperial sporting culture
at socially elite public (private) schools. Immersed in an educational
curriculum that emphasized the history and importance of the British
empire, public schools like Eton, Harrow, and Rugby reinforced imperial
qualities of manliness, service, discipline, and patriotism.[1] Public school
magazines, sporting narratives, popular fiction, and juvenile literature
also served specific purposes by constructing the archetype of the imperial
man and presenting him for moral and physical emulation. This included
participation in manly sports. Through colonial hunting expeditions, these

men sought exercise for moral improvement and to further exploration and scientific progress through natural history. Magazines and books told of harrowing adventures, great campaigns, and the exhilaration of sport, all on the colonial frontier. Writers made the connections between sportsmen and public schools explicit. Leading big-game hunters themselves trained in public schools where they learned the athletic imperative, or sporting ethic, and the importance of physical activities for character formation.[2] Indeed, the specific act of big-game hunting was considered good training for warfare. Young upper-middle- and upper-class boys received these lessons in regular doses, ensuring that they held an appropriate imperial world view before assuming their rightful place as soldiers, scientists, and administrators of the British empire.

From the mid-nineteenth century onwards, English public schools espoused a mixture of harsh Social Darwinism and pious Christian gentility. This led to a dual perspective, structured through an unapologetic ethnocentrism and a staunch belief in the God-given right of the white man to dominate the globe. This ideological blending merged into a single combined perspective with the former taking precedence.[3] Drawing from Social Darwinism, public school headmasters instilled in their boys a belief in the eminence of imperial Britain. They inculcated them with a belief in militarism, obedience, loyalty, and teamwork. These students believed in racial and gender superiority, with the foundation being the physical health, manly vigour, and athletic prowess of the white man. Public schools used Christianity to impress upon their students the divine rightness of their civilizing mission. The Christian rightness of their global quest presented British imperialism not as a simple economic endeavour but rather as a moral and cultural crusade sanctified by God Himself. The Christian tenets of seriousness, self-denial, morality, and rectitude played a central role in the education of mind and body in English public schools.[4]

These social values found expression in the nineteenth-century British sporting ethic. Athletic culture emphasized the superiority and total victory of Social Darwinism on one hand and the propriety of Christianity on the other. The "games ethic" referred to the English tradition of athletic participation but also to the educational role of sport in cultivating morals, values, and imperial ideology in young men. When combined with the new pillar of Social Darwinism, the games ethic emphasized values that contradicted a Christian upbringing, such as supreme victory, male aggression, and ruthlessness.[5] Christianity nevertheless played an important role in tempering these behaviours. Christian tenets reinforced the belief that one must triumph, but only from within established rules of conduct. Young men must display humility in triumph and compassion for the defeated: the mantra of a good Muscular Christian gentleman. As the nineteenth century advanced, this belief system coalesced into notions of fair play and sportsmanship. Public school headmasters championed these values as the keys to the moral education of young men through team and field sports.

Based in the games ethic learned at public schools, upper-class big-game hunters from England, Scotland, and Ireland espoused a specific code of conduct for their sport. The accepted methods of bagging game date back at least to the medieval period and the hunting culture of the landed nobility.[6] However, the specific origins of the code of conduct for field sports like hunting and angling during the nineteenth century probably stem from English writer and sportsman Izaak Walton and his book *The Compleat Angler; or The Contemplative Man's Recreation* (1653).[7] Walton's book provided an early archetype for later nineteenth-century sporting narratives, containing equal parts travelogue, sport manual, natural history, and landscape aesthetics.

The hunter's code delineated preferred methods for bagging game which, for the hunters, attested to the respectable character of their sport. The code emphasized the difficulty of the hunt and the establishment of a clean kill. The legitimizing language of fair play and Muscular Christianity, common to the gentlemen's cricket ground or public school rugby pitch, found expression in hunting codes and guidelines. Big-game hunters and their fraternal hunting clubs claimed that the "true" sportsman hunted for the intellectual aspects of the chase and for the love of nature – not for the kill itself.[8] The hunting code called for sporting gentlemen to shoot wildfowl on the wing to provide a sporting chance, and to never shoot an injured animal or an animal trapped in snow. When angling, the sportsman favoured the familiar skill and strategy of fly-fishing over indigenous methods deemed crude and wasteful, such as spearing.[9] Sporting gentlemen hunted only during the appropriate season, and gentlemen hunters restricted their hunting to stags and bulls to conserve wildlife.[10] British hunters considered the killing of females, particularly with young, as decidedly unsporting. Paradoxically, the "true" hunter discharged his weapon to avoid the needless waste of wildlife. Hunters approached close enough to identify the sex and trophy quality of their prey prior to delivering the kill. This implied that they possessed the skill, stealth, and prowess to approach within point-blank range.[11] Of course, these parameters existed for sport hunters only and conflicted with subsistence and commercial gunners. British big-game hunters abhorred the idea of the subsistence or commercial hunt. Even though some collected specimens on official behalf of museums or scientific organizations, elite sporting gentlemen claimed no material interests – game provided a source of amusement and scientific education, not income.

Best described as a class-based ethos, the code of gentlemanly hunting highlighted the elite social character of British hunters for the purpose of exclusion. British hunters used the code to enforce a hierarchy of class, race, and gender privilege to legitimize their actions. In this way, the connection of the hunting code to social class legitimized their own position while also excluding the underclasses.[12] The elite sporting code constructed and maintained these social and cultural divides by vilifying the techniques of Native peoples, Métis, and lower-class settlers during the mid- to late nineteenth century. In both the colonies and in England, the code served the interests of the upper class. When game became scarce, the imperial and colonial elite forwarded a policy of protectionism to ensure the continuation of their ritual pastime. British elites made the protection of colonial game and the exclusion of lesser races and classes a legislative priority across the British empire by the mid- to late nineteenth century.[13]

Upper-class British hunters used the sporting code to ensure their socially exclusive hunting activities remained within the confines of respectable manly leisure.[14] For British hunters, the terms "sportsman" and "gentleman" existed synonymously. The sporting code increased the difficulty of the hunt by ensuring, at least in the minds of the hunters, that they adhered to some semblance of fair play. This placed the activities of lower-class pothunters and Native peoples, or individuals who hunted for mere subsistence, as uncivilized and unmanly.[15] Through the hunting code, British big-game hunters tied their sport to the activities of respected and adventurous empire-builders, not uncivilized butchers. Big-game hunter Frederick Ulric Graham relayed his disgust at the cold-blooded actions of his Métis and Native guides in 1847. He wrote, "the half-breeds and Crees ran the last band [of buffalo], and killed three more. I saw the brutes cut up one cow alive – a most cruel operation."[16] Through his utter abhorrence to Native practices as they related to the hunting code, British gentlemen such as Graham appeared humane. By refraining from causing excessive pain, withholding shots with little success of a kill, or delivering a decisive death blow to minimize suffering, elite sportsmen who adhered to the code paradoxically appeared compassionate.

British hunters opposed non-sporting methods that contradicted the code with religious zeal. They expressed particular disdain for lead-shooting. When lead-shooting, the hunter camped near a deer or caribou path or

3.1 "Close Quarters with a Grisly Bear." Good sport included an opportunity for the hunter to test his personal mettle. Through the ritual of imperial hunt, British men cultivated moral improvement and built character. John Palliser, *Solitary Rambles and Adventures of a Hunter in the Prairies* (London: J. Murray, 1853), frontispiece.

lead and simply awaited their prey.[17] Instead, big-game hunters preferred stalking, also known as creeping or still-hunting, over lead-shooting because the hunt involved the active pursuit of game. Celebrated hunter Frederick Selous, during a slightly later period, articulated succinctly the mid-nineteenth-century British revulsion to lead-shooting. He wrote, "I must say that I felt thoroughly disgusted with the whole business. In the first place to sit in one spot for hours lying in wait for game is not hunting ... It is not a form of sport which would appeal to me under any circumstances ... I could see no redeeming point in it whatsoever."[18] The techniques of animal baiting, elevated shooting platforms, killing zones with overlapping fields of fire, and lead-shooting contradicted every aspect of the idealized hunting code.[19] These techniques raised the hunter from the ground and removed him from imminent danger. Only mere assassins, such as commercial poachers and subsistence pothunters, engaged in such despicable practices.[20] Upper-class hunters and sporting gentlemen rejected these practices outright. Nefarious techniques like these stripped the gentleman hunter of his role as the active pursuer, and placed him in a passive role. This contradicted the sporting code that prompted elite British men to use their superior intelligence, force, and technology in the active pursuit of their prey. Having levelled the odds, the gentleman hunter established victory in a final one-on-one confrontation in the wilderness (Figure 3.1).[21] Through the hunting code, the new imperialists appeared courageous but rational, strong yet civilized, armed with rifles, modern science, and a clear sense of entitlement.

The elite cult of hunting positioned those who disregarded the sportsman's code, by hunting out of season, by taking females, or by using less-desirable techniques, as irrational and uncivilized. Although hunters described Native hunting and fishing methods in a neutral way in the late eighteenth century, they denigrated these same techniques with the continued decline of game stocks in the mid- to late nineteenth century. Gentlemen hunters vilified poachers and pothunters for using illegitimate hunting tactics and constructed them as the enemies of hunting and the environment.[22] White hunters conducted their sport in a husband-like manner, they argued. Lower racial and social classes, not elite British hunters, destroyed colonial game. Ignoring their own role in the destruction of wildlife, hunters condemned these groups as the principal transgressors of their sport. Without the benefit of British technology, subsistence hunters relied on techniques such as traps, pits, snares, poisons, arrows, and spears, which horrified elite British sensibilities. These techniques, designed to produce meat for the pot rather than good sport, provided the cultural markers through which hunters condemned poachers and pothunters as the defilers of the environment.

Despite their claims of adherence to the sportsman's code, British big-game hunters engaged in wholesale bloodshed and committed heinous transgressions of the code. They cried havoc and gave way to indiscriminate slaughter by firing into herds, shooting females, shooting by water holes at night, or expressing indifference to the escape of wounded animals.[23] Big-game hunters employed specific discourses to legitimize their hunting improprieties. In their view, killing for science, sustenance, defensive purposes, and for either vermin or nuisance destruction all fell outside the boundaries of the British hunting code. Other hunters contravened the code in the interests of mere slaughter. In 1859, James Carnegie justified his buffalo butchery in the western interior with the following apologetic statement: "Yesterday's shooting was successful enough, especially in regard to my chief object – fine heads; and a man who travels thousands of miles for such trophies may be excused for taking part in one day's rather reckless slaughter."[24] Strewn with inconsistencies, the elite hunting code accommodated additional infringements based on arguments of evolutionary theory. Hunters accepted violations of the code relating to the slaughter of animals they viewed as being on the lower end of the evolutionary ladder, such as game birds and reptiles. Although British hunters used moral, masculine, scientific, class, and racial discourses to uphold their exclusive guidelines for sport, they abandoned the hunting code repeatedly.[25]

Although imperialists in Great Britain viewed the removal of large predatory animals as crucial to the initial stages of imperial appropriation, some expressed fear that the British hunters might abandon civilized social conduct in the colonial wilderness. They believed the ritual of hunting, with its focus on violence, aggression, and bloodshed, unleashed primal urges in civilized men. In the face of these urges, could the white hunter remain in control? Without societal structure, the unobstructed gentleman hunter became the master of all he surveyed and answered only to himself.[26] When exposed to savage cultures and bloodthirsty beasts, could he maintain the rational qualities that kept him British? Could he overcome the inner challenges of morality and character invoked by the hunt?

By the mid- to late nineteenth century, restraint and self-control evolved into the cardinal virtues of the imperial hunting cult. British hunters displayed their character and moral fibre through a test of their rational restraint. Compared with hunting in England, colonial frontiers, without game laws and with an overabundance of game, presented an inner test of a hunter's ability to exercise restraint. By demonstrating their coolness in the face of danger and their ability to exercise self-control, big-game hunters reaffirmed the superiority and rightness of British character, conduct, and ideals. This reassured imperial readers at home that white hunters remained civilized in the face of primitive cultures and the savage frontier.

While hunting buffalo, Carnegie made a special point to remind his readers of his self-control. "Had slaughter been the chief object, we might have slain hundreds of bulls and lean cows – nothing could have been more easily done; but such cruelty would have weighed heavy on my conscience ... Not counting two or three bulls shot after a fine run and allowed every chance for their lives, or slain under some sudden excitement, I could safely say that no buffalo had been killed by myself or my men except for good, or at all events definite and sufficient, reasons."[27] Even though he might occasionally give in to "some sudden excitement," Carnegie reaffirmed his personal calm and coolness. By allowing the buffalo "every chance to run for their lives," Carnegie and other British hunters invoked the elite hunting code to demonstrate their restraint and to situate themselves diametrically from indiscriminate potshooters. Manly, educated British hunters refused to engage in bloodlust or buck-fever and offered their prey a sporting chance. They selected and stalked their prey, purposefully extending as much personal risk to themselves as to their quarry.

The issue of rational restraint was connected to prominent cultural issues and themes in mid- to late-nineteenth-century England. During this period, the British exhibited anxiety over their place as an advanced imperial nation. Part of this fear resulted from scientist Charles Darwin (1809-82), his theories, and his widely read treatise on evolution, entitled *The Origin of Species* (1859). Darwin's theory argued against the divine creation of man in God's image and forwarded the idea that human beings existed as part of an evolutionary chain. This presented a direct challenge to men who embodied dominance and rationality in British Victorian society. Rather than being created divinely, man evolved from the animal kingdom. Other scientists, like Herbert Spencer (1820-1903) furthered this view. Spencer conceived the advancement of mankind as an evolutionary ladder that allowed movement either to the top (civilized, rational, ordered, technologically advanced Europeans) or the bottom (savage, irrational, chaotic, primitive Native peoples). Hunters and explorers who failed to demonstrate the British quality of rational restraint in the midst of such wild and primitive peoples themselves reverted to savages. By losing self-control or by turning "Indian," British hunters regressed to a savage, animal state.

The connection with the animal world suggested that man waged a constant internal battle against his primitive evolutionary beginnings. Contemporary Victorians feared that the animal in man would overcome the rational and moral British hunter, a fear so prominent that nineteenth-century author Robert Louis Stevenson personified the idea years later in his *Dr. Jekyll and Mr. Hyde* (1885) – the rational scientist and the ferocious savage embodied within the same civilized man.[28] British men must seek to maintain the highest personal standards of morality and character. If usurped by irrationality and chaotic primitivism, British men would degenerate, and with them, the degeneration of the British empire. In this way, the sport of big-game hunting expressed the social and cultural concerns of its time. The activity paradoxically promoted both the rational and the irrational, the civilized and the primitive, the modern and the anti-modern, the scientific and the romantic. Big-game hunting provided an exercise in social and cultural contradiction. The sense of masculine identity embodied and celebrated through big-game hunting underscored the cultural inconsistencies of the sport. The gentleman hunter was cool and calm in the face of danger; yet the *coup de grâce* highlighted aggression and brutality. The blood, gore, and sheer violence of the kill contradicted any such rationality.

The belief in moral degeneration also worked in reverse. If the loss of rational restraint threatened to usurp the morality and genteel manliness of the British hunter from within, the effeminacy of domestic civilized industrial society threatened to usurp him from without. Victorian imperialists and social reformers, during the mid- to late nineteenth century particularly, connected the degradation of empire with the deterioration of British men and their moral and physical strength. They promoted hunting at home and along the colonial frontier as an antidote to the effeminacy of their urban civilization.[29] For them, big-game hunting offered a natural training regime related specifically to warfare, conflict, and expansion into foreign territories. The hunting and athletic ethos espoused at British public schools exposed boys and young men to the readiness to kill. This included the determination and character to see to the inevitable conclusion of the hunt – the complete domination and victory of British men.

The rational and rugged British hunter possessed a masculinity both civilized and primitive. By possessing both, he brought the values of one to bear upon his activities in the other. On campaign to a wilderness frontier, the hunter celebrated a civilized masculinity informed by social class, race, technology, science, and the values of industrial civilization.[30] The hunter then returned to England altered by his wilderness frontier experience. He now possessed an almost feared, rugged, gritty, colonial masculinity. This imperial hunting masculinity inspired awe in some men, apprehension in others, and a desire to emulate in the rest. Imperialists held these men aloft as symbolic of the British masculine ideal in Victorian England. Part of this ideal hinged on the return of the hunter with trophies representative of his symbolic appropriation of the frontier. Imperialists feted returning hunters as empire builders. Savages, wilderness chaos, and irrationality confronted the hunter at every turn, yet he retained a staunch commitment to his Britishness. Exposed to the animal within and to effeminacy from without, the British hunter survived the test of his inner character and returned triumphant. His exposure to the edges of empire made him rugged, but he retained his moral, rational, imperial masculinity for which Victorian society lauded him as heroic and courageous.

In addition to stalking game with their rifles, British sporting gentlemen hunted with their pencils and sketchbooks. Indeed, the study of animals and their environment, or natural history, formed an integral part of the nineteenth-century British imperial hunting cult.[31] One of the fascinations with natural history was the opportunity for immortality. By identifying never-before-seen animals, hunters and explorers reserved the right to christen new species after themselves – a great prize during the period. The discovery of additional species and subspecies accelerated the collecting fever during the nineteenth century, and leading museums employed hunters to gather specimens of all kinds. Understanding the markings and behaviours of new colonial species allowed hunters opportunities to study nature and creation through scientific observation and to verify or criticize other sportsmen's narratives regarding the correct Latin classification of flora and fauna.[32] The study of natural history grew dramatically in the second half of the nineteenth century. Social Darwinism, discussions of evolutionary theory, and the opening of the new Natural History Museum in London brought natural history to the forefront of public discourse. The British applied natural history to animals, the environment, and even indigenous peoples – distinguishing advanced from primitive cultures.[33] The classification and ordering of species related to the imperial urge to order colonial nature. The science of classification included the science of killing, and killing en masse for museums, collections, and scientific progress.

The hunters' preoccupation with the science of natural history led them to rationalize the killing of game and the seizing of trophy heads and skins for themselves and the empire under the auspices of British science. Through the natural sciences, hunters renamed meat and carcasses as specimens, and heads and horns as trophies. This modernist rationalization and creation of scientific knowledge, which validated the processes of killing, categorization, and dispossession, constructed British hunters as non-invasive, gentleman naturalists. Hunters also invoked evolutionary theory to justify their sport. They viewed themselves engaged in the process of natural selection by hunting and killing dominant males and allowing younger, more vigorous males to take their place. The hunters argued that their activities ensured the survival of the fittest. They merely assisted the natural processes of nature.

The connection of hunting with the advancement of natural history and imperialism rationalized big-game hunting by emphasizing the educated and civilized nature of the sport. Through these discourses, big-game hunters positioned their activities within the anti-conquest. The integration of classification with killing separated the hunters from the act of appropriation while, at the same time, conferring scientific morality upon trophy hunting and game butchery. In this way, British hunters enveloped killing, collecting, and displaying under the umbrella of morality, respectability, and rationality. The scientific association of hunting with zoological and botanical research provided the foundation of the sport's social acceptability, particularly among late Victorians.[34]

Under the guise of natural history, British hunters engaged in an endless search for trophy heads and skins. Securing and maintaining the integrity of a good trophy began in the field. British hunters conducted the demanding tasks of drying and skinning hides and trophy heads in the wilderness. If they mismanaged their trophies during this initial stage of preservation, hunters could destroy the trophy value of their kill. In addition to the possible destruction of their prizes though skinning and drying, hunters needed to prevent insects from consuming and rotting their trophies. A mutual admiration existed between hunters who conducted the skinning of an animal with as few holes as possible. Both art and science, the skinning process required an understanding of animal anatomy and biology.

Enlisting a good taxidermist ensured the preservation of a good trophy. Hunters brought their trophies to a taxidermist who immortalized the animal as a vicious beast and thus offered testimony to the heroism and courage of the hunter. However, depending on the skill of the hunter, the process of skinning, and the art of the taxidermist, excellent specimens sometimes made for inferior trophies. Acknowledged as the foremost taxidermist of Victorian England, Rowland Ward (1848-1912) also published wildlife manuals, wrote books on natural history, and contributed trophy specimens to museums. Ward operated a highly successful taxidermy business in Piccadilly, and by publishing record books of game, Ward linked taxidermy to imperialism by tapping into the enthusiasm for collecting natural history trophies.[35] He wrote a *Record of Big-Game Comparisons* in the 1890s, which remains the standard book for hunters and naturalists registering game across the world (as of 2007, in its twenty-seventh two-volume edition). He wrote other books, such as *The Sportsman's Handbook to Collecting, Preserving, and Setting-Up Trophies and Specimens,* in which he offered advice for hunters and taxidermists.

Taxidermists like Ward focused on the illusion of realism. They sought to capture the living image of the dead, but ultimately the illusion mattered most.[36] By focusing on ferocious realism, animals demonstrated a reason for their death and displayed the vicious characteristics they exhibited in life.[37] By reanimating the animal, taxidermy linked the kill with the hunter's masculine prowess. Hunters viewed taxidermists as essential to conveying the spirit of their exploits, and in some cases, mere stuffing failed to provide sufficient realism. Ward developed a process, referred to as Wardian taxidermy, whereby he mounted an animal skin on a model base. This offered him greater manipulation of detail in highlighting the subtleties of expression and gesture.[38] Taxidermists sought to understand the animal's habitat, and in museum exhibits they recreated the landscape of the colonial frontier within the safe confines of British museums. The hunter and the taxidermist collaborated in the cultural appropriation of nature: controlling, reinventing, and redeploying the colonial frontier complete with ferocious wildlife.

The process of trophy appropriation objectified antlers, horns, and skins as specimens, while also imbuing them with masculine meaning. The process of objectification reduced animals to trophies that rendered standardized game statistics. Instead of conceiving game as living, breathing animals, trophies, skins, and horns existed as quantifiable objects. Trophy objectification allowed hunters to assess, correlate, and contrast their kills against those of other sportsmen. Hunters focused on the number of points on deer antlers, for example, an indicator of the age and virility of their male prey. During the later nineteenth century, the emphasis on statistics continued, with hunters distinguishing themselves through exactness of their trophy measurements. The process of measuring itself became a quality respected within the hunting fraternity. Among hunters, measuring reinforced the importance of exactitude and honesty. Some hunters sought to combine aesthetic appraisals of their trophies alongside quantitative measurements. This identified hunters as possessing a discriminating elite taste, distinguishing their bag by both beauty and by the number of points. Qualitative and aesthetic measures produced angst for some, as they failed to offer a fixed and verifiable means of comparison.[39]

British hunters expressed periodic regret and, on these rare occasions, allowed their game to revert from object to subject status. In these instances, the rugged and manly hunter revealed his compassion and humanity. One downtrodden hunter wrote, "There was too much slaughter, and [my] conscience rather reproached me."[40] Another observed the *coup de grâce* in vivid Shakespearean terms. "He [the deer] was so near me that I could see his eyes quite plainly, and it seemed to me that they were full of a dreadful terror – the terror which unnerved Macbeth at the apparition of Banquo's ghost."[41] Some hunters engaged in broader philosophical examinations of the hunt within their narratives. Carnegie wondered in his travel narrative about the consequences of his actions when hunting buffalo. "Still there is something repugnant to the feelings in carrying death and anguish on so large a scale amongst beautiful inoffensive animals. One thinks little – too little – of the killing of small game, but in shooting large game the butchery of the act comes more home, one sees with such vividness the wounds, and the fear, and the suffering. But it does not do to look at things too narrowly – one grows morbid – and no thinking will ever bring one

3.2 "Head of a Cabree." Trophy heads like this highlighted the masculine prowess of the British hunter. James Carnegie, *Saskatchewan and the Rocky Mountains: A Diary and Narrative of Travel, Sport, and Adventure, in* 1859 *and* 1860 (Edinburgh: Edmonston and Douglas, 1875), 83.

to the root of the matter."[42] Selous, the more experienced veteran hunter, communicated his reflection in anti-modern terms: "Did I feel sorry for what I had done, it may be asked? Well! No I did not. Ten thousand years of superficial and unsatisfying civilization have not altered the fundamental nature of man, and the successful hunter of today becomes a primeval savage, remorseless, triumphant, full of a wild exultant joy, none but those who have lived in the wilderness and depended on their success as hunters for their daily food, can ever know or comprehend."[43] Although hunters rarely considered the devastation wrought by their sport, they ensured that their game regained its object status as either a specimen, trophy, or meat so the hunt could continue anew.

British elites displayed their trophies on the walls of their upper-class homes and country estates. Graham sought a buffalo head to hang proudly in his estate in Cumberland, England. He wrote, "got among the buffalo. I opened ... by flooring an old bull with 'Kill-bull,' [his rifle] and took his head for Netherby."[44] For British hunters like Graham, trophy heads, skins, and horns embodied the totality of the British imperial experience and reveal a process of cultural signification (Figure 3.2, also see Figure 4.3,

p. 74). Trophies signified the hunter's masculinity, class, and social privilege to engage in the elite ritual of the hunt. They signified the dominance of imperial culture and the subordination of non-white cultures. Trophy heads symbolized the foreign service offered by the elite towards the advancement of the British empire. They signified the advanced technology and scientific progress of industrial society through natural history. They signified the appropriation and exploitation of colonial resources. Indeed, static, immovable trophies merely served to underscore the appropriation and violence of imperialism.[45] The visualization of the trophy in the country home, with its many and varied cultural significations, stoked the imperial mentality. Through ostentatious display of their trophies, as a form of interior decoration, the socio-economic elite of British society captured the essence and substance of hunting and imperial appropriation during the mid- to late nineteenth century.

The requisition of hunting trophies and their display by the upper classes reveals an emphasis on collection as well as objectification. British hunters amassed hunting trophies whose rarity and practical uselessness ultimately drew attention to their class status and the social and economic position of the hunter.[46] Some hunters exhibited a collecting impulse that likely grew from the natural history craze during the nineteenth century but also served as a representation of their own personal role in the appropriation of colonial territories. Some hunters collected all the game from a specific region or collected both sexes of the animals in a given area. Some personal trophy collections, like that of hunter Selous, rivalled those of leading natural history museums.

The collection of trophies, as well as the size of the trophies, testified to the hunters' masculine prowess. Hunters measured horns and antlers meticulously. They sketched their trophies and compared them to the kills of their Native companions and to the recorded kills of fellow British hunters in published hunting books. These comparisons reveal feelings not only of competitiveness but also of inferiority and insecurity among British hunters – to these men, trophy size mattered. Carnegie seemed particularly focused on the quality and size of his trophies compared to those of his fellow hunters. He wrote, "an admiring contemplation of the beautiful [ram] horns carried by Antoine's [his guide] sheep made me anxious to get some other specimens to match them."[47] Later in his narrative, he referred to the travel book *Solitary Rambles of a Hunter in the Prairies* by Captain John Palliser and compared the horns of his ram with those of the British hunter-explorer.[48]

This attitude towards trophies changed along with the hunting code during the later nineteenth century. The emphasis on distinguishing one's trophy based on both qualitative and quantitative measures heightened dramatically with the application of hunting laws in the colonies and the general decline of game as a result of overshooting. But while measurements and their relative importance evolved throughout the nineteenth century, the criteria of size remained a hallmark and related directly to the strength and prowess of the hunter. Carnegie noted his success relative to his hunting companions and how they admired his bag of game. He wrote, "my own success I considered very satisfactory. I had picked out from an immense herd a bull with a head that everybody admired ... I had killed one ... which was acknowledged to surpass any animal shot by the hunters at either encampment."[49] Although big-game hunters sought trophies for their own personal collection, they shot additional trophies to bestow upon women. Viscount William Milton and Dr. Francis Cheadle conducted their sport hoping they might secure trophies for the "fair sex at home."[50] The violence required to secure these trophies, and their connection to the prowess of the hunter, positioned them as manly and courageous. Hunters used this cultural currency in their travel writing to validate their virility and authority.

British hunters gave human personalities to their prey, and in some cases these characteristics validated their destruction. Hunters identified game that provided good sport with characteristics they associated with themselves, such as nobility, pluck, courage, and boldness.[51] Anthropomorphizing trophies reveals a fascinating cultural process of construction, consumption, and reconstruction of game. British hunters used their culture to construct and designate game appropriate for their social class: elite gamesmen hunted first-class game only. The important process here relates to consumption: by consuming noble animals, big-game hunters symbolically consumed the virtues they attributed to their game. Hunters then reconstructed trophies based on these same qualities. This process of anthropomorphization resulted in the construction of human-like, class-based game before death; the reversion to object status for the kill, trophy appropriation, and/or consumption as meat; and the reconstruction through taxidermy of those same pre-death qualities to valorize the hunter's prowess.

Much like the red deer in Great Britain, the moose provides an example of the British hunter's anthropomorphism of game. British hunters identified with the work of artist Sir Edwin Landseer, especially his widely acclaimed painting *Monarch of the Glen* (1851).[52] Landseer's painting depicts a broadly antlered deer stag against a sublime background of the windswept Highland landscape in Scotland. Landseer depicted the stag as a noble, powerful, independent, and sexually dominant animal because the stag held special class resonance amongst the British and European elite.[53] The red deer represented nobility but also became an associated feature of the Scottish Highland estate. Across nineteenth-century Canada, British hunters referred to the moose as the Monarch of the Forest.[54] Many big-game hunters desired a broad set of moose antlers – a much-sought-after trophy. Like the red deer of Scotland, hunters associated the moose with the Canadian forest landscape. The size of the creature, its great antlers, and the evocative autumn hunting technique referred to as "calling the moose" endeared the sport to British hunters.[55] By referring to the moose as the Monarch of the Forest, British hunters made an explicit association with their social class and Landseer's famous painting. These associations endowed the moose with similar cultural significations to construct elite game suited to the hunters' discriminating taste. Rather than the noble red deer within a misty Highland landscape, British hunters considered the tall, stately moose, set against the dark primeval Canadian forest. By constructing game with elitist cultural significations, and thereby populating colonial sporting landscapes with the "right sort" of game, British hunters constructed the colonial moose with a sense of cultural familiarity and class exclusivity, much like the red deer in Scotland or the tiger in India.[56]

Ironically, hunters rarely made explicit reference to meat as the ultimate by-product of their imperial sport. They sought to distance themselves from the meat-hunting activities of commercial poachers and subsistence pothunters. If British hunters had highlighted meat consumption, they would have likened themselves to lower-class gunners – an unthinkable act. Despite their denial, however, the elite hunt included two essential elements: the ritual of the chase and, most important, the ritual of meat consumption. Indeed, if hunting rests at the centre of the imperial experience, meat eating rests at the centre of hunting.

We rarely scrutinize the interconnectedness of, and the cultural meanings produced by, hunting, meat eating, and masculinity. So ingrained are these concepts in Western culture that the idea of the great white British vegetarian seems inconceivable. This speaks to the social entrenchment of these concepts and their cultural constructedness. Similar to the process of trophy appropriation, the objectification of game both during the kill and after death made the consumption of meat possible. Objectification removed the issues of death and butchery from meat. Objectifying game made the killing of animals acceptable and reduced them to a sanitized and abstracted cut of meat. By renaming meat to conjure cuisine, rather than butchered animals, game became referents, signifiers of the hunter's masculine prowess in the hunt.[57] The evocation of maleness for upper-class British hunters rests on the interconnection of hunting, meat eating, and masculinity.[58]

British hunters imbued meat possession and consumption with meaning. Meat consumption remained the crowning, celebratory ritual of big-game hunting, but gentleman hunters walked a paradoxical line between the need for consumption and the need for celebration. On one hand, they deemed the consumption of their kill improvident and below their social class, and on the other viewed the practical uselessness of trophy hunting as provident.[59] Although hunters displayed their masculinity during the chase, the reward of consumption and control of meat related to masculinity and class. The spoils remained in the hands of the victor, and through the division of spoils, meat produced other meanings. Hunters constructed and used meat as a cultural currency. Through the distribution of spoils to their entourage and Native peoples, hunters displayed their noblesse oblige, which was as important as meat consumption. By distributing meat, British hunters drew attention to their social rank and their beneficence to the lower orders. Hunters used meat as a symbol of British dominance, and its presentation to groups deemed their social and racial inferiors served to reaffirm the class and racial divide they created. With every bloody meal, British hunters reinscribed their racial, class, and gender superiority. Within the cultural confines of big-game hunting, meat served as a means of social and cultural control.

The provision of meat held class-based meanings. Only second-class citizens ate second-class, meatless meals. From the perspective of the upper class, only the lower classes could conceive of a meatless meal. For the social elite, grouse, pheasant, chicken, and beef adorned every plate and signified the social status of its consumers. The importance of meat lay in the symbolic act of consumption. Men ate meat but real men hunted and killed their own meat. Real men hunted and ate big game.[60] British hunters ate red meat, and the rarer and bloodier the better. They consumed red meat voraciously and in as many different forms as possible: ground, sliced, ribs, rump, and steaks.[61] Hunters also signified their social class through conspicuous meat consumption. Hunters ate only the best cuts of meat and left behind lesser meat. After killing a large buffalo stag, one hunter wrote, "we took his *depouilles* [skin] and tongue, and left some thousand pounds of good meat to the wolves."[62] By wasting large quantities of meat, big-game hunters drew attention to their ostentatious affluence, noble privilege, and largesse. Wastefulness drew sharp attention to social status.

Meat eating and the ability to provide meat formed the foundation of the hunters' sense of masculinity. Highly carnivorous, British hunters extolled the value of meat eating. Meat eating enhanced their masculinity and provided them with the sustenance required to conduct their manly activities. Hunters believed in a "law of meat" that provided them with strength and vigour.[63] The hunters believed men needed meat for physical strength. If they ate the muscle and sinew of strong animals, they themselves became strong – akin to the process of anthropomorphization discussed earlier. Men achieved a level of masculinity by consuming meals that imperial hunting culture constructed as masculine.[64] For them, meat provision and consumption linked directly to the masculine activity of hunting; just as the ability to provide meat signified social class, hunting and supplying meat signified male prowess and virility. Meat provision and consumption lay central to hunting masculinity.

British big-game hunters who hunted in the western interior of Rupert's Land aspired to a specific imperial hunter-explorer masculine archetype modelled by Gordon Cumming (1820-66) and Frederick Selous (1851-1917) – the two most well-known imperial big-game hunters in the British empire during the nineteenth century.

The second son of minor nobility, Roualeyn George Gordon Cumming grew up in Elginshire and spent his life in the military and as a big-game hunter-explorer. Cumming developed a passion for sport during his days at the Eton public school. At the age of eighteen, he was a subaltern in the Madras Light Cavalry of the East India Company, later serving in Africa before initiating five hunting campaigns into the African interior between 1843-48. He returned to England in 1848 and wrote *Five Years of a Hunter; Life in the Far Interior of South Africa* (1850). A much heralded sporting narrative, and widely read during his time, *Five Years of a Hunter* combined big-game hunting, natural history, and exploration. Subsequent editions were published posthumously throughout the nineteenth century and as late as 1904.

Frederick Selous began his education at the Rugby public school. At the age of nineteen, he travelled to Africa and spent the better part of 1872-92 hunting big game and exploring the continent. Selous started his hunting career as a commercial hunter, then turned to collecting specimens for natural history museums in the 1870s and 1880s. Of modest birth, Selous elevated himself into the ranks of the social elite through his hunting prowess and contributions to scientific progress. During the 1890s, Selous fought in several South African conflicts and settled in England by 1896. In addition to stories and notes in publications like the *Geographical Journal* and *Field*, Selous wrote numerous travel narratives that combined sport, exploration, and natural history: *A Hunter's Wanderings in Africa* (1881), *Travel and Adventure in South-East Africa* (1893), *Sunshine and Storm in Rhodesia* (1896), *Sport and Travel in the East and West* (1900), *Recent Hunting Trips in British North America* (1907), and *African Nature Notes and Reminiscences* (1908). Following Cumming's example, Selous used his books, trophy collection, and lectures to validate and publicize his prowess. In his narratives, Selous expanded on kills that emphasized risk and violence, reaffirming his dominance over noble game. Selous developed a museum of his own trophies at his house in Worplesdon, England, and he connected explicitly the result of his hunting exploits to the advancement of British colonial expansion and colonization of Africa.[65]

British men emulated the powerful masculine images projected by Cumming and Selous. Less prolific Victorian gamesmen and stay-at-home imperialists looked to Cumming and Selous as skilled and courageous masculine role models.[66] Nineteenth-century fiction author H. Rider Haggard, for example, used Selous as inspiration for his popular imperial adventurer-hero character Allan Quartermain.[67] British men idealized them for their prowess as hunters but also for the manner in which they wrote and conveyed their experiences in their narratives. British big-game hunters lionized both the travelling etiquette and style employed by Cumming and Selous. Their prowess and bravery in hunting and in the British military added to their reputations as icons of British imperialism and as the consummate sporting gentlemen.[68] On returning from their trips, they wrote multiple travel books documenting their manly exploits and took transportable trophy displays on a lecture circuit to further celebrate their successes as the vanguard of Britain.[69] Similarly, other hunters wrote books and lectured, communicating and celebrating specific masculine images interwoven with gender codes, expectations, and the ever-present concepts of duty, imperialism, and empire.

Cumming used his African expeditions to create a profitable reputation, marketing himself as the "Lion-Slayer." When he returned to England during the late 1840s, he carried over thirty tons of trophies from Africa.[70] Cumming used his trophies as testimony of his hunting prowess, and imperialists heralded him as the greatest hunter of his time. In addition to his hunting narratives, he used a trophy circuit to popularize his reputation. He reinforced to readers and lecture audiences the extraordinarily terrifying beasts he hunted and killed, and the feats of strength and intelligence required to slay them. During this early phase of exploration in Africa, Cumming rarely adhered to the sporting code. He admitted to shooting two sleeping rhinos from the saddle.[71] Cumming shot into herds, he shot females, he shot at long range, he shot at water holes at night, he shot to lame instead of kill, and he listened to the death throes of his prey.[72]

If imperialists considered Cumming the greatest hunter in the British empire, they viewed Frederick Courtenay Selous as his protégé. Selous also transgressed the code of the sportsmen, but in a different manner from Cumming: Selous hunted during a later period, when game stocks started decreasing during the second half of the nineteenth century, and the code became increasingly important. With the moral high ground of scientific progress firmly beneath him, Selous disregarded the guidelines of the hunting code and killed game to advance the field of natural history. For his lifetime of accomplishments, the Natural History Museum in South Kensington, England, erected a bronze statue of Selous to immortalize one of the greatest hunters of the British empire.[73] Africans also honoured Selous, ironically by naming a game reserve in Tanzania after him.

British hunters constructed themselves within the archetype of the imperial hunter as set forth by Cumming and Selous. The archetypical big-game hunter, or Nimrod, demonstrated, over the course of his narrative, enterprising qualities such as independence, loyalty to God (most hunters observed the Sabbath during their expeditions), and the British empire. Bold, dashing, and disciplined, the imperial Nimrod also possessed the style, grace, and etiquette of his social class. He possessed wit, a sense of adventure, eternal optimism, and courage in the face of danger. The great white hunter was young, able, adventurous, hardy, brave, resolute, and skilled. He exuded poise, self-possession, and calm. He possessed a broad knowledge of science, geography, hunting, British sporting etiquette, and he formed part of a larger class-based culture of imperial big-game hunters.

Narrating the ritual of the hunt to the hunters' best advantage required literary style and grace. In order to present themselves within the imperial hunter archetype, British hunters situated the hunt as a thrilling and exceptionally dangerous sport involving vicious wild beasts only they possessed the qualities to overcome – a literary strategy employed by British fur traders for decades before them.[74] Hunters like Graham made sure readers understood how the buffalo made "the earth tremble" with their "galloping and roaring" and how they "shook the prairie." He highlighted their courage through brief, terse statements that circumvented any thought of intimidation. Graham used simple yet emphatic comments like, "the open plain to the left, black with animals" or "saw buffalo in herds upon herds all day." On one occasion, he pulled out his double-barrelled muzzle-loading rifle he named "Kill-Bull" and went to work. His comments suggested brevity, bloodlessness, and control. Graham commented matter-of-factly, "a very large band. Ran them, killed twelve fat cows." Another element of this dangerous activity included the holes of prairie dogs that dotted the landscape. When the British hunters were running buffalo at top speed, these holes presented potentially life-threatening obstacles, and the hunters made sure to inform readers of the danger. Graham observed, "a large wooded plain perfectly covered with buffalo for miles and miles ... the ground frightfully dangerous from badger holes, and the dust so thick that we were blinded before we had run half a mile."[75]

British hunters positioned themselves within the exhilarating and life-threatening sporting landscapes of the western interior. Just like Cumming and Selous, the hunt provided them with an opportunity to comment unabashedly on their own hunting prowess. Graham congratulated himself, stating that he had "stalked a herd, picked out a cow, and placed two balls behind the shoulder ... a very sporting shot."[76] Carnegie wrote, "my own success I considered very satisfactory. I had picked out from an immense herd a bull with a head that everybody admired; and, besides shooting several good cows, I had killed one – the fine barren cow that Morgan had out-raced so gallantly."[77] Other important elements of an exhilarating sporting experience included presenting their willingness to dash off into harm's way. "Took 'Kill-Bull' out of the cover, and put caps on, and as all the party seemed shy, McKenzie and I dashed off towards them."[78] The hunters reiterated the omnipresence of Native war parties and the necessity of avoiding them in the midst of their sport. "This lake is rarely visited, on account of the danger, and from what I hear, no white man has ever been there. I expect great sport, and hope to dodge the war-parties."[79] Of all the examples of buffalo hunting, Milton and Cheadle captured the essence of the sport and the ways through which British hunters used the opportunity to establish and reaffirm their authority. "Buffalo running is certainly a most fascinating sport. The wild charge together into the thick of the herd, the pursuit of the animal selected from the band, which a well-trained horse follows and turns as a greyhound courses a hare; the spice of danger in it from the charge of a wounded animal, or a fall from the holes so numerous on the prairies, contrive to render it extremely interesting."[80] Their description encapsulated the menacing size of the herd, the thrill of the charge, the extreme skill, strength, and courage required, the bravery needed to withstand a charge of a wounded bull, and the dexterity to avoid prairie holes. Each of these elements served to reinforce the British hunters' construction of self within the archetype of the imperial hunter and empire builder, as set forth by Cumming and Selous in the mid-nineteenth century.

Big-game hunters who travelled to the British North American frontier hired Native men and Métis "half breeds" as hunting guides. Without guides who possessed local knowledge to advise them and direct the hunt, British hunters met with little success. In addition to their own personal servants, they filled out their entourage by hiring Native men and women to cook, carry, and set up camp. Consider, for example, Carnegie's 1859 entourage in the western interior while he was travelling with the well-known fur trader and Scotsman Sir George Simpson on his journey west. In addition to Carnegie and Simpson, the company consisted of Mr. Hopkins (Simpson's secretary), and Mr. Cameron (an officer in the Hudson's Bay Company's service). There were four attendants: James Murray (Simpson's servant and a Shetland Highlander), Duncan Robertson (a Perthshire Highlander, who served as Carnegie's gamekeeper at home in Scotland), and Baptist and Toma, two Iroquois voyageurs employed by Simpson as canoe men on previous expeditions to the Red River Settlement.[81]

British hunters found little game without the skills of their Native and Métis guides. They acknowledged repeatedly the tracking and animal-calling prowess of their companions. In some cases, big-game hunters relied on their guides for the totality of their colonial expedition – the guides took them into the bush or onto the plains, led them to their prey (and in some cases drove their prey to them), and led the hunters out again with trophies intact. The British hunter was both dependent on and vulnerable to his Native or Métis guide.[82] To British hunters, an accomplished guide resembled one of their domestic servants.[83] A good servant demonstrated competence, dependability, and an understanding of his lower-class position relative to his employer. To the guides, the British hunter represented an economic opportunity. As the nineteenth century advanced and game laws that excluded Native and Métis from hunting and fishing were introduced, guiding became increasingly important for their economic survival. Guiding paid well in relation to other forms of wage labour. Both pushed and pulled into the profession, these men asserted their own agency within the sport hunting industry and developed reputations for their skill.[84]

British hunters hoped their guides would lead them to "good sport." Good sport meant several things but always included an opportunity for the hunter to test his personal mettle one on one with the stalked animal.

3.3 "Our Party across the Mountains." Milton, Cheadle, their guide, and his family. William Fitzwilliam Milton and W.B. Cheadle, *North-West Passage by Land* (London: Cassell, Petter, Galpin, 1875), frontispiece.

This required that he confront and defeat danger in the form of ferocious big game. The quality of the sport depended ultimately on the animal and the degree of immediate personal danger posed to the hunter. By testing his mettle, the sportsman cultivated moral improvement, built character, and combated effeminacy in young British men. Good sport allowed the hunter to display deadly aggression.[85] Expeditions in search of good sport went awry occasionally and, unable to feed themselves, British hunters resorted to slaughtering their horses to stay alive. After an extremely hard trek across the Rocky Mountains in the 1850s, Milton, Cheadle, and their Native guide, whom they called "the Assiniboine," resorted to killing their horse Blackie when their hunt failed.[86] Milton and Cheadle both shirked the responsibility of killing their equine companion until the Assiniboine finally dispatched the horse with a quick shot.[87]

Examining the experience of Native and Métis guides and their relationship with British hunters is a difficult task. The information gleaned from British hunting narratives reveals more about the racial and cultural predispositions of British hunters than about the guides.[88] The central problem relates to roles within the narrative. British hunters wrote their guides into their narratives, but not as central figures – they used this rhetorical strategy to place their guides on the periphery of the reader's experience. In this sense, readers learn about guides only when the British

hunters allowed. While piecing together the experiences of Native and
Métis guides appears daunting, an array of published narratives written by
British hunters exists that reveal insight into their experiences. Together
these narratives provide detail and offer entry points into the role and
agency of Native guides and their relationship with British sportsmen
(Figure 3.3).

Elite hunters believed the character of indigenous guides varied little
within the empire's colonies. They viewed their guides as lazy, insubordinate,
primitive, and without restraint.[89] To British hunters the limited, broken, or
incorrect English of their guides only reaffirmed the cultural inadequacies
of Native peoples. Native or Métis men greeted each other with bonjour
as "bo jour," they used "mebbe" for maybe, and "praps" for perhaps.[90] In
some narratives, guides reveal no voice whatsoever. By highlighting their
cultural naiveté, hunters demonstrated Native impotence in the face of
British colonization and industrial civilization. This set Native and Métis
men firmly within their restricted roles as domestic servants in the sport-
hunting industry.[91]

Big-game hunters viewed Native and Métis peoples as a culture on
the verge of extinction. The hunters' belief in their racial superiority, the
civilizing process, and the moral crusade of Christianity influenced how
they interacted with Native people and understood their culture. Even
when hunters praised the ability, strength, or attitudes of their guides,
they matter-of-factly presented Native culture as descendant in the face
of British colonization. Big-game hunter and explorer William Butler
believed strongly in the inevitable extinction of the North American Indian
and "half-breeds." These people, he wrote, were "destined to disappear
before the white man's footprint."[92] He added that doctors may "differ as
to what he is, or who he is, or whence he came," but nonetheless "the red
man withers and dies out before our gaze: soon they will have nothing but
the skulls to lecture upon."[93] Some British hunters, so convinced of the
inevitable extinction of the North American Indian, objectified Native
culture like any other aspect of the colonial landscape. They sought to
collect everyday Native tools and implements as artifacts or souvenirs of
the soon-to-be-extinct culture. During the late 1850s, Carnegie included
numerous sketches of Cree artifacts he collected, including a Red River
fire bag, patterned beadwork, a whip, an Assiniboine pipe and stem, and
a decorative knife sheath.[94]

The longer elite British men sat at their desks surrounded by paperwork,
the more they craved the manly exercise provided by colonial big-game
hunting. British hunters engaged in big-game hunting because they drew

a number of class-based and often contradictory meanings from the sport. On one hand, big-game hunting provided an anti-modern wilderness escape from the effeminacy of urban society. On the other hand, the sport offered a means to express their modernist preoccupation with science and the advancement of natural history. In both cases, the hunters used their elite hunting code to position their activities in specific ways. By hunting game through techniques they claimed minimized suffering and emphasized preservation and conservation, British big-game hunters constructed themselves as compassionate and humane. Through the discourse of science, these men used the hunting code to legitimize their trophy appropriation and butchery of game. British hunters also mediated class relations and through their hunting methods demarcated themselves from their Native guides and colonial potshooters. Their class-based code of masculine honour served to construct their imperial whiteness and class position, but also to exclude and limit access to game and resources. In these ways, the code of imperial big-game hunting emphasized the "modest warrant" of the hunters – as expressed by William Shakespeare at the opening of this chapter – instead of those instances when they cried havoc and gave in to the irrationality of the hunt.

4

The Science of the Hunt:
Map Making, Natural History,
and Acclimatization

THROUGH THE CREATION OF MAPS, the application of natural history, and the acclimatization of wildlife, British hunters constructed an anticipatory geography of colonization in the western interior. Maps and natural history allowed British hunters to chart and systematize the land. Based on scientific and other cultural codes of representation, the hunters' maps identified the resources of the colony for the British empire. They created space by erasing existing cultural formations while projecting a new settlement geography.[1] In addition to mapping, they used the science of natural history to catalogue and systematize flora and fauna. By applying the Linnaean system of Latin nomenclature, British hunter-explorers used natural history to extract plants and animals from their environments and christen them with new scientific names. They invoked the Linnaean system in a larger process of cultural signification – plants and animals became symbols of imperial possession and proprietorship. Through maps and natural history, hunters naturalized their colonial images as familiar, and most importantly, as British. Both maps and the Linnaean system suggest Ornamentalist processes designed to apprehend and represent unfamiliar lands through a discursive negotiation of similarity and difference. These men also advocated the physical exchange of wildlife, or acclimatization, between England and the western interior.

As much as their rifles and pistols, imperialists used maps as weapons in their cultural appropriation of the western interior. Rather than viewing maps as a set of objective scientific or geographical "facts," maps are cultural constructs. Maps provide an image of a culture's relationship with land

and reveal a discourse of control.[2] Like literary or pictorial constructions of landscape, maps are cultural texts that illustrate the process of cultural appropriation.[3] When framed within familiar modes of understanding, the map-as-text facilitated the construction and dissemination of imperial space (and the need to appropriate that space continuously) to the British public. These representations formed the controllable and communicable images of the British empire. By taking possession of terrain on paper, maps preceded exploitation and colonization: maps anticipated empire.[4] The construction of maps highlighted the indispensable nature of cultural symbolism in the establishment of imperial authority.[5] What imperialists failed to appropriate physically, they appropriated symbolically through their imperial culture. Only those who possessed the cultural construction of space through maps possessed the physical space represented. For imperialists, the map breathed life into their empire and facilitated the key phases of imperial possession-taking, such as exploration, appropriation, exploitation, and colonization. Maps allowed for the control of the periphery from the safe confines of the imperial metropole. A fundamental precept of empire during the nineteenth century was the use of maps to construct and control the geography of the British empire geopolitically.[6]

Maps drip with the discourse of scientific positivism. British hunters used the tenets of positivism to construct an absolute Cartesian space. They viewed space as fixed through coordinates of latitude and longitude. Through geographical and scientific methods they denied their subjective role in the construction of maps and thereby privileged the objectivity and truth value of their constructions. Map making and positivism reinforced each other and denied that non-scientific or non-objective methods were used in their construction. By supporting their maps with facts constructed through the discourse of science and modern technology, British hunters appeared transparent and objective. Cartographic epistemology centred on the transparency of the map maker, who acted as an unbiased medium for the collection of objective cartographic knowledge.[7] Constructed through objective means, imperialists at home viewed maps and cartographic information as both positive and comprehensive. They saw maps as a collection of facts or individual pieces of positive knowledge. These pieces of information appeared both objective and verifiable and led to a belief in the broad applicability and comprehensiveness of knowledge. Comprehensive knowledge emphasized absolutism, not plurality, completeness over partialness, and universalism over regionalism or locality.[8]

The term "verisimilitude," defined as the appearance of truth, or possessing the quality of appearing truthful, best describes the purpose of maps. Viewing maps with this in mind prompts scrutiny of the inevitable cultural selectivity contained within the cartographic process. By sifting through the layers of positivist discourse, careful examination of maps as cultural texts reveals their ideological, political, economic, and appropriative intentions – viewing maps as simple depictions of facts ignores their complex textuality. Maps exist as texts of possession, and imperialists used maps to validate and legitimize their appropriation of land.[9] These texts constructed the way in which imperialists like big-game hunters applied their imperial culture to colonial space. Maps functioned as appropriative constructs, but only human agents such as big-game hunters, fur traders, and other imperialists imbued maps with meaning.

Any critical appraisal of maps must deny their commonsense foundational assumptions and intended scientific positivism.[10] The authority of the map rests in its perceived ability to represent an objective, fixed space. Yet they fail to represent space in such a simplistic way; they exist as geopolitical abstractions of imperial appropriation.[11] Map readers typically accept the commonsense methods and codes for representing space, such as shading for elevation or colouring for vegetation, as "true" when viewing maps. Indeed, maps establish authority in their taken-for-grantedness. The application of cartographic codes for elevation, vegetation, resources, and landmarks ensures that the reader conceptualizes the map as a real, fixed, and identifiable space.[12] Cultural codes provide a set of interrelated indexes that reinforce meaning, unity, and the truth value of maps. By examining maps as discursive tools, or as weapons of imperialism, we can scrutinize their assertions of accuracy and truth in the construction of space.

Maps represent an extension of the appropriative, proprietary gaze of imperialism. They emphasize appropriated space, but they also possess a temporal quality and look forward into time.[13] This temporal view glances ahead of the imperial appropriation by highlighting exploitable resources and the future potential of the landscape for colonization. By privileging an elevated viewer position, maps also exert other forms of authority. Looking down on space distances the reader from the processes of dispossession. The reader views himself as a non-invasive observer enjoying an innocent, disinterested overview of colonial landscape brought together as a coordinated set of geographical facts. Alongside the commanding top-down overview or macro view of space, maps present a micro or closer view of specific landmarks and toponyms to distinguish the character of the space appropriated.[14] However, while maps represent constructed "realities," maps on their own cannot make such a claim in an unmediated way. Maps fail to provide a complete outline of any space. Only through symbolism can a map allege any relationship to land – the epistemological basis of representational cartography requires the cultural construct of the map in order to appropriate the cultural construct of the seen.[15] The perceived relational claim of positivism between the construct and the seen attested to the scientific authority of the map.

Big-game hunters used their maps to construct an anticipatory geography with a self-legitimizing view of space. The anticipatory geography of the frontier consisted of a geographical space of measurable and divisible components that imperial positivist science and superior technology could identify, classify, and exploit. Their sense of superiority and entitlement dispossessed Native peoples of the land by highlighting their inability to identify or exploit the material resources that advanced imperial culture recognized immediately as exploitable and profitable.[16] The creation of new positive knowledge through maps contributed to the construction of a scientifically accurate geography for the colonial frontier, which in turn allowed for the production of a set of verifiable place images that imperial culture packaged and disseminated to readerships in England through hunting and exploration narratives. British hunters used maps and positivism to bring their anticipatory geography into focus – a clear vision of the landscape depended on both geographical reconnaissance, presented in the form of travel writing and maps, and on scientific discourse such as natural history.[17] Imperial administrators and British diplomats then used these cultural constructions of space to appropriate colonial territories on paper.[18] Their appropriation established control of the anticipatory geography of imperialism rather than the physical colonial geography in the form of rocks and trees. The construction of the British empire unfolded as much on paper as anywhere else.

Much like the early maps of Rupert's Land constructed by the Hudson's Bay Company, big-game hunters imbued their cartographic representations with legions of messages, meanings, and symbols that paid close attention to available resources.[19] Hunters charted colonial resources whenever possible. They noted the presence of gold along the banks of the Saskatchewan River and branded specific regions with terms like "Rich Soil and Fine Pasture." Just as important, they labelled uncharted or unidentified regions as "Unexplored" – a direct affront to the appropriative westward gaze of imperialists.[20] Other labels identified vast tracts of land simply as "The Great Plains," or "The Great Forest."[21] Hunter James Carnegie even took the time to label the "Valleys for the First Time

Explored" by him on his map, reaffirming the interest of imperialists to peer into every colonial corner.[22] Each of these acknowledgments hinted at the potential for resource exploitation, colonization, and further exploration. The hunting and exploration maps also displayed the author's route as he blazed a trail across his colonial frontier.[23] During the mid-nineteenth century, hunter-explorer William Butler identified the approximate locations of Native peoples on his maps, such as the "Beaver," "Cree," "Chipewyan," "Black Feet," and "Assiniboine."[24] Wherever possible, they noted abandoned Hudson's Bay Company outposts, fur trading houses, and forts, such as "Ft. Pitt" on the North Saskatchewan River, "Edmonton House," or "Ft. Carleton," or they used simple generic references like "Old H.B. Post."[25] British hunters also highlighted British and French colonial history in the region by noting geographical features or places like "Portage la Loche," "Qu'appelle Fort," or "Isle a la Crosse House."[26] Of course, Butler noted the English alternatives to French place names and rivers whenever possible.[27] Some maps highlighted the Christian missions set up throughout the West, such as the "Qu'appelle Mission," "Nipowewin Ch. Mission," "Wesleyan Mission," and "St. Albert R.C. Mission."[28]

Hunters outlined key portages, portage lengths, the locations of rapids, and identified, described, and pictured key landmarks in their narratives, like the "Forks of the Athabasca River" or the "Height of Land."[29] They constructed enough space to outline the history of their expedition and enclosed all of these points of detail within a homogenizing grid of latitude and longitude. This grid allowed readers to identify the exact position of the western interior from the Prime Meridian (zero degrees), located at the geographical centre of the world – Greenwich, England. British hunters also used their maps to convert colonial spaces into English miles. Bracketed by borders and grids, the unknown blank spaces were incorporated as known, enabling the British hunters to set up future incursions while displaying their possession of space. With their maps properly bordered, ordered, and rendered homogeneous, the hunters signified their colonial space by highlighting names and places illustrative of British colonial history. Made benign through imperial mapping practices, occasional Native and French place names merely added a sense of past otherness to the new, and secure, British colonial landscape.

The application of Anglo-Christian toponyms to maps and colonial spaces reveals the hunters' proprietary vision of the frontier. Indeed, the naming of landscape features with familiar British place names formed the centrepiece of imperial map making during the nineteenth century. They

4.1 "Mount Dalhousie, North River Valley." Carnegie christened Mount Dalhousie, Alberta, after his friend the 11th Earl of Dalhousie. James Carnegie, *Saskatchewan and the Rocky Mountains: A Diary and Narrative of Travel, Sport, and Adventure, in* 1859 *and* 1860 (Edinburgh: Edmonston and Douglas, 1875), frontispiece.

reveal the appropriative process through which British hunters attempted to remake the land in their image. For them, place naming took on a personal dimension as they named landmarks after themselves and other upper-class men, such as British royalty, military figures, and political leaders.[30] During his excursion to hunt the buffalo in 1859, Carnegie named a peak in the foothills of the Rocky Mountains after himself. As he entered the region, he wrote, "I am the first European who has visited this valley," and that he wished "the geographical honour of giving my name to some spot of earth." Carnegie climbed his mountain, and once at the top constructed a stone cairn to commemorate his territorial conquest. He added that his construction was "a sort of rough tower, or cairn, some six feet high, on the highest and most commanding point, as a memorial of our visit." Having immortalized his triumph in the form of "Southesk's Cairn," an edifice that symbolically "commanded" the surrounding landscape, he noted, "I have therefore taken leave to designate [the mountain] on the maps by my own name, as raiser of the cairn that crowns its summit." After naming the first peak after himself, Carnegie named mountains nearby after Sir Coutts Lindsay (Baronet of Balcarres) and Lord Panmure (11th Earl of Dalhousie) (Figure 4.1) who first suggested Carnegie travel to British North America for a rest-cure and colonial big-game hunting.[31]

Travelling for sport, exploration, and adventure across the Rocky Mountains, Viscount William Fitzwilliam Milton and Dr. Francis Cheadle named numerous landscape features after themselves. Their map entitled *The Western Portion of British North America* reveals Mount Milton, Mount Fitzwilliam, Mount Cheadle, and Mount Bingley.[32] Milton and Cheadle also named other features, such as Mount St. Anne, Murchison's Rapids, Rockingham Falls, and the Wentworth and Elsecar Rivers.[33] Maps with place names like these, which highlighted nobility, served to confirm the *royal* and *hierarchical* nature of the British empire. Royal and noble place names also naturalized the cultural unification of the empire under a sovereign who symbolized the order, control, and class hierarchy of British imperial society. Across the British empire, imperialists routinely named places after Queen Victoria, who reigned for sixty-four years (1837-1901). They christened almost anything after their beloved queen: capes, bays, beaches, bridges, coves, points, peaks, flowers, and even entire colonies. So pervasive was place naming after nobility that the process has been tabbed a geographical deification or earthly apotheosis.[34] In this way, British royalty and British class hierarchy appeared ubiquitous across an empire on which the sun never set. Like the places named after their queen, the place names of the nobility christened by Milton and Carnegie commemorated and venerated the British empire. They also celebrated the act of colonial possession and dispossession.[35] Royal place names and colonial maps branded an Ornamentalist cartography of command into the new colonial consciousness. Many of the place names christened by British hunter-explorers during the nineteenth century remain etched into the fabric of Canadian history and geography today – the legacy left to us by big-game hunters as they travelled across the western interior.

The naming of places served various functions beyond making specific reference to royalty and hierarchy. Naming provided a medium through which to understand space. As an act of appropriation, naming secured and fixed the land both spatially and temporally. Place naming identified and proclaimed ownership of land. Naming acted as a stamp of authority, as a seal of ownership over place. Naming facilitated the construction of a visual vocabulary for maps, a vocabulary that evoked a set of images to facilitate exploitation and settlement. British big-game hunters used naming to normalize and naturalize the western interior.[36] By labelling prominent landmarks, these men transformed space into place. In this way "the namer inscribed his passage permanently on the world, making a metaphorical word-place which others may one day colonize and by which, in the meantime, he asserted his own place in history."[37] Place naming transformed a formerly unknown space into a communicable place that imperialists could travel to, explore, exploit, and colonize. This process established proprietorship, not geographical position. Place names like those christened by big-game hunters branded themselves into the history of Rupert's Land and immortalized the act of British cultural appropriation. The hunters' acts represent an expression of the elite landed values and their understanding of land and land ownership in England. British hunters stamped their maps with familiar names to signify British cultural possession.

In their attempt to depict colonial space, British hunters used the cultural media at their disposal to anchor specific colonial sites, or landmarks, in the minds of their imperial readership. They employed narrative tropes and descriptions, aesthetic landscape principles, colonial and Native history, maps, various sciences, and sketches of colonial sport. By producing spaces through multiple media, British hunters created an image of the colonial frontier in their travel writings through multiple points of orientation. Sketches, narratives, and maps combined to construct an integrated representation of the frontier designed and arranged specifically for imperial audiences. These integrated frames of reference worked to construct images of space, that, when read at home in England, served as a form of legitimation, as a stamp of authenticity on the hunter's depiction of the frontier. The British hunters' many and varied representations contributed to the anticipatory geography of imperialism. Each cultural code and system of meaning shared in the meaningful construction of space.[38]

The hunter's coordinated set of visual representations included the integration of maps alongside both descriptive and pictorial sketches of specific locations. This illustrative approach emphasized both a micro, or narrow, view and a broad, or macro, overview. Hunters strove to balance the two in their descriptions of space. The combination of view and overview within travel narratives allowed readers to examine individual points of interest in more aesthetic or scientific detail.[39] The construction of specific sites connected the macro overview of colonial space to the micro view on the ground. The ability to envisage the anticipatory geography of the frontier depended upon the construction of such landmarks to ground the overview or map. The overlapping of a grid of latitude and longitude afforded imperialists the opportunity to gaze across the entire territory while also focusing in on points to read or view specific landmarks highlighted by the hunter-explorers. Coded with aesthetic, scientific, historical, or Native meanings, these specific landmarks added colonial character by highlighting unique features that broke the homogeneity of the colonial wilderness.

British big-game hunters used a series of overlapping techniques to construct specific landmarks and invest them with meaning. They used specific systems of meaning, such as the Linnaean Latin of natural history, and forms of representation such as the aesthetics of the picturesque and the sublime to saturate landmarks with meaning, making them British within multiple fields of cultural reference. Landmarks became geographic, symbolic, and literary vantage points through which British hunters and explorers extended their proprietary colonial gaze. In this way, landmarks became stable geographical sites constructed through numerous fields of vision.[40] By organizing space through various frames of reference, landmarks cultivated a sense of colonial proprietorship while highlighting the exploration history of the colonizers. British hunters constructed almost anything into landmarks: mountains, hills, cliffs, trees, or glens. Hunter-explorers even landmarked trees as they went – literally blazing a trail through the colonial wilderness. Landmarks served as literary and cultural anchors, grounding the hunters' symbolic and conceptual representation of space. They used images and narratives to saturate specific sites with meaning, and in doing so, made them into reproducible and consumable landscape images. Landmarks both constructed and consolidated the hunters' appropriation of the territory. Such landmarked sites, in all the British colonies, invoked the power to evoke the look and feel of the frontier.[41]

Landmarks also served a variety of other purposes. They indicated passage through wilderness terrain, marked directions on the route, identified points of previous passage, and offered a glimpse of the upcoming terrain. These sites offered geographical vantage points in the thick and disorienting wilderness. Without these sites, the explorers appeared lost, unable to take an aesthetic bearing. Landmarks acted as references and designated routes into, through, and out of colonial space. They inscribed a territorial history to emphasize British colonial possession. The construction of landmarks created a history of imperial passage and established the threshold of colonial exploration by marking key starting points, mid-points, or end points. William Francis Butler used a specific sublime landmark construction, the Spathanaw Watchi (see Figure 5.2, p. 94), to symbolize the beginning, or gateway, into the western interior.[42] Constructing and using landmarks became a means of geographical, but also literary and symbolic, navigation.

On some occasions, landmarking included the physical construction of objects at the landmarked site. British hunters christened sites with place names, fixed flora or fauna with Linnaean designations, or erected cairns to commemorate and appropriate colonial space. Some explorers inscribed their passage in the landscape on trees or rocks, while others left bottles containing accounts of their passage and the names given to sites. One hunter, for example, stamped the land as his own by shaving the bark off a fir tree and burning his name into the wood. He observed enthusiastically that the resin from the tree would preserve his inscription for decades.[43] Similar to landmarks designated by geographical formation, British hunters used specific types of flora and fauna in their construction of colonial landmarks. Alongside these sites, the identification of flora, fauna, and other particulars created a set of cultural markers in the construction of place.

British hunters used the landmarking strategy to appropriate and redeploy Native mythology. Prior to European contact, Native peoples viewed specific geographical formations as the "petrified remnants of animals, plants, men, and food from a heroic age of giant ancestors."[44] In one case, Butler created his own sublime, quasi-Native, spiritual landscape. He described the Spathanaw Watchi in detail and suggested the hill represented the half-buried head of an ancient giant. Other British hunters either overwrote or incorporated Native mythology in their construction of colonial landmarks. By incorporating these myths, hunters assumed possession of the mythological history of the landmark. The spaces that bristled with Native myth and rumour British hunters reproduced as an extension of familiar ground. Spirit names became toponyms attached to hills, lakes, and cataracts. Through this sort of cultural appropriation, imperialists claimed these names and used Native myths as landmarks in the construction of their colonial territory.[45] British hunters assimilated and redeployed Native mythology and spiritual geography in the cultural construction of space.

Just as God sent Adam to take possession of the biblical Garden of Eden, big-game hunters and explorers went forth and appropriated the western interior of Rupert's Land. The bible relayed the Christian sanctity of this ritual in detail: "And out of the ground the LORD God formed every beast of the field, and every fowl of the air; and brought them unto Adam to see what he would call them: and whatsoever Adam called every living creature, that was the name thereof. And Adam gave names to all cattle, and to the fowl of the air, and to every beast of the field."[46] As a first act of possession during the nineteenth century, British explorers employed the gaze and discourse of scientific positivism to name and inventory plants and animals systematically.[47] This tightly focused perspective scrutinized the minute features and individual resources of unfamiliar land, such as geological, botanical, and zoological details.[48] British big-game hunters expressed their scientific gaze through the discourse of natural history and the codifying framework of the Linnaean system of Latin nomenclature.

The Linnaean system, created by Swedish naturalist Carl Linnaeus in his *Systema Naturae* (1735), classified and codified all the plants of the world. Linnaeus chose Latin as the formal language of the system and based the classificatory framework around the reproductive parts of plants. By identifying stamens and pistils, along with characteristics such as form, number, size, and position, naturalists incorporated all known and unknown plant life into the language of the *Systema Naturae* by identifying their genus and species.[49] In later books, *Philosophia Botanica* (1751) and *Species Plantarum* (1753), he created additional systems for animals and minerals.[50] On his own, Linnaeus added 8,000 species to the system, including his name for humans (homo sapiens).[51] Previous attempts by scientists and naturalists to construct a broad-based classification system for nature with international appeal met with little success or failed. The simplicity of the *Systema Naturae*, combined with the use of Latin, met with instant success across Europe. Imperial Britons considered his framework a medium through which they could change the chaos of nature into scientific order.[52] By the end of the eighteenth century, scientific communities accepted the Linnaean system as the principal mode of classification for the natural world.

With the popularization of the Linnaean system, new themes emerged in travel, hunting, and exploration narratives. Whether British travellers, surveyors, explorers, or hunters toured for scientific reasons or not, natural history played an important part in their expeditions. While on tour, authors wrote extensively on the capturing of foreign plant and animal specimens, made drawings in sketchbooks, took measurements, recorded observations, built and contributed to collections, and, of course, looked forward to the excitement of finding and naming new species.[53] The Linnaean system initiated "a knowledge-building enterprise of unprecedented scale and appeal."[54] British imperialists returned home with new specimens and observations, and built their own natural history collections or contributed to the collections of natural history museums.

As they travelled across the western interior of Rupert's Land, British big-game hunters and explorers applied the Linnaean system to impose order onto the land. Although these activities appear benign, big-game hunters used the Linnaean system as an appropriative, systematizing framework

4.2 "Prairie-Hen (*Cupidonia Cupido*)." Sportsman and naturalist William Ross King brought the prairie-hen to the attention of the British Acclimatisation Society and advocated the game bird's appropriation to Great Britain. William Ross King, *The Sportsman and Naturalist in Canada* (London: Hurst and Blackett, 1866), facing 144.

– a schema through which to inventory their colonial landscape. As they extended and explored the interior, big-game hunters applied the Linnaean system to identify and systematize unfamiliar game.[55] Carnegie, for example, identified the American bison (*Bos Americanus*), mule-deer (*Cervus Macrotis*), and the Rocky Mountain goat (*Capra Americana*) during his 1859 expedition, and Major William Ross King noted the presence of the prairie-hen (*Cupidonia Cupido*) (Figure 4.2), wapiti (*Cervus Canadiensis*), and the caribou (*Cervus Tarandus*) in his natural history of British North America.[56] These examples illustrate the univocality of the processes of naming, claiming, and reorganization.

The British hunters' systematizing of game naturalized their imperial presence in the colonial territory. Based on an egocentric imperial world view, big-game hunters and other upper-class Britons considered little-known colonial territories as a chaos onto which they must impose order.[57] This process, whereby the British naturalized their own presence in, and appropriation of, unfamiliar territories is referred to as the anti-conquest. The anti-conquest, as discussed in the introduction and employed in this book, refers to any strategy of cultural representation whereby empire builders sought to demonstrate the innocence of their cultural appropriation while simultaneously underscoring their proprietorship and domination of foreign lands.[58] Although they appeared innocent, imperial representations of colonial lands, peoples, and resources ultimately contributed to the imperial fashioning of space. Natural history reveals the anti-conquest at work. The imperial British hunter, trained in modern scientific methods, conducted his expedition while implementing a set of benign, objective systems with no hint of domination or subordination. In these subtle but meaningful ways, natural history provided a central outlet for the expression of imperial appropriation.

The systematization of the land through natural history provided a medium through which big-game hunters narrated their anti-conquest of the western interior. By familiarizing and incorporating new animals into the language of the system, British hunters naturalized their presence in the colonial landscape. Big-game hunters thus provided an image in their travel writings that reorganized and reinvented colonial spaces from a distinct perspective. Although natural history appeared benign and abstract when compared to more overt expressions of appropriation, the underlying purpose remained the same. By incorporating unfamiliar elements of the land through imperial systems of meaning like the Linnaean system, these men reaffirmed the presence of previously identified game in terms of similarity and difference while, at the same time, familiarizing and naturalizing the unknown as known.

Imperialists used natural history to encode their colonial ambitions. The collecting of natural history specimens was part of a larger systematizing of nature, and this impulse continued as the nineteenth century advanced. Imperialists viewed natural history as a means through which to impose order on colonial lands. As they tramped through the wetlands, prairies, and mountains of the western interior, British hunters and explorers extracted plants and animals from their environment and inserted them, both physically and symbolically, into their vision of colonial order. Armed with the modernist science of natural history, they familiarized and naturalized "new sites/sights immediately upon contact, by incorporating them into the language of the system."[59] The naming aspects of natural history relate directly to the issue of imperial transformation, of remaking the image of the land from a wilderness into an anticipatory geography of colonization – a transformation that possessed inferred temporal qualities, including the change from ignorance to knowledge creation, from chaos to order, from raw nature to *Systema Naturae*. In this way, naming brought advanced scientific order to colonial spaces. Natural history reveals an imperial discourse about colonial worlds, a civilized discourse about savage worlds, a metropolitan discourse about peripheral worlds, all made recognizable through the Ornamentalist discourse of similarity and difference. Applied across the empire, the application of the Linnaean system "specified plants and animals in visual terms as discrete entities, subsuming and reassembling them in a finite, totalizing order."[60] The application of natural science to this region extended well beyond the frontier period in the West, as the new Dominion of Canada used inventory science in similar ways after Confederation to help envision a transcontinental nation.[61]

In conjunction with the Linnaean system, British hunters systematized game through pictorial modes of representation. As cultural constructs, their graphic representations suggest certain underlying discourses and the application of the hunter's appropriative, imperial gaze. The British hunters' sketches of game reveal a fascinating connection to the systematizing process. Their representations reveal no ambiguity. The hunters' bifurcation of space in these images objectified and appropriated nature by dissociating game from the environment. Big-game hunters emphasized the specificity and detail of the scientific object in the foreground by ignoring the background landscape altogether.[62] The figure "Head of a Rocky Mountain Ram" (Figure 4.3) illustrates this point and reveals a distinct bifurcation of space. In this example, Carnegie objectified and appropriated the ram by removing the background landscape and dissociating the specimen from its environment. This sketch also centres attention on the details of the head, and valorizes trophies as the fruits of the hunter's imperial appropriation. British hunters used Latin nomenclature, in conjunction with pictorial representations, to order, designate, and reorganize the colonial wilderness.

4.3 "Head of a Rocky Mountain Ram." In displaying trophy heads, British hunters emphasized the modernist advancement of natural history through hunting. James Carnegie, *Saskatchewan and the Rocky Mountains: A Diary and Narrative of Travel, Sport, and Adventure, in 1859 and 1860* (Edinburgh: Edmonston and Douglas, 1875), 215.

Although outright classification identified and situated each aspect of nature into the proper Linnaean category, big-game hunters used associationism, or comparative discussions of natural history, in their systematization of game.[63] Natural history formed an integral part of the British science during the nineteenth century, and it involved gathering specific details on foreign wildlife, collecting specimens, and identifying new species. After the development and adoption of the Linnaean system amongst scientific communities, a shift occurred in travel and exploration literature. The British began narrating the accumulation and systematization of nature. Travel authors used natural history to produce a storyline for their narratives.[64] As one might expect, comparative discussions of natural history formed an important feature of hunting narratives. These comparisons, which I refer to as game associationism, compared and contrasted the specific attributes of wildlife with those of Great Britain based on similarity and difference. This expression of Ornamentalism contributed to the hunter's systematization by elucidating the specific differences between familiar and unfamiliar game.[65] Indeed, explanation added a level of cultural depth overtop the application of Latin nomenclature.[66] British big-game hunters compared and contrasted attributes, behaviours, and characteristics through game associationism. While hunting Rocky Mountain rams, Carnegie wrote, "At this season the rams are in their best condition ... in October they become uneatable, as in the case with the red-deer stag in Scotland."[67] In their widely popular travel narrative, *North-West Passage*, Milton and Cheadle stated, "The pine partridge is rather larger than the willow grouse, darker feathered, like an English grouse."[68] William Ross King described the wapiti (North American elk) and added that it "stands about four and a half feet high at the shoulder, or nearly a foot higher than the red-deer of Scotland, though in general form both are very similar."[69] The Linnaean system placed each animal within the broader system of nature, but it failed to provide the descriptive specificity required to explicate the differences and similarities of species. Instead, British hunters aimed their educated, naturalist's eye towards the size, colour, organization, habitat, and behaviour of game. Comparing and contrasting game with that at home reveals the discourse of Ornamentalism and provided hunters with an appropriate cultural medium to communicate these aspects of natural history. The distinctions made through game associationism contributed to the big-game hunters systematizing of nature.

Upper-class readers of travel literature in England, many of whom possessed knowledge of natural history, expected these discussions and a detailed examination of the finer points of colonial venery. In several cases, British gentleman hunters had read the narratives of the hunters that preceded them and took issue with their descriptions of game.[70] British hunters were especially familiar with Sir John Richardson's *Fauna Boreali-Americana* (1829), the first natural history of northern British North America. However, these comparative observations provided more than a mere functional purpose. Having designated and depicted game, these descriptions reveal a natural extension of the British hunters' scientific systematization of the land. Natural history provided hunters with a framework to discuss descriptions, classifications, and the behavioural aspects of game, further incorporating unfamiliar and exotic otherness into their proprietary understanding of the territory. It contributed to the systematizing of game and facilitated the construction of a colonial hierarchy of nature.

Not all big-game hunters remained content systematizing and codifying game. At least one, Major William Ross King, advocated the physical exchange of game between Great Britain and the colonies during the nineteenth century. The British referred to the introduction and propagation of species between the colonies as acclimatization.[71] The British Acclimatisation Society, an ecological extension of imperialism, facilitated British attempts to physically remake new colonial landscapes into something that resembled Great Britain.[72] North American animal species lacked the cultural familiarity necessary to make them suitable elements of the new British territory. The British Acclimatisation Society existed largely for the purposes of sport and aesthetic landscape ornamentation and provided the stimulus for the introduction of a variety of domestic British game in the colonies. Indeed, the introduction of new animal and plant species went hand in hand with colonial exploitation and settlement. This sort of imperial or environmental engineering created a zoological mélange, particularly in New Zealand.[73] The presence of English skylarks in Tasmania, Scottish red deer in New Zealand, and the ring-necked pheasant in Canada today are the results of the British Acclimatisation Movement during the third quarter of the nineteenth century.[74]

A small group of elite private animal collectors, domesticators, and sportsmen founded the British Acclimatisation Society in 1860. The idea for the society developed from discussion by sportsmen and anglers in *The Field* – a London-published newspaper devoted to hunting and sport fishing – and from small-scale acclimatory efforts by the Zoological Society of London established in 1826. The new society sought to combine the efforts of individuals and groups already engaged in acclimating and propagating exotic species from overseas. The most famous of which was Edward Smith Stanley, the Earl of Derby, a founding member of the Zoological Society. The list of members and benefactors to the British Acclimatisation Society represents a who's who of the social elite in England during this period. Among the group were three dukes, three marquises, seven earls, and seven viscounts. The society included university professors, medical doctors, scientists, museum curators, and a chief justice. Many of these men counted among the other British "Noblemen, Agriculturalists ... Travellers, Sportsmen, Landed Proprietors, and Scientific Men" who attended their meetings.[75] The roots of the acclimatization movement lay with British royalty and the landed elite in England who sought the sport provided from imported colonial game as early as the seventeenth century. King James I (1566-1625) acclimatized Scandinavian fallow deer, King Charles I (1600-49) brought wild boar and partridge, and Charles II (1660-85) sent his gamekeeper to France in 1673 to import red-legged partridge specifically for hunting, consumption, and sport at the royal game park at Windsor.[76] This game bird exists today across south, central, and eastern England.[77]

Despite the group's narrow support base, the society's elite members held positions of social influence and possessed connections across the empire. Although the society existed for a mere six years (it amalgamated in 1866 with the Ornithological Society of London), its 270 members worked feverishly at importing new exotic species for domestication and exporting domestic British species around the globe.[78] The Acclimatisation Society also sought to naturalize and perfect these exotic species through hybridization. The first formal gathering of the society included a grand banquet at which members consumed rare and exotic colonial meats ravenously.[79] The Acclimatisation Society's desire to obtain specific colonial animals suggests it was directed more by the whim and fancy of its elite members than by any attempt at systematic organization of imports and exports. The acclimatizers celebrated imperial possession and the place of Great Britain at the forefront of all European nations.[80] As they captured, controlled, and consumed colonial animals, they captured, controlled, and consumed colonial territories. The symbolism of appropriation and consumption is unmistakeable.

The society sought connections both at home and abroad. It established contact with gentlemen of the Société Imperiale d'Acclimatation in Paris, also an exclusive and explicitly colonial organization. Members used the offices of *The Field* for their initial meetings and promoted themselves and their endeavours through the paper. In accordance with its stated objectives, the Acclimatisation Society hoped to establish a liaison with the Zoological Society of London. Representatives of the society spread the word of their efforts through lectures at Oxford University and to the Council of the Society of Arts. The acclimatizers worked in conjunction with natural history museums and societies. Indeed, the Kew and other botanical gardens provided the "hub" for the acclimatization and the global dispersal of plant species throughout the empire.[81] The British Acclimatisation Society corresponded with agents across the British empire, including the British Honduras, British North America, India, Australia, and Scotland, to obtain unique species for introduction in Great Britain. It focused on obtaining game fowl and fish species from these correspondents, probably for the hunters and sportsmen within the society. For example, Lieutenant Campbell Hardy of Halifax offered to ship the society young tree and prairie grouse, and F.J. Stevenson of Montreal offered to send additional game birds.[82]

Although no acclimatization society developed in British North America, individual hunters and naturalists, like William Ross King, contemplated the acclimatization of various game to Great Britain. King called for the introduction of the prairie-hen specifically. While discussing its natural history, he brought the prairie-hen to the attention of the British Acclimatisation Society. King considered the ability of the game bird to survive in Great Britain despite the obvious unsuitability of the British environment. The "continual recurrence of the cold winds, rain, and fogs, characteristic of English weather, would probably be less likely to be endured with impunity [by the prairie-hen] than the normal state of the Canadian winter," wrote King. He added, "there are also few districts suitable to its habits, for as the Prairie-hen always avoids high grounds and hilly tracts, and is exclusively a denizen of the driest plains, our Scottish Moors and mountains are necessarily excluded."[83] Even if acclimatizers could find an appropriate habitat, King observed that the prairie-hen might drive away the smaller British red-grouse.

King contemplated the acclimatization of other British North American game and fish for the enjoyment of all British sportsmen. In addition to the prairie-hen specific to the West, King called for the introduction of the colin. He found it "worthy of the attention of the Acclimatisation Society" because the bird was "pugnacious enough to defend itself anywhere, yet from its size not likely to drive away any other gamebird."[84]

Beyond game fowl, King advocated the appropriation of the black bass and whitefish because they offered excellent angling for the British piscator. He found the black bass particularly sporting when hooked. The fish "will run a lot of the line at once, shooting away with extraordinary fury and impetuosity, leaping madly out of the water ... with such strength and activity as demand all the care and address of its captor." King extolled black bass fishing. "Except the salmon, there is hardly any other fish that affords more thorough sport, or deserves to rank higher in every way, than that prince of fresh-water fish, the Black Basse (*Huro nigricans*)." So taken by the fish, King called for the introduction of the fish into the lakes of Great Britain for the benefit of British sport fishermen. He wrote, "I have not the smallest doubt that the Black-Basse is quite capable of acclimatisation in our own country [England], and I believe that this might be accomplished with less amount of trouble and expense than would be incurred in the transport of most other foreign fish, or their ova, and certainly with the amplest reward in the event of success." Regarding the acclimatization of the whitefish, King stated, "were it possible to introduce this fish into some of our larger Scottish Lakes, and find suitable subsistence for it, it would indeed be an acquisition to our waters."[85]

King's efforts to bring North American game to the attention of the

British Acclimatisation Society reveals a specific class-based aspect of the process of possession-taking. He did not advocate the introduction of game to sustain human life or to replace extinct British species. He called for the introduction of game from the western interior purely to provide the upper-class British hunter with unique colonial sport. The acclimatization of game reveals an obvious effort to appropriate, and thereby physically and symbolically incorporate into the empire the most desirable game from the colonial frontier for sport and symbolic consumption.

As they made their way across the western interior of Rupert's Land, British hunters employed modernist scientific discourse in their cultural construction of space. They used cartography to construct maps, used the science of natural history to fill their maps with rich imperial detail, and encompassed both with the discourse of scientific positivism to present their images and descriptions as accurate and objective. Through the application of scientific cultural codes, systems of meaning, and forms of representation, they also constructed cultural landmarks that remain a part of the history of Rupert's Land. As part of a larger ecological extension of imperialism, they also sought to remake colonial lands by introducing proper English game for sport through acclimatization. They also imported colonial game into England to physically possess, and in some cases consume, the best colonial fish and game. These representations reveal the extent to which imperialists like big-game hunters brought their appropriative culture to bear in the construction and appropriation of colonial space. Together they also served, in conjunction with the prefatory positivism at the beginning of their books or the class-based discourse behind the elite hunting code, to construct and set a proprietary vision of the western interior of Rupert's Land within multiple frames of reference.

5

Hunting for Landscape:
Social Class and the Appropriation
of the Wilderness

I N CONTRAST TO MODERNIST SCIENCE, British big-game hunters also
used romantic aesthetics to appropriate the wilderness landscape of
the western interior. Their books contained lengthy literary descriptions as well as sketches and engravings to reaffirm the British-looking
character of Rupert's Land. The hunters constructed these images through
the application of two distinctly British aesthetic landscape principles:
the picturesque and the sublime. Composed of specific cultural codes,
these two forms of landscape description allowed big-game hunters to
construct and organize the natural world in a way that created meaningful landscapes for imperial-minded readers at home.[1] Although different in their constituent codes and rules of application, British hunters used the picturesque and sublime in their narratives – preceded by
prefatory truth statements that spoke to the veracity of narrative landscape
descriptions – to appropriate the wilderness of the western interior.[2] I
employ the term "appropriation" in two ways throughout this chapter:
to refer to the upper-class hunters' proprietary outlook on their colonial
lands, and also to refer to the sustained application and production of
British-looking landscapes through the aesthetics of the picturesque and
the sublime. As an Ornamental strategy, the construction of British-
looking landscapes worked in a two-pronged manner: picturesque landscapes served to emphasize similarity and the domestic, while sublime
landscapes focused (seemingly) on difference and the exotic.

British hunters imposed the elitist aesthetic principle of the picturesque
to appropriate the frontier landscape of the Rupert's Land interior. Drawing

on themes in landscape gardening and the work of classical painters such as Claude Lorrain and Salvator Rosa, the aesthetic of the picturesque emerged as the primary way to consider nature amongst the landed elite in England during the eighteenth and early nineteenth centuries. During this period, the picturesque found two forms of expression: estate landscaping and landscape painting. Both forms of the picturesque evolved through literary debates among leading British landscape designers Capability Brown (1716-83), William Gilpin (1724-1804), Humphry Repton (1752-1818), Richard Payne Knight (1750-1824), and Uvedale Price (1747-1829).[3] Although their debates have been adequately summarized elsewhere, the important point in this chapter is that they used these debates to determine which specific elements constituted the picturesque and which did not.[4] Although each developed their own views, these aestheticians agreed that a landscape must emphasize proprietorship and remind them of a painting to be deemed picturesque. Gilpin himself stated, "with regard to the term *picturesque*, I have always myself used it merely to denote *such objects, as are proper subjects for a painting*."[5] Although the picturesque had its component objects, Gilpin emphasized that the picturesque did not have a reductive gaze. "The province of the picturesque," wrote Gilpin, "is to *survey* nature; *not anatomize matter* ... It examines parts, but never descends to particles."[6] These parts defined the application of the aesthetic during the eighteenth and nineteenth centuries and led to the development of a specific set of picturesque codes.

By the late eighteenth and early nineteenth centuries, the picturesque had a well-established set of codes and rules of application. A picturesque landscape typically consisted of three planes to provide depth of perspective, with the foreground, midground, and background containing a variety of elevation, vegetation, and light. A river often provided further depth by connecting the three planes, while trees or rocks acted as coulisses (side scenery on a theatre stage to focus audience attention towards the centre of the scene). The foreground invited leisurely habitation by providing some human or animal presence, and viewers typically considered the scene from an elevated prospect to look down on nature and command the landscape. On a broader level, the landscape enthusiast looked for roughness, an essential feature to ensure visual variety, within an organized landscape. The play of light and shade contributed to the harmonization of the overall scene – particularly at sunset. This created a singular picture with a composed effect and gave rise to a sense of comfort or contentment. Employing these constituent codes, the landed elite adopted the picturesque as "the authoritative, socially acceptable way of apprehending the external world between 1770 and 1840 in England."[7] The picturesque, grounded for the English elite in literature and art, ordered the land into a composed picture to adhere to the cultural construction of the aesthetic. These guidelines formed a complex set of components that had to exist for purveyors of the aesthetic to deem an image picturesque.

The picturesque was a class-based, cultural construction. This elitist landscape preference stemmed from perspectives in nature, literature, art, and land ownership. For those of socio-economic privilege in British society, land represented something to be composed, improved, and constructed into a landscape. In this regard, the picturesque reveals the politics of exclusion because only the members of the upper class, educated in art and landscape touring, held the capacity for ordering and controlling the land. The picturesque suggested the reiteration of social hierarchy and the stability of caste. Repton, one of the leading estate aestheticians in the early nineteenth century, emphasized the importance of this proprietary class-based perspective as viewed from the centre of the estate. He believed that the manor-view of one's estate should celebrate social class and ownership: "The views from a house, and particularly those from the drawing-room, ought rather to consist of objects which evidently belong to the place. To express this idea, I have used the word *appropriation*, by which I mean such a portion of wood and lawn as may be supposed to belong to the proprietor of the mansion, occupied by himself, not so much for the purposes of gain as pleasure and convenience."[8] For Repton, the proprietary perspective provided a central feature of the picturesque aesthetic: the picturesque should display that which one owned. Moreover, stemming from Gilpin, an important part of the picturesque included the physical modification of the land, which in some cases involved the removal of trees, rivers, or entire villages, to fit the cultural construction of the aesthetic on estate lands. Indeed, during the late eighteenth and nineteenth centuries, the landed elite believed it had a right to change the land to suit its tastes.[9] In this way, the picturesque reinforced to the elite the personal views and perceptions of its members as the owners of nature. By emphasizing the owning and controlling of the land, the elite imbued the picturesque with an inherently proprietary outlook. The aesthetics of landscape emerged from the values of leisured culture and from those who possessed a natural, appropriative view of land.[10] For the landed elite, the ideological import of landscape thus developed from an emphasis on land ownership as a signifier of British privilege, exclusivity, and social class.

The picturesque held other discursive implications. Because the aesthetic emerged during a time of rapid agrarian change in England, the landed elite used the picturesque to recreate pre-industrial rural England within their private estates.[11] By restructuring their estates into picturesque parklands, the landed classes sought to return to pre-enclosure England, and in doing so they drew attention to their social status as landowners – only the British upper class possessed unproductive land.[12] On the other hand, the emphasis on class, snobbism, and the aestheticization of rural poverty in picturesque landscape paintings sanctioned the consequences of agricultural industrialization.[13] The picturesque, as displayed through landscape or landscape painting, thus had special ideological resonance and application to the private estates of rural England.

The application of the picturesque within colonial landscapes included a material appraisal of the land. In Great Britain, estate owners used the picturesque to celebrate land ownership. In a slight colonial adaptation of the term, the British used the picturesque to accord resource value to the new land. The picturesque presents an amalgamation of both aesthetic value but also an appraisal of the land's resources and use value.[14] For upper-class Britons, the picturesque provided the primary interpretive paradigm for understanding landscape both at home and abroad. However, upon travelling to unfamiliar colonies, big-game hunters, like other elite British travellers, modified the picturesque to address imperialist issues of order, control, and the acquisition of resources. British hunters readily applied their proprietary schema for understanding and appraising space to make sense of their new landscapes, and in doing so used their imperial culture to construct and appropriate the western interior.

Perhaps the big-game hunter's most common aesthetic construction of landscape involved landscape associationism, which is similar to the game associationism discussed in the preceding chapter. British hunters used landscape associationism to compare and contrast picturesque landscapes in the western interior with picturesque landscapes in Great Britain. Knight originally popularized landscape associationism, and it provided an important aesthetic strategy for representing space.[15] As part of the larger discourse of Ornamentalism, British hunters often used landscape associationism to compare and contrast the foreign landscapes of the West with the familiar landscapes of home.

Examples of landscape associationism can be grouped into two categories: general and specific. British hunters used associationism to refer in general terms to the landscapes of Great Britain. For example, in the West during the 1850s, Carnegie stated, "Soon after starting we crossed Pembina River [Alberta], a shallow stream about sixty yards wide, flowing in a rapid current over a bed of stones and gravel. The banks were very pretty; not monotonous, but broken and varied like those of a Highland river."[16] The second category of landscape associationism identified landscape by its specific likeness to landscapes at home in Great Britain. Carnegie wrote, "Old Bow Fort [Alberta], outside the mountains, and at the edge of the plains, is 4100 feet above the sea, nearly equalling Ben Nevis, the highest point in Great Britain."[17] Similarly, Graham compared the landscape around Battle River (Alberta) to Netherby, his family estate in Cumberland, England: "[We] camped at a lovely little plain surrounded by wood, which reminded me of 'Jack's Pasture' at dear old Netherby."[18] British hunters also used the Thames River, arguably the most prominent landscape feature in England, as a comparative reference for streams and rivers in the western interior. While fording the North Saskatchewan River in 1847, Graham described the broad nature of the river as "about the width of the Thames at Westminster."[19]

Whether employed in a general or specific manner, these examples of landscape associationism, drawn from a veritable legion of references, reveal an effort to characterize the landscape as British. By likening one landscape to another, particularly a well-known landscape feature such as the Thames River in London, England, British hunters constructed and appropriated the cultural landscapes of the interior in understandable terms. Cultural associationism made colonial landscapes intelligible visually. British readers may not have been able to identify the location of the North Saskatchewan River on a map, but through the British big-game hunter's experience, they could appreciate the feel and tone of the landscape by way of associationism.

Beyond examples of associationism that teetered along an axis of similarity and difference, British hunters imposed their elitist aesthetic principle of the picturesque to construct landscapes that resembled their estate parklands in England. The identification of the land as a park, or as park-like, created an analogy between the big-game hunter's private estate parks and naturally occurring parks in the colonial wilderness. The parkland along the North Saskatchewan River embodied the nineteenth-century British landscape preference for "undulating, well-watered parkland of delimited scope and scale, and exhibiting only moderately-sized geographical features."[20] Openness of terrain provided an additional component of the park-like landscape, as it identified both agrarian and pastoral uses for land. The association of picturesque parklands with potential use value represents a colonial adaptation combining material production with aesthetic pleasure.[21] Indeed, a number of British explorers and traders helped perpetuate the image of the land in park-like terms.[22]

The construction of picturesque parklands in the western interior did indeed contain an inherent evaluation of its material resource value. Constructing the land as an ordered British estate park suggested that the land was both familiar and well-suited for colonization.

While in search of buffalo in 1847, Graham described the landscape as a picturesque English park – much like his family estate at home in Netherby. He wrote that the landscape near Eagle Tail Creek (Saskatchewan) was "studded with clusters of poplar bushes doing duty for timber; but the effect very good for the western summit. I thought many a nobleman at home would be glad for such a park for his house." He provided a similar landscape description when he stated his company "camped on a hill with a beautiful plain below us, studded with clumps of trees like a park, and a range of wooded hills on the other side." The term "clumps" became an essential component of the picturesque during the eighteenth century and, combined with an open plain, made particular reference to the classical estate parks designed by landscape aesthete Lancelot Capability Brown. Graham's third reference to the landscape as a picturesque park reaffirms his longing to see familiarity in the foreignness of the western interior:

> Some of the views of the noble river, with its steep wooded bluffs and long reaches through the forest vista, very, very bonnie! While every now and then we look down from a high bluff upon a large "holme" [a grass meadow] by the water side, studded with clumps of fine timber and single trees; like an English park. At one of these, at "la riviere de la terre blanche," [White Earth Creek River, Alberta] the remains of two old forts of the rival [Hudson's Bay and North-West] companies were situated, in a lovely spot, which would have made a Belvoir or a Chatsworth [estates in Leicestershire and Derbyshire respectively] had it been in England.[23]

Graham's literary pictorial of the English park imposed a stock application of the picturesque. His perspective looked down onto nature in order to command the landscape and the grass meadow, properly diversified with Brownian clumps of trees, and presented a view that resembled an estate lawn. Beyond the construction of the landscape to match familiar English parks, Graham emphasized British ownership and history in the region by highlighting the ruined forts of the British Hudson's Bay and North-West fur-trading companies, and by associating the landscape with the picturesque English estates of Belvoir and Chatsworth.

In addition to Graham, other British hunters described the West in park-like terms during the early 1860s. While gazing into a valley near

5.1 "The Rocky Mountains at the Sources of the Saskatchewan." Butler's picturesque parkland of the western interior used stock elements of the aesthetic, including coulisses, to draw the eye to the midground. William Francis Butler, *The Great Lone Land* (London: Sampson Low, Marston, Searle, and Rivington, 1872), 274.

Jasper House, Alberta, sportsman Viscount William Fitzwilliam Milton stated, "Following the river-valley, we travelled through thick timber marshes, and boggy ground, pleasantly varied occasionally by beautiful park-like oases of an acre or two in extent."[24] Milton produced a landscape representation, "View from the Hill Opposite Jasper House," that reveals the emphasis on the picturesque despite the remote desolation of Rupert's Land. The perspective looks down onto the Athabasca River, and Jasper House is located in the right midground. Milton and Cheadle, reclining in the foreground, convey a sense of ease in the midst of the wilderness. Their posture suggests a relaxed tone and their expedition as the harbinger of future British colonization. While travelling through similar country, another hunter, William Butler, commented in *The Wild North Land* that as he neared the east side of the Rocky Mountains, he travelled "through a park-like land of wood and glade and meadow, where the jumping deer glanced through the dry grass and trees."[25] In addition to narrative images, Butler used pictorial images in his other travel book, *The Great Lone Land,* to convey the park-like landscape motif (Figure 5.1).

Although these park-like accounts hint at materialist concerns, several other picturesque descriptions reveal an explicit appraisal of the future resource value of the landscape. Beyond outright observations on the bounty of game within these parks, sportsmen were interested in indicating the land's capacity for supporting colonization. The hunters commented on the fertility of the land, the abundance of trees and game, and the presence of rivers and lakes. In particular, the term "rich" was employed to identify potential resource-producing lands. During the early 1860s, Milton wrote, "Having crossed the Assiniboine River [Alberta] above the Fort [Ellice], we now left it to the right, travelling for several days through rich, park-like country, similar to that we had previously traversed. Innumerable lakes and pools, swarming with wild-fowl, supplied us with constant shooting." The abundance of game in these estate-like parks amazed Milton. He stated, "The broods of prairie grouse were already full grown, and very plentiful. When driven into the little round copses of aspen which are such a prominent feature of the 'park country,' they afforded capital sport." While traversing west from the Shell River (Manitoba), Milton combined the term "rich" with the prospect of colonization. He observed, "As we crossed it, we remarked to one another what a magnificent site for a house one of the promontories would be, and how happy, many a poor farmer who tilled unkindly soil at home [England] would feel in possession of the rich land which lay before us."[26] Carnegie also used the term "rich" to describe the use value of the land near Fort Edmonton (Alberta) in the 1850s. He stated, "The view was exceedingly pretty, for the elevated banks which confined the channel were picturesquely broken, and richly covered with an abundant growth of wood."[27] Like the other hunters, he connected the resource value of the land to a picturesque estate park when he observed that "the opposite banks of the river [at Fort Carleton] seemed like an English park" and that the "gradual slopes luxuriantly clothed with wood, disposed by nature in groups and gladed masses, as if some skilful hand had been cutting the forest into forms of symmetry."[28]

The British big-game hunter's construction of park-like lands combined both aesthetic and material appraisals of the land. The connections drawn between estate parks in England and naturally occurring wilderness parks transformed a strange and foreign land into a familiar and distinctly British landscape. The narration and depiction of big-game hunting in these landscapes, the cultural activity typically conducted on exclusive and picturesque estates, further familiarized and valorized the hunter's appropriation of the land. This imperial appropriation justified the possession and occupation of the land by those who could appreciate its picturesque character. If colonial lands resembled private British estate parks, then surely their appropriation had been validated. Milton and

Cheadle summed up both the imperial appropriation and resource value of the land while hinting at forthcoming colonization. They described the parklands near Fort Pitt (Saskatchewan) as "rolling hills and fertile valleys, of lakes and streams, groves of birch and aspen, and miniature prairies; a land of kindly soil, and full of promise to the settler to come in future years, when an enlightened policy shall open out wealth now uncared for or unknown."[29]

Although big-game hunters used the picturesque aesthetic to appropriate the landscape of the western interior of Rupert's Land, not all landscapes lent themselves to an English-like appraisal. When the terrain presented geography unknown in England, such as vast level prairies or impenetrable forests, big-game hunters imposed the aesthetic of the sublime to construct landscapes based on dissimilarity – or did they? Like the picturesque, the aesthetic of the sublime consisted of an identifiable and constructed set of cultural codes. British big-game hunters applied these codes to construct, and thereby appropriate, the landscapes of the western interior. Although the aesthetics of the sublime and the picturesque varied considerably, I suggest that the sublime held similar appropriative ideology.[30] In contrast to the picturesque, which created familiar landscapes, big-game hunters employed the sublime to construct images of foreign landscapes. By employing the sublime, which was a specific British cultural aesthetic used to describe the foreign, hunters paradoxically naturalized the landscape in British terms. For the British, the sublime corresponded to an established but flexible cultural conception of the foreign, and I argue that its use paradoxically appropriated landscapes within the parameters of the familiar in a manner similar to the picturesque.

The sublime emerged as a widespread element of elitist aesthetic taste in England during the eighteenth and early nineteenth centuries.[31] Unlike the various aestheticians involved in the creation of the picturesque, Irish politician Edmund Burke (1729-97) merged the different threads of sublime theory in his widely popular *Philosophical Enquiry into the Origin of Our Ideas of the Sublime and Beautiful* (1757).[32] The sublime encouraged a new appreciation for the frightening or unattractive in landscape and emerged as part of the gothic architectural movement in the eighteenth and early nineteenth centuries.[33] Unlike the limited application of the picturesque, the sublime extended beyond natural phenomena to any structure found within a landscape that inspired fear or a sense of history. These usually included images of decay, like ruins or battlefields, and encouraged a sense of vastness, darkness, or obscurity.[34] Burke defined the sublime as "whatever is fitted in any sort to excite the ideas of pain, and danger, that is to say, whatever is in any sort terrible, or is conversant about terrible objects, or operates in a manner analogous to terror, is a source of the *sublime*."[35] Understanding the aesthetic meant understanding the ability of a sublime landscape to inspire fearful emotions.

Other than the Scottish Highlands, Great Britain offered only limited opportunities to experience the sublime. Instead, upper-class travellers applied the sublime on grand tours of Western European countries and expeditions to their own British colonies in Africa, New Zealand, Canada, or Australia. Britons travelling though Europe often employed the sublime to describe foreign landscape features, such as the Alpine Mountains and the fjords of Scandinavia.[36] To find the sublime at home, the English upper class transformed their own private landscape gardens into miniature fantasy-like worlds to satisfy their sublime aesthetic taste.[37] After the successful defence of British North America and the defeat of the Americans during the Anglo-American War of 1812, upper-class British tourists and big-game hunters directed their attention across the Atlantic to their British North American colonies. As they travelled to the West, these upper-class travellers ensured that they paid a visit to the epicentre of the sublime in North America – Niagara Falls.[38]

The codification of the sublime included specific parameters for its application. Burke highlighted the various components of the sublime through subtitles in his book, identifying terror, darkness, obscurity, power, vastness, suddenness, startling sounds, and feeling as integral to the aesthetic.[39] By the late eighteenth century, the sublime took root in British culture and led to a specific set of codes and applications to describe foreign or non-British landscapes. The sublime cultivated appreciation for the scars of nature, such as ravines, vertical mountains, dense forests, cascading rapids, and bleak moors.[40] Unlike the picturesque, uninhabited foregrounds became a hallmark of the sublime landscape.[41] The sublime reduced human agency in the face of nature by portraying desolate landscapes occupied by animals, animal or human bones, or diminutive human figures.[42] Rather than looking down on the scene, landscape enthusiasts typically looked up to the sublime phenomena, which further contributed to a sense of human vulnerability.[43] Excessive variety, or excessive uniformity, of light and vegetation contributed to the sublimity of a landscape.[44] This led to an inability to harmonize the overall scene and encouraged an almost artless appearance. When considered collectively, the sublime inspired vastness, infinity, and power.[45] Landscape viewers and exponents of the aesthetic during the eighteenth and nineteenth centuries equated these characteristics with God or Mother Nature and the manifestation of His or Her power in nature.[46] Unlike the cultural specificity of the picturesque, the sublime became a broad term readily applicable to various types of landscapes.

Although the sublime and the picturesque resulted in decidedly different landscapes, the appropriative discourse behind their application remained the same. Put differently, big-game hunters applied the sublime, paradoxically, to familiarize and naturalize the landscape of the western interior not as *strangely alien* but rather as *identifiably foreign*. This resulted in the creation of negotiated landscape images that appeared frighteningly new in some ways and yet oddly familiar in others. The hunter's construction resulted in the creation of foreign, yet surmountable, colonial landscape images based on the cultural construction of the sublime. Like the picturesque, I view this act as part of the discourse of imperial appropriation. Hunters created images of foreign lands that resembled images constructed and disseminated previously to British imperial culture. These images provided non-threatening consumable images and suggested that sublime landscapes merely required settlement and colonization to transform the sublime wilderness into picturesque colonial landscapes.

The construction of a sublime landscape first required a declaration of speechlessness. Employing a hallmark application of the aesthetic code, British big-game hunters described themselves so astonished at the sublime nature of specific landscapes that they professed themselves incapable of describing the experience. Regardless of their initial claims, the hunters immediately followed their declaration of ineffability with a code-based application of the sublime. The declaration of speechlessness firmly placed the landscape within the aesthetic and also reaffirmed the authority of the travel narrative and the narrator. Despite the initial rejection of their proprietary gaze and their subsequent declaration of speechlessness, British hunters overcame their claims of language inadequacy to triumphantly appropriate the landscape for the British empire. By identifying one's inability to describe the sublimity of the scene, and then describing it anyway, the hunter-explorer portrayed himself as capable of overcoming both literary and geographical boundaries. The British big-game hunter's declaration of speechlessness arose from the notion that the forest, barren, or prairie held either a physical or aesthetic obscurity or impenetrability arising from either sheer density or dimness. By initially rejecting the hunter's gaze, the inviolability of the landscape defied identification and exploration while also offering a surmountable challenge.[47]

Speechlessness resulted from the overpowering emotions brought forth by sublime astonishment, and astonishment provided the foundation from which one experienced all other sublime emotions, such as fear, apprehension, terror, and melancholy. Astonishment of the great and the sublime in nature stirred the most powerful and primal of emotions, such as horror and fear.[48] When astonished by a sublime landscape, the mind appeared so transfixed that it became impossible to describe the nature of the sublimity.[49]

A sampling of these claims of speechlessness illustrates their prevalence and importance as part of the sublime code. During his hunting trip to the West in 1859, hunter and sportsman Carnegie attempted to describe a pine forest. He wrote, "I wish some painter had been there, to paint what I so vainly attempt to describe. Never had I seen such an effect represented in art."[50] Butler, also hunting and travelling in the West, doubted if he could "place before the reader's mental vision anything like a true picture of the sense of solitude, of endless space, of awful desolation which at times comes to the traveller's mind as he looks over some vast prairie and beholds a lonely herd of bisons." Some exaggerated their declarations of speechlessness to reinforce to readers the sense of sublimity. Butler claimed speechlessness three times while recording his first impression of the Rocky Mountains in 1872. He exclaimed, "Alas, how futile it is to endeavour to describe such a view!" Butler further added that the sublimity of the mountains "is as much above my poor power of words, as He who built this mighty nature is higher still than all." Finally he wrote, "We cannot put in words the things that we see from these lonely mountain-tops when we climb them in the sheen of evening."[51]

British big-game hunters employed a codified, taxonomic understanding of the sublime. By claiming speechlessness, the sportsmen placed the forthcoming landscape description firmly within the aesthetic of the sublime. However, these descriptions did not construct the land as *strangely alien*. Instead, they used identifiable markers to distinguish the landscape as recognizably foreign based on the British cultural construction of the sublime. Like their picturesque appropriations, imperial-minded British hunters invoked the sublime code to construct variations of landscape to meet a preconceived expectation of the foreign in imperial culture.

The vast level prairies of the western interior and the arctic barrens of the Northwest confronted British hunters with landscapes unlike anything in England. They responded by describing the landscape as ocean-like. Their construction of ocean landscapes emerged from Burke's understanding of the sublime aesthetic. In his own work, he reinforced the sublimity of vastness and suggested that a level plain or barren presented a similar perspective to that of an ocean: "To things of great dimensions, if we annex an adventitious idea of terror, they become without comparison greater. A level plain of a vast extent on land, is certainly no mean idea; the prospect of such a plain may be as extensive as a prospect of the ocean."[52]

The construction of ocean-like landscapes on vast level prairies, plains, and arctic barrens emerged more from the scarcity of recognizable landscape features than from anything else. The prairies, plains, and barrens of Rupert's Land lacked two of the essential elements of the picturesque aesthetic: trees and elevated prospects.[53] These flat landscapes provided little or no foliage, and this presented problems for the aesthetic tastes of upper-class Britons. Without trees, which played an essential picturesque screening role, these long, flat expanses of country appeared dismal and lifeless.[54] With no elevated prospect to look down on nature, landscape viewers failed to establish a distinct midground – another key element of the picturesque.[55]

Another crucial difference relates to the sublime and its application in Rupert's Land. During the nineteenth century, British explorers, hunters, and fur traders possessed a vertical understanding of sublimity similar to that used to construct mountain landscapes on the European Grand Tour or the Highlands of Scotland. The British North American prairies provided an aesthetic conundrum for the British. British hunters, like the explorers and fur traders before them, modified the sublime code to emphasize horizontal sublimity rather than vertical sublimity. By applying the horizontal sublime to depict ocean-like landscapes, British hunters constructed and appropriated landscape images that fit within their cultural understanding of sublime foreign landscapes.

Hunter and naturalist William Ross King employed the horizontal sublime to construct the grasslands and prairies of the interior as ocean-like, while also reinforcing the importance of landscape aesthetics to the British hunter:

> As the mountain scenery of our [Scottish] Highlands forms so great a portion of the enjoyment of grouse shooting, so does the majesty of these ocean-like plains add to the fascination of prairie-hen shooting. There is something even supernaturally impressive in their vastness, everlasting silence, and solitude, and in no other situation perhaps does man feel more strikingly what an atom he is on the face of the earth than when fairly launched on the prairie ... Indeed, so utterly destitute of any landmark is the face of the plain that a person unused to move alone in these regions would quickly lose his way, and might wander on with a hundred miles of prairie before him, in vain search of the point he had started from, each

moment serving only to increase his distance from it, and every weary step leading him further away from human aid, fainting with fatigue and parched with thirst. No one should venture alone for any distance on the prairie until thoroughly able to trust himself to steer his own way by the aid of the sun.[56]

King stated that while travelling across these ocean-like landscapes one occasionally views "stunted trees or a patch of brushwood, but these can hardly be said to break the uniformity of the surface, for they are completely lost in the immense space and are rarely noticed at all till close at hand."[57] King's description of ocean-like prairies relates the importance among nineteenth-century sportsmen of enjoying the aesthetics of hunting in addition to the sport itself. He made the experience of prairie-hen shooting analogous to the experience of grouse shooting and deer stalking in the sublime windswept Scottish Highlands. Employing key elements of the sublime code, such as solemn silence, vastness, and solitude, King firmly placed his landscape description within the aesthetic.

Butler offered similar depictions of the landscape. During his 1872 exploring and hunting expedition, Butler wrote in *The Wild North Land*, "It was the last of October, just one day after my arrival at the Forks [of the Saskatchewan River], when we turned our faces westward in quest of buffalo." He added, "They were said to be a long way off – 200 miles nearer to the setting sun – out somewhere on that great motionless ocean, where no tree, no bush breaks the vast expanse of prairie." Butler made several other references to ocean-like landscapes on his journey, describing the landscape as "wild, treeless, and ocean-like in everything save motion." Butler continued his aesthetic appropriation of the land by making particular reference to familiar seas in Europe – a form of landscape associationism. He wrote, "What the Irish Sea, the Channel, the Baltic, and the Mediterranean are to the Atlantic, so are these various outlying regions of plain to the vast rigid ocean of the central continent. It is true that on the Red River, or the Qu'Appelle, or along the line I have lately passed, one may frequently 'get out of sight of land;' there are spaces where no tree or bush breaks the long monotony of the sky-line; but all these expanses are as nothing compared to the true prairie."[58]

Butler also used the ocean-like theme in his sketches and engravings to describe the prairies of the interior. The pictorial images of landscape included in his travel narrative reveal his emphasis on the sublime aesthetic. Although not an illustration of an ocean-like prairie itself, Butler used "View from the Spathanaw Watchi" as his gateway image to the vast prairie

5.2 "View from the Spathanaw Watchi." Located between the South Saskatchewan and
Qu'Appelle Rivers, the Spathanaw Watchi, or Dog Knoll, represented Butler's gateway
image to the ocean-like landscapes of the interior. William Francis Butler, *The Wild
North Land* (London: Low, Marston, Low, and Searle, 1873), 31.

oceans of the West (Figure 5.2).[59] Located between the South Saskatchewan
and Qu'Appelle Rivers, the Spathanaw Watchi, or Dog Knoll, represented
the only landmark prior to entering the vast level prairie. For Butler, and
fur trader Sir George Simpson decades before him, the hill presented the
only elevated prospect from which to attain a commanding view of the
surrounding landscape.[60] Standing atop the hill with his faithful Inuit
sled-dog, Cerf-Vola, Butler contemplated the sublimity of the ocean-like
landscape that lay ahead on his journey.

> Alone in a vast waste the Spathanaw Watchi lifts its head, thickets and lakes
> are at his base, a lonely grave at top, around four hundred miles of horizon;
> a view so vast that endless space seems for once to find embodiment, and
> at single glance the eye is satiated with immensity. There is no mountain
> range to come up across the sky-line, no river to lay its glistening folds along
> the middle distance, no dark forest to give shade to foreground or to fringe
> perspective, no speck of life, no track of man, nothing but the wilderness.
> Reduced thus to its own nakedness, space stands forth with almost terrible
> grandeur.[61]

5.3 "Tent in the Great Prairie." This ocean-like landscape emphasizes desolation and the horizontal sublime. William Francis Butler, *The Wild North Land* (London: Low, Marston, Low, and Searle, 1873), 69.

The idea of the mound lifting its head – as if a partially unearthed giant lay long buried – connected the site with Native legend and folklore, which viewed specific geographical locations as the remains of giant ancestors or great battlefields.[62] Butler continued his narration, straining to describe the limitless character of the ocean landscape that lay before him: "One is suddenly brought face to face with that enigma which we try to comprehend by giving to it the names of endless, interminable, measureless; that dark inanity which broods upon a waste of moorland at dusk, and in which fancy sees the spectral and the shadowy."[63] To Butler, the ocean landscapes of the West held no mountains, forests, or signs of life. They even appeared to Butler as grave-like and spectral, key descriptors in the ruins motif of the sublime. He extended his use of the horizontal sublime further by describing the ocean landscapes as endless, interminable, and measureless.[64]

After leaving the Spathanaw Watchi, Butler's following pictorial representation, "Tent in the Great Prairie," and corresponding narrative account illustrate his use of the horizontal sublime in his construction of sublime, ocean-like landscapes (Figure 5.3). This picture reveals several interesting features. Due to the lack of an elevated prospect, this image has no background – the landscape appears endless. Moreover, the buffalo merge with the midground horizon line to give a sense of the enormity

of the herd. Despite the presence of the animals, however, desolation
provides the overriding theme of this picture. While in the midst of this
ocean landscape, Butler described the feeling of utter isolation:

> Those who in summer or autumn visit the great prairie of the Saskatchewan
> can form but a faint idea of its winter fierceness and utter desolation ...
> Should they really wish to form a true conception of life in these solitudes,
> let them go out towards the close of November into the treeless waste; *then,*
> midst fierce storm and biting cold, and snowdrift so dense that earth and
> heaven seem wrapped together in indistinguishable chaos, they will witness
> a sight as different from their summer ideal as a mid-Atlantic mid-winter
> storm varies from a tranquil moonlight on the Aegean Sea. During the
> sixteen days in which we traversed the prairie on our return journey, we
> had not seen one soul, one human being moving over it; the picture of its
> desolation was complete."[65]

Butler's final narrative and sublime landscape image depicts buffalo-
hunting on the Great Prairie during the winter of 1872. Butler first prepared
his sublime sporting landscape with a declaration of speechlessness. He
wrote that he doubted whether he could possibly "place before the reader's
mental vision anything like a true picture of the sense of solitude, of endless
space, of awful desolation which at times comes to the traveller's mind as
he looks over some vast prairie and beholds a lonely herd of bisons trailing
slowly across that snow-wrapt, endless expanse, into the shadows of the
coming night."[66] The corresponding sublime landscape picture, "Sunset
Scene, with Buffalo," reinforces the sublimity of the western interior of
Rupert's Land (Figure 5.4). Like the "Tent in the Great Prairie," Butler's
image reveals no background whatsoever. These ocean-like landscapes
do indeed appear endless, and the buffalo again appear so vast that the
herd merges with the horizon line. The presence of trees in this picture
does not suggest the possibility of shelter or warmth. Instead, these trees
appear withered and broken, reinforcing the motif of lifelessness and utter
desolation.

The British big-game hunters' construction of ocean-like lands illustrates
the flexible manner in which they applied the sublime in the western
interior. With the vast prairies of the West presenting no opportunity to
employ the picturesque or the vertical sublime, British hunters resorted
to an application of the horizontal sublime to construct and appropriate
the landscape for their British audiences. The emphasis on desolation, the
complete removal of the background, and the lack of elevated prospects

5.4 "Sunset Scene, with Buffalo." This image illustrates Butler's view of horizontal sublimity. Like the "Tent in the Great Prairie," the buffalo herd merges with the background; these ocean-like landscapes do indeed appear endless. William Francis Butler, *The Wild North Land* (London: Low, Marston, Low, and Searle, 1873), 57.

contributed to the hunters' ocean-like construction of the landscape. Unlike the picturesque estate parklands discussed earlier, British hunters did not view the broad expanse of the interior as ready-made for imperial purposes. Instead, their construction of ocean-like landscapes portrayed specific areas as desolate and interminable. These landscapes did not fit the aesthetic of the picturesque, so British hunters constructed foreign landscapes that yet required exploration and appropriation. As the harbingers of empire, British hunters made sure to describe the land as sublime, but also to depict themselves *within* these sublime landscapes courageously hunting buffalo and going boldly into unfamiliar and dangerous colonial expanses.

The application of the sublime continued with the depiction of primeval forests as ancient, dark, dank, overgrown, murky, and impassable. In the forests of British Columbia during the 1850s, Milton and Cheadle called attention to the motif of the primeval forest. They reflected, "No one who has not seen a primeval forest, where trees of gigantic size have grown and fallen undisturbed for ages, can form any idea of the collection of timber, or the impenetrable character of such a region."[67] Beyond the vast nature of these wooded landscapes, British hunters imbued the forest with a temporal

5.5 "Cutting Up the Moose." Butler accentuated the vertical sublimity of the Rocky Mountains in this construction of primeval forest. The extreme vertical nature of the cone-shaped mountain reduces the agency of the British hunter and guides in the foreground. William Francis Butler, *The Wild North Land* (London: Low, Marston, Low, and Searle, 1873), 271.

untouched quality seemingly unknown to English forests. The primeval forest represented an ancient virgin woodland unspoiled by the presence of mankind. In addition to designating the forests as primeval, these examples reveal that the hunters also portrayed the woodlands as "impenetrable." This impenetrable obscurity, so crucial to the sublime, blocked their aesthetic gaze and created an obstacle for the hunter to overcome.[68]

British hunters used the vertical sublime in their construction of primeval forests. Rather than focusing on the horizontal sublimity of a vast level plain, the hunters concentrated on the vertical grandeur of trees, wooded cliffs, and mountains encircled by forest. The vertical sublime, transposed from European and colonial grand tours, emphasized straight perpendicular landscape features to convey the dominance of nature and to reduce human agency. Sublime enthusiasts during the nineteenth century argued that the presentation of nature's overwhelming power would lead to a sense of powerlessness, fear, and terror. The straighter the vertical lines, the stronger the emotional response to the landscape. A dramatic perpendicular line heightened the feeling of sublimity more than an inclined plane.[69]

The vertical sublimity of the primeval forest found expression in the hunters' sketches and pictures that accompanied their literary descriptions. Butler's images "Cutting Up the Moose" (Figure 5.5) and "Alone in the Wilderness" (Figure 5.6) reveal the recurrent emphasis on the vertical sublime in the construction of primeval forests. Butler also incorporated and accentuated the vertical sublimity of the Rocky Mountains in his construction of primeval forests. His pictorial representations, as well as Milton and Cheadle's "View of the North Thompson, Looking Eastward" reveal this emphasis (Figure 5.7). The extreme vertical nature of the cone-shaped mountain "some eight or nine thousand feet" in the background of "Cutting Up the Moose" stands out from the surrounding mountains and forest.[70] This mountain, as the central feature of this forest landscape, completely diminishes the presence of Butler and his Native guides in the foreground: the image embodies the British hunters' aesthetic and appropriative ideology in landscape. Butler employed a similar technique in "Alone in the Wilderness." This landscape image depicts his camp along the Peace River near the Rocky Mountains. Here again, the focus on the vertical sublime, with the precipitous perpendicular cliffs, contrasts with and diminishes the animated foreground. Like Butler's representations of the prairie, "Alone in the Wilderness" reinforced the absolute solitude of the sublime wilderness of the interior. Milton and Cheadle's "View of the North Thompson, Looking Eastward" presents a construction similar

5.6 "Alone in the Wilderness." This landscape shows Butler's camp along the Peace River near the Rocky Mountains. The use of precipitous perpendicular cliffs to contrast and diminish the animated foreground reveals the vertical sublime in nature. William Francis Butler, *The Wild North Land* (London: Low, Marston, Low, and Searle, 1873), 181.

5.7 "View of the North Thompson, Looking Eastward." This image illustrates the vertical sublime as experienced in the forests of Rupert's Land. William Fitzwilliam Milton and W.B. Cheadle, *The North-West Passage by Land* 6th ed. (1865; repr; Toronto: Coles Publishing, 1970), 275.

5.8 "The Look-Out Mountain." Butler used the horizontal sublime in his construction
of the primeval, sea-like forest. William Francis Butler, *The Wild North Land* (London:
Low, Marston, Low, and Searle, 1873), 327.

to "Cutting Up the Moose." They emphasized the vertical sublime in
this picture by contrasting the two figures in the left foreground against
immense trees in the midground and a mountain in the background.
Milton and Cheadle drew attention to the sublime in this image by
depicting the overgrowth, obscurity, and impenetrability of the primeval
forest. The trees in the midground reduce human agency by enveloping
them with an overarching canopy of branches.

The horizontal sublime also contributed to the hunters' aesthetic
vision and construction of primeval forests in the interior. Alongside
his application of the vertical sublime, Butler used the ocean-like motif
reserved typically for plains, barrens, tundra, and prairies to portray
the forest canopy in the dense woodlands of New Caledonia (British
Columbia). He stated, "over the sea of forest, from the dark green and
light green ocean of tree-tops, the solid mountain mass lay piled against
the east. Below my stand-point the first long reach of the canyon opened
out."[71] He continued, "I stood high above the canyon, high above the vast
forest which stretched between me and the mountains; and the eye, as
it wandered over the tranquil ocean upon whose waves the isles of light
green shade lay gold-crested in the sunset."[72]

The following image illustrates the use of obscurity, in conjunction with the horizontal sublime, to construct primeval forests. The landscape image entitled "The Look-Out Mountain" by Butler, depicting New Caledonia in 1872, reveals an attempt to convey the vast and impenetrable character of the primeval forest (Figure 5.8). The Rocky Mountains enclose the background of the picture and confine the British hunter's westward expansionist gaze. The image again confirms his sense of desolation while travelling through the primeval forest landscapes of the West and Northwest. The bear and the skull and bones that occupy the foreground of this image reveal a clear message: only desolation and death await those who dare to penetrate the primeval forests of British North America.

Beyond the vertical and horizontal sublime, the construction of primeval forests centred on two additional motifs: the supernatural and decay.[73] Although Burke did not discuss the supernatural extensively, he commented on the presence of ghosts and the propensity of supernatural phenomena to inspire sublime fear and terror. He wrote, "Night adds to our dread, in all cases of danger," and that "notions of ghosts and goblins, of which none can form clear ideas, affect minds, which give credit to the popular tales concerning such sorts of beings."[74] When the hunters referred to ghosts, they did not use the term literally but rather referred to landscape features that resembled the supernatural. Big-game hunters suggested the presence of ghost-like phenomena in the landscape to hint at the unknown and to further invoke sublime fear. While moose hunting, Edward Wyndham-Quin, Earl of Dunraven, peered into the forest and stated, "An occasional dwarfed pine, encumbered with hanging festoons of moss, strives to grow in the wet soil; and on drier spots, two or three tall, naked, dead firs, that have been burned in some bygone fire, look pale, like ghosts of trees in the deepening twilight."[75] On another occasion, he recalled that the moon shone "white upon the birch trees, throwing into black shadow the sombre pines, dimly lighting up the barren, and revealing grotesque ghost-like forms of stunted fir and grey rock. The tree trunks stand out distinct in the lessening gloom; the dark pine boughs overhead seem to stoop caressingly towards you."[76]

In addition to landscape features that resembled the supernatural, British hunters referenced images of decay in their code-based construction of primeval forests. To British eyes, the forests of British North America appeared in a perpetual cycle of life and death unaffected by human agency.[77] King attempted to convey the image of ancient overgrown woodlands. He observed, "The Grand forests, free of all brushwood, present a more striking appearance than anything else to the eye of one just arrived from the Old World. No one can enter their shadows or tread their long-drawn vistas of tall grey stems, spanned by over-arching roof of dark leaves, without the idea of a vast cathedral involuntarily rising in the mind. Like ruined columns, huge prostrate trunks lie strewn around, some but newly fallen, others moss-grown and verdant, with creeping plants; while many show only a dark line of decayed vegetable mould, the last and rapidly disappearing vestige of their former stateliness."[78] King's description of the forest made use of several aspects of the sublime code. The "over-arching roof" of trees dwarfs the presence of the hunter and reduces his power in the face of nature. The experience seems like a religious one for King who, awed by and revering the sheer power of the forest, worships in nature's "vast cathedral."

Of all the hunter's descriptions, Milton and Cheadle's offered the sublime literary archetype of the primeval forest. "No one who has not seen a primeval forest, where trees of gigantic size have grown and fallen undisturbed for ages, can form any idea of the collection of timber, or the impenetrable character of such a region. There were pines and thujas [cedar] of every size, the patriarch of 300 feet in height standing alone, or thickly clustering groups of young ones struggling for the vacant place of some prostrate giant" wrote Milton. In addition to drawing the reader's attention by outright labelling his description a "primeval forest," Milton also employed themes crucial to the aesthetic of the sublime. Oversized growth, a temporal prehistoric quality, impenetrability, obscurity, and vertical sublimity – all were key elements in the construction of a primeval forest. He continued his description, emphasizing the motif of decay:

> The fallen trees lay piled around, forming barriers often six or eight feet high on every side: trunks of huge cedars, moss-grown and decayed, lay half-buried in the ground on which others as mighty had recently fallen; trees still green and living, recently blown down, blocking the view with the walls of earth held in their matted roots; living trunks, dead trunks, rotten trunks; dry, barkless trunks, and trunks moist and green with moss; bare trunks and trunks with branches – prostrate, reclining, horizontal, propped up at different angles; timber of every size, in every stage of growth and decay, in every possible position, entangled in every possible condition.[79]

Milton concluded his description by acknowledging the impassable character of the landscape. The wilderness rejected the physical passage of the British hunter and his gaze. The theme of decay so forcefully described by

Milton in this archetype of the primeval forest gave rise to the emotions of sublime melancholy, fear, and apprehension.

The description of solemn silence within the ocean-like plains and primeval forests of the West reveals another aspect of the sublime. British hunters used either excessive loudness or excessive silence to invoke the sublime. Excessive loudness in nature, such as the sound of a waterfall or thunder, could inspire sublime terror.[80] In addition to the sound of nature in extreme, animal sounds formed part of the sublime, particularly sounds that imitated those of humans or animals in danger or pain. The angry noise of wild beasts and big game also inspired the sublime.[81] Although they commented on the sublime sounds of the wilderness, British hunters also used the solemn silence of the wilderness to invoke feelings of sublime fear.[82] Employing this understanding of the sublime, British hunters emphasized the silence of the wilderness to reinforce their complete withdrawal from the safety of civilization.

Butler discussed the silence, solitude, and loneliness of the wilderness. Most found the silence unnerving, but Butler, on the other hand, found communion and companionship with nature's isolation: "The great silent river, the lofty ridge darkening against the twilight, yon star burning like a beacon above the precipice – all *these* were friends, and midst them one could rest in peace. I was there almost in the centre of the vast wilderness of North America, around, stretched in silence, that mystery we term Nature."[83] Travelling through the Rocky Mountains, Butler again observed that the landscape "was stillness; forest, isle, river and mountain – all seemed to sleep in unending loneliness; and our poles grating against the rocky shore, or a shot at some quick-diving beaver, alone broke the silence; while the echo, dying away in the vast mountain canyons, made the relapsing silence seem more intense."[84] The emphasis on solemn silence reveals a key component of the sublime aesthetic code. This silence reinforced the hunter's sublime construction of the landscape as desolate and completely removed from the comforts and safety of civilization. By corresponding to the sublime, claims of solemn silence further contributed to the overall sense of foreignness of the colonial landscape.

The presence of God in nature lent further credence to the sublimity of the landscape. The power of the vertical and horizontal sublime in nature prompted spiritual reflection. Burke justified the ability of the sublime to inspire visions of God through a discussion of the Bible: "In the scripture, wherever God is represented as appearing or speaking, every thing terrible in nature is called up to heighten the awe and solemnity of the divine presence."[85] The association of God with the sublime ultimately hinted at a new appreciation for God's omnipotence. The British made grandiose references to the presence of God and Mother Nature when first confronted with Niagara Falls. The pilgrimage to the Falls and subsequent experience with the sublime was so strong that "it was not unusual for tourists to describe their reaction to the falls as a profound religious awakening."[86] Whether Britons viewed God incarnate in nature or not, spiritual claims provided an important and powerful aspect of the sublime. The presence of God or Mother Nature, like the feeling of sublime melancholy or a claim of speechlessness, contributed to the veracity of the sublime landscape description and the feelings of awe and reverence inspired by it.

In addition to referring to God, hunters used religious references to Mother Nature and Heaven. While standing on an ocean-like prairie landscape, Carnegie stated, "it is strange to find oneself on an apparently flat disc of grass, nothing but grass meeting the plain horizon-line all around. One feels as if crawling about in view of high Heaven on a circular table punched out from the world and stuck on a spike."[87] At the Grand Fork of the Fraser River in present-day British Columbia, Milton and Cheadle described Robson's Peak: "When we first caught sight of it, a shroud of mist partially enveloped the summit ... and we saw its upper portion dimmed by a necklace of light feathery clouds, beyond which its pointed apex of ice, glittering in the morning sun, shot up far into the blue heaven above, to a height of probably 10,000 or 15,000 feet."[88] Butler invoked the presence of God: "Not more wooden are the ark animals of our childhood, than words in which man would clothe the images of that higher nature which the Almighty has graven into the shapes of lonely mountains!"[89] He continued by comparing the sublime mountain landscape to a church where one could offer reverence and worship God and Mother Nature: "You expect me to tell you about this church, whose pillars are the mountains, whose roof is the heaven itself, whose music comes from the harp-strings which the earth had laid over her bosom, which we call pine-trees; and from which the hand of the Unseen draws forth a ceaseless symphony rolling ever around the world."[90]

Hunters made references to Mother Nature and her omnipotence as part of a quasi-religious sublime experience inspired by landscape. Wyndham-Quin observed that in the midst of the wilderness, "surrounded by a majesty that is appalling, he shrinks not, nor is he dismayed. In a scene of utter loneliness he feels himself not to be alone. A sense of companionship, a sensation of satisfaction, creep over him. He feels at one with Nature, at rest in her strong protecting arms."[91] Butler wrote, "I was there almost in the centre of the vast wilderness of North America, around, stretched in silence, that mystery we term Nature, that thing which we see in pictures, in landscapes, in memory; which we see and hear in the voice of wind-swept forests and the long sob of seas against ocean rocks."[92] He added, "This mother, ever present, ever mysterious, sometimes terrible, often tender – always beautiful – stood there with nought to come between us save loneliness and twilight."[93] Spiritual claims, be they directed to God or Mother Nature, provided an important part of the sublime code. Like speechlessness or assertions of solemn silence, the religious component of the sublime provided an important aspect of the aesthetic code that, for British readers, contributed to the veracity of the sublime in landscape.

The application of the sublime code, as revealed through hunting narratives, focused on the construction of ocean-like landscapes and primeval forests in the western interior. The repeated application of the vertical and horizontal sublime, the primeval forest, references to the supernatural, and the motif of decay illustrate their efforts to appropriate the landscape through the sublime. Since the British landed elite owned most of the remaining forests in England during the nineteenth century, the construction of the forest in British North America within their travel narratives reveals as much about the discourse of class as it does the forest as a marker of the sublime. Only those with the material means and education of the social elite could encode wilderness lands into sublime landscapes. More important, Victorians believed that imperialists and their culture would ultimately break the impenetrability and obscurity of the primeval forest in North America. As a resource, they believed the colonial landscape would ultimately yield to the needs of British civilization. Big-game hunters would wipe out large wilderness predators, leading the way for British settlers to thin out the primeval forests, or plant clumps of trees on the ocean-like prairie, to transform the sublime wilderness into picturesque colonial landscapes.

British big-game hunters encoded their wilderness visions of the western interior into the picturesque and the sublime. Far from offering innocent descriptions, they generated images of unknown lands with their class-based landscape preferences. Through these forms of representation, they appropriated the landscape but also *naturalized* their appropriation by constructing landscapes that fit within pre-existing British cultural codes. Although the aesthetics of the sublime and the picturesque consisted of identifiable codes, they required a degree of negotiation in their application. The hunter-explorers used the familiar construct of the sublime to other the wilderness, but they did so within specific parameters. Their representations depicted the foreign from within their cultural conception of foreignness. The British hunters' constructions, specifically of the sublime, corresponded to a set of loosely conceived and adaptable cultural representations of the foreign within British imperial culture. In this paradoxical way, the sublime familiarized and appropriated the interior. Alongside the specific colonial adaptations of the picturesque and the sublime, British hunters also employed stock elements of these aesthetics, such as picturesque estate parklands, that had particular resonance with their elite readerships. Whether describing the picturesque or the sublime, they used their modified colonial renderings to approximate a set of familiar and recognizable *British* landscapes for readers at home. As we shall see, these class-based picturesque and sublime sporting landscapes continued to inform tourists' perceptions of the Canadian West for decades to come.

6

From Colonial to
Corporate Landscapes

Not pen, nor brush, nor tongue can convey the proper idea of the sublimity of those marvelous mountains; they are something too imposing for mere words; they must be seen and studied. One must live among them and watch the glories of sunlight upon their everlasting snows and glaciers; must climb their steeps and breathe the cold, thin atmosphere of those dizzy elevations, and train his eyes to measure soaring pinnacles and dark abysses ere he can realize their stupendous grandeur. One must hear the thunderous voice of the whirling storms amid their peaks; the avalanche tearing the forests from their native slopes; the avulsion of crag and giant boulder from buttresses frowning darkly above the clouds, and the booming echoes of waves of mighty sound breaking against the walls of unmeasured ravines, ere the full power of those matchless monuments of the old-time war of forces is impressed upon the mind. And then the glory of laying low the game that haunts them. Right well did the Indian hunter know what tested manhood, when first he wrenched the great scimitar-shaped claws from the broad fore-paw of the dead grizzly, and strung them around his neck as a token to prove a man. Time has changed many things, the rifle has supplanted the bow, but nothing has supplanted the grizzly; he is there yet, and king of the wilds; his claws are yet the proudest ornament the savage can wear, and his skin the most valued trophy of the white sportsman.[1]

To portray the grandeur of the Canadian Rocky Mountains, the author set this scene firmly within the aesthetic of the sublime. He began, as one typically would, by providing a declaration of speechlessness to ensure readers of the veracity of the forthcoming account. The author reinforced the importance of experiencing the landscape first-hand in order to appreciate the absolute awe-inspiring effect. The literary motifs consistent with the sublime, such as storms, avalanches, crags, boulders, and ravines suggest an almost alien landscape. Only within this sublime landscape could the white hunter stalk the mighty grizzly bear with his scimitar-like claws. There, in the solitude of the primeval Canadian wilderness and far from a paper-filled desk, the big-game hunter could test his mettle against the king of the wilds, claim his trophy, and reclaim his manhood.[2]

So closely does this sublime hunting landscape description follow the literary conventions of British travel literature that the passage seems like a quote taken directly from the pages of a mid-nineteenth-century big-game hunting narrative. However, the author of this passage was no big-game hunter – he wrote corporate advertising brochures for the Canadian Pacific Railway (CPR) in the late 1880s. Entitled *Fishing and Shooting along the Line of the Canadian Pacific Railway*, this popular CPR promotional brochure, and others like it, appropriated and redeployed sporting landscapes from published big-game hunting narratives to market the Canadian West during the late nineteenth and early twentieth centuries. In the years that followed the passing of the frontier and the development of transcontinental railroad service in 1885, the CPR targeted elite British sportsmen specifically with their advertising, and they invoked culturally recognizable literary devices, sporting scenes, and landscapes, similar to those discussed throughout this book, as the central motifs of the campaign. Grounded in the cultural conventions of British travel discourse, the CPR tapped into sublime themes to invoke the image of a primeval romantic wilderness.[3] They also employed the aesthetic of the picturesque to construct an antimodern escape from the hustle and bustle of modernity. In these ways, the CPR leaned on the previously published colonial landscapes of the western interior as their "new" corporate landscapes of the Canadian West.

Like the sublime account that opened this chapter, the CPR's use of cultural landscapes provided a backdrop for the specific depiction of sport and the marketing of sporting holidays. The CPR populated sublime and picturesque landscapes with class-appropriate game, such as grizzly bears and Rocky Mountain ram. They demonstrated places where British hunters could hunt game in a sportsmanlike manner, consistent with the hunting ethos.[4] The CPR used landscape and game associationism and drew parallels with hunting tourism in Europe, Africa, and India. One promotion read, "If you are a sportsman, you will meet with unlimited opportunities and endless variety, and no one shall deny you the right to hunt or fish at your sweet will. If you are a mountain climber, you shall have cliffs and peaks and glaciers worthy of your alpenstock, and if you have lived in India, and tiger hunting has lost its zest, a Rocky Mountain grizzly bear will renew your interest in life."[5] Strategies like these found repeated expression in the CPR advertising of the Canadian West. The CPR took aim at the next generation of elite British hunters and sportsmen in the 1880s and 1890s, and redeployed colonial images for capitalist purposes.[6] The CPR, through the explicit appropriation and implementation of colonial discourse, marketed back to elite British sportsmen and tourists a series of images already grounded in the conventions of British travel literature.

The corporate landscape most often marketed to British hunters by the CPR leaned on the motif of the Canadian West as the empire's Eden or a picturesque sportsman's paradise.[7] The CPR's literary and pictorial construction of the sportsman's Eden rested on an amalgam of everything the British hunter might find ideal in a sporting vacation, which included landscape images filled with overabundant game. Although hunters throughout British North America and nineteenth-century Canada referred to various regions in Edenic terms, the West and Northwest appear most closely associated with this construction.[8] Western promoters, expansionists, and the CPR engaged actively in boosterism and produced pamphlets, brochures, displays, pictures, and photographs constructing Western Canada as the sportsmen's paradise.[9] Many of these images leaned on the theme of wildlife superabundance, and tied into the "back to nature" and urban reform movements of the late 1800s. Although the image of the Canadian West as the sportsmen's Eden remained a part of CPR advertising, the motif of the mountaineer's playground, emphasizing the Selkirks and the Rockies, supplanted the sportsmen's Eden as the CPR's dominant corporate landscape in the early twentieth century.[10]

Between the 1840s and the 1870s, prior to the arrival of the CPR and the creation of advertising brochures, the western interior of Rupert's Land presented an evocative destination for imperial sporting adventure. During this fascinating period of change, the influence of the Hudson's Bay Company (HBC) continued to wane, and the CPR had yet to replace the HBC as the dominant economic, social, and cultural engine that would integrate the region into the British empire. Also during these decades, the popular perception of the frontier began to evolve from that of a vast desolate wilderness to a potential region for settlement. The buffalo, the British hunters' primary attraction to the region, provided excellent sport and still crossed the plains in numbers. No longer the hinterland of the fur trade, the western interior of Rupert's Land appeared to big-game hunters as a familiar, resource-rich land ready-made for expansionists, settlers, and the coming of the railroad.

The writing of a travel narrative was a central expression of imperial culture. Indeed, elite education, social position, and literary ability to encode hunting and exploration experiences into text were as crucial as sport itself. Early in their narratives, British hunters employed specific literary strategies to encourage the commonsense acceptance of their authorship of travel narratives. Instead of simply relaying the scope and purpose of their books, the prefaces of hunting texts served to construct the author and his literary authority. Through specific linguistic codes set at the beginning of their prefatory remarks, big-game hunters like Charles Alston Messiter asserted the truthfulness of their forthcoming colonial accounts. The authors of sporting narratives, like most travel narratives, worked feverishly to this end. Despite their truth claims and positivistic language, the hunters often contradicted themselves through statements of self-deprecation, pandering, highlighting errata and omissions, or acknowledging the influence of individuals and institutions in the development of their books. In these glancing but fundamental ways, authors undermined their statements of truth and the commonsense acceptance of their narratives.

Within their travel and exploration texts, British hunters expressed their imperial culture of "sport," in the form of the elite hunting code, for the purpose of exclusion and to take possession of colonial game. Through their code, men like James Carnegie, the Earl of Southesk, mediated colonial class relations. They used their gentrified notions of hunting etiquette to identify their moral inferiors, such as lesser colonists and Native peoples, and restricted them from access to game. British hunters invoked the legitimizing language of class, the games ethic, and respectability to highlight their social character and to enforce a hierarchy of class, race, and gender privilege. Through the hunting code, they identified "scientific" methods of taking game and vilified the methods of others as cruel and uncivilized. Despite their claims of adherence to the code that emphasized discretion and rationality, however, British big-game hunters routinely gave in to their less rational impulses and slaughtered colonial game. On these occasions, the hunters excused their behaviour through the discourse of science and the advancement of natural history.

As much as knives, rifles, or bullets, British hunters used science – in the forms of cartography and natural history – as weapons in their cultural appropriation of the interior. Through their maps, British hunters constructed an anticipatory geography of imperialism. Like explorer and hunter

William Butler, they constructed images of space and lined their cultural constructions with grids of latitude and longitude to indicate the position of the western interior of Rupert's Land in the British empire, constructed landscapes and landmarks, and christened them with familiar British place names. These images, superimposed over existing cultural formations, constructed new images of seemingly British-looking places. In addition to maps, British hunters used the science of natural history in their construction of place. As part of a larger process of cultural signification, the plants and animals identified through the Linnaean system of Latin nomenclature, symbolized imperial possession. British sportsman William Ross King also advocated the acclimatization of colonial fish and game to England for upper-class sport and consumption. Through these multiple frames of cultural reference, British hunters brought the western interior into focus.

In concert with their creation of maps, British hunters invoked the aesthetic landscape principles of the picturesque and the sublime to construct "nature." Composed of specific British class-based cultural codes, only those with the education and an understanding of landscape principles possessed the ability to encode and decode meaningful images of place. They employed the picturesque to depict landscapes that resembled England. Through the proprietary code of the picturesque, Sir Frederick Ulric Graham, the Baronet of Netherby, and other British hunters, constructed landscapes that resembled the parklands of their English estates. Specific to their colonial context, they also used the picturesque to highlight resources and use value. When the terrain appeared strange, British hunters imposed the aesthetic of the sublime to construct images of primeval forests and ocean-like landscapes. By identifying the terrain as foreign, hunters paradoxically familiarized the landscape and portrayed themselves as the harbingers of empire. Although the implementation of these two principles resulted in decidedly different landscape images, I argue that both landscape principles reveal a discourse of proprietorship, and that the act of applying these cultural constructs to the wilderness landscape was an act of appropriation. Big-game hunters sought to represent the landscapes of Rupert's Land, but also to represent themselves undertaking imperial activities in those landscapes. They naturalized their presence *within* these seemingly British landscapes by depicting themselves engaged in big-game hunting – the exclusive pursuit of the landed and leisured elite. In this way, the hunter-explorers constructed and signified their representations of the interior. Set within a British-looking landscape, surrounded by game identified through British science, and flanked by new landmarks with familiar British place names, elite sporting gentlemen engaged in and depicted themselves in the ritual of the upper-class hunt, and in doing so wrote themselves into the colonial history of Rupert's Land. This proprietary process of representation dispossessed, appropriated, and possessed the frontier in one swift literary motion.

In the preceding chapters, I used the themes of authorship, sport, science, and nature to provide a critical analysis of imperialism as revealed through big-game hunting narratives from the western interior of Rupert's Land. I began by situating these travel books as cultural texts, positioned as part of a broader imperial literary tradition, and proceeded to offer a reading of the specific linguistic codes, systems of meaning, and forms of representation embedded within their pages. The extent to which travel books are laden with textual and pictorial representations, and to which these images are bound by specific symbols and codes, reveals much about their importance within British hunting culture. Instead of simple descriptions that chronicled their adventures, British hunters invoked proprietary discourses that produced cultural meaning while framing their depiction of sport within a context of imperial appropriation. Not all of these strategies worked to their advantage. The class-based sport of big-game hunting and the structure of hunting narratives are beset, indeed saturated with, contradiction and incongruity. Many of these incongruities served to weaken the authority and position of the hunters as they attempted to bring the terrain under the aegis of British control.

Although we will never have a complete understanding of the codified ritual of imperial big-game hunting, we do know that British hunters drew several class-based meanings from the sport. Through big-game hunting and the hunting code, men constructed their imperial whiteness and expressed their class position to exclude lesser classes and racial groups from access to resources. Through the sport, these men found an anti-modern wilderness escape from the hustle and bustle of professional urban life, and yet they also used the sport to express the rationality of modern science. The activity provided meaning by combatting effeminacy and allowing the hunters to constitute themselves as men. As they hunted game across the interior, British men found meaning in the landscape and constructed visions of the wilderness based on familiarity and difference. They even took meaning from the act of travel writing. Their writings evince great care, particularly in the form and style of their narrative and literary authority. Through words, texts, symbols, rituals, and systems of power, big-game hunters invested and drew multiple meanings from the lived discourse of imperial big-game hunting.

Examining big-game hunting in Rupert's Land during the mid-nineteenth century required something of a departure from conventional approaches to and interpretations of primary sources. The varied motivations of the imperial-minded men, along with an early context for expeditions devoted exclusively to sport, required a malleable application of the term "hunter" during the period under discussion. Although I used the label "big-game hunters" as shorthand, these individuals represented a group of *men who hunted for sport* rather than a definable group of *sport hunters* more commonly found in the later nineteenth or early twentieth century. Big-game hunting as a sporting pursuit in the western interior during the mid-nineteenth century was often embedded within, or existed alongside, other cultural activities; as a form of sport tourism, big-game hunting was only beginning to be expressed for its own sake in this region.[11] Moreover, there has been a tendency in the historiography to view the men who travelled to the interior – hunters, explorers, surveyors, and scientists – in their strictly defined roles. Focus on these classifications has narrowed our understanding and, in this context, peripheralized the study of big-game hunting in favour of other topics.[12] Throughout this book, I attempted to blur these definitions by positioning them as men of both science, sport, and nature. Lastly, the period examined in this book represents a transitory stage between the early expression of sport hunting in the narratives of British fur traders and the popular rise of the middle- and upper-class sporting holiday in Western Canada during the late nineteenth and early twentieth centuries.

British hunter-explorers used depictions of otherness and sameness to represent the western interior of Rupert's Land. The negotiation of this Ornamentalist dynamic offered British hunters ways of visualizing the colonial frontier for their readerships in England. In addition to Ornamentalism's focus on class and social hierarchy, I examined the hunter's negotiation of the foreign and the domestic by discussing their cultural preconceptions and analyzing the culture of adaptability through which they framed their pictures of the interior. They shifted back and forth between sights and sounds they perceived as unfamiliar and strange and those they viewed as similar and domestic – a choreographed form of representation that played itself out across countless pages of hunting narratives. They employed specific forms of geographical reconnaissance to construct a set of homogenizing parameters applicable across numerous colonial frontiers where little or no homogeneity existed.[13] These images normalized their appropriation in a form of representation known as the anti-conquest and presented the hunters as removed from the act of proprietorship. This form of representation further included a malleable cult of associationism with enough peripheral variety to present a new landscape image, and yet was reminiscent enough of previous colonial constructions to be recognizable as familiar or foreign to their British imperial audience. Taking possession in this manner facilitated the representation and appropriation of colonial frontiers across a vast and diverse empire. The British hunters' representation of otherness and sameness emerged from deep-seated and culturally mediated beliefs of land ownership, social class, and loyalty to the British empire.

In *Hunting for Empire,* I suggest that the process of cultural appropriation, as revealed through hunters' writings, was a part of an ongoing process of cultural vision and revision of the interior, rather than a single event or act. This process involved the repeated representation of the land through British cultural systems that reaffirmed to the imperial centre the nature and Britishness of the territory and its resources. In this sense, hunting and exploration narratives represent how British hunters imagined Rupert's Land, rather than presenting an exact description of the territory. They reveal a series of discourses set forth by the British hunter and his imperial imagination. When examining these books, we are left with the difficult task of scholarly explanation – examining the signs, textuality, and cultural meanings associated with nineteenth-century narratives of sporting adventure. At first glance, hunting books and their positivistic language appear to represent some sort of positivistic truth. Their multiplicity of interpretation, however, disrupts any effort to characterize them as accurate reflections of historical realities. Rather than making a record of truthful observations, British big-game hunters used their travel narratives to construct and signify the western interior of Rupert's Land.

Big-game hunting and exploration narratives fascinate us today for the same reason they captivated readers during the nineteenth century. As they turned the pages of hunting texts, stay-at-home imperialists experienced the sport of big-game hunting vicariously. Readers imagined themselves riding alongside heroic men, stalking ferocious game, traversing the vast frontier, and making geographical discoveries, all in the name of the British empire – or, as I reminisced at the opening of this book, under the watchful eye of the Queen. The capacity of these narratives to render such vivid images provides us with opportunities to examine the cultural history of hunting, travel writing, and empire in the western interior of Rupert's Land. These evocative themes provide a point of departure that speaks to the memories of a shy freckled lad, sitting quietly on a chair, daydreaming in the Sportsman's Barbershop.

Notes

FOREWORD

1 This despite Thomas L. Altherr and John F. Reiger, "Academic Historians and Hunting: A Call for More and Better Scholarship," *Environmental History Review* 19, 3 (1995): 39-56.
2 Several of these items are noted in Jean L. Manore, "Introduction," in *The Culture of Hunting in Canada*, ed. Jean L. Manore and Dale G. Miner (Vancouver: UBC Press, 2007), 7. See also J.A Swan, *The Sacred Art of Hunting* (Minocqua, WI: Willow Creek Press, 1999); Randall Eaton, *The Sacred Hunt: Hunting as a Sacred Path* (Ashland, OR: Sacred Press, 1998) and Jose Ortega y Gasset, *Meditations on Hunting* (New York: Charles Scribner's and Sons, 1972); S.R. Kellert, "The Attitudes and Characteristics of Hunters and Antihunters," in *Papers of the Forty-Third North American Wildlife Conference,* ed. Kenneth Sabol (Washington, DC: Wildlife Management Institute, 1978); Thomas L. Altherr, "The American Hunter-Naturalist and the Development of the Code of Sportsmanship," *Journal of Sport History* 5, 1 (1978): 7-22; J. Ward Thomas, "Fair Chase and Technology: Then, Now and Tomorrow," *Proceedings of the Western Association of Fish and Wildlife Agencies* (Jackson, WY: Western Association of Fish and Wildlife Agencies, 1998), 35-40; Roderick Nash, *Wilderness and the American Mind* (New Haven, CT: Yale University Press, 1967); John F. Reiger, *American Sportsmen and the Origins of Conservation* (New York: Winchester, 1975); E.P Thompson, *Whigs and Hunters: The Origin of the Black Act* (New York: Pantheon Books, 1975); William K. Stoery, "Big Cats and Imperialism: Lion and Tiger Hunting in Kenya and northern India, 1898-1930," *Journal of World History*, 2, 2 (1991): 135-73, Edward I. Steinhart, *Black Poachers, White Hunters: A Social History of Hunting in Colonial Kenya* (Athens, OH: Ohio University Press, 2006); Roderick Neumann, *Imposing Wilderness* (Berkeley: University of California Press, 1998).
       Boys' adventure stories focused on hunting constitute a small library in their own right. Any search of works by R.M. Ballantyne, G.A. Henty, W.H.G. Kingston, or Captain Mayne Reid will yield numerous examples. Malaspina College BC historian Patrick Dunae wrote his PhD dissertation for the University of Manchester (1975) on British juvenile

literature in the age of empire, 1880-1914, and the theme is further explored in John M. MacKenzie, "Hunting and the Natural World in Juvenile Literature," in *Imperialism and Juvenile Literature*, ed. Jeffrey Richards (Manchester: Manchester University Press, 1989), 144-72; Stephen Taylor, *The Mighty Nimrod: A Life of Frederick Courtney Selous, African Hunter and Adventurer, 1851-1917* (London: Collins, 1989); Frederick C. Selous, *A Hunter's Wanderings in Africa* (London: Richard Bentley, 1890); and Frederick C. Selous, *African Nature: Notes and Reminiscences* (London: Macmillan, 1908).

    For a general overview see Matt Cartmill, *A View to a Death in the Morning: Hunting and Nature through History* (Cambridge, MA: Harvard University Press, 1993). See also Heidi Dahles, "Game Killing and Killing Games: An Anthropologist Looking at Hunting in a Modern Society," *Society & Animals: Journal of Human-Animal Studies* 1, 2 (1993): 169-89.

3 John M. MacKenzie, *The Empire of Nature: Hunting Conservation and British Imperialism* (Manchester: Manchester University Press, 1988), 7.

4 C.H. Stigand and Denis D. Lyell, *Central African Game and Its Spoor* (London: H. Cox, 1906), 2, cited in MacKenzie, *Empire of Nature*, 37; Jan Morris, *Pax Britannica: The Climax of an Empire* (London: Faber, 1968).

5 Kingsley cited in Bruce Haley, *The Healthy Body and Victorian Culture* (Cambridge, MA: Harvard University Press, 1978), 119.

6 William C. Oswell, *William Cotton Oswell, Hunter and Explorer*, vol. 1 (London: Heinemann, 1900), 83, cited in MacKenzie, *Empire of Nature*, 101.

7 Harriet Ritvo, "Destroyers and Preservers: Big Game in the Victorian Empire," *History Today* 52, 1 (2002): 33-39; see also Harriet Ritvo, *The Animal Estate: The English and Other Creatures in the Victorian Age* (Cambridge, MA: Harvard University Press, 1987); Jane Carruthers, *The Kruger National Park: a Social and Political History* (Pietermaritzburg: University of Natal Press, 1995); and James R. Ryan, "Hunting with the Camera: Photography, Wildlife and Colonialism in Africa," in *Animal Spaces, Beastly Places: New Geographies of Human–Animal Relations*, ed. Chris Philo and Chris Wilbert (London: Routledge, 2000), 203–21.

8 Tina Loo, *States of Nature: Conserving Canada's Wildlife in the Twentieth Century* (Vancouver: UBC Press, 2006); John Sandlos, *Hunters at the Margin: Native People and Wildlife Conservation in the Northwest Territories* (Vancouver: UBC Press, 2007); George Colpitts, *Game in the Garden: A Human History of Wildlife in Western Canada to 1940* (Vancouver: UBC Press, 2002); James A Burnett, *A Passion for Wildlife: The History of the Canadian Wildlife Service* (Vancouver: UBC Press, 2003).

9 Manore and Miner, eds., *Culture of Hunting*.

10 Tina Loo "Of Moose and Men: Hunting for Masculinities in British Columbia, 1880-1939," *Western Historical Quarterly* 32, 3 (2001): 296-319; John Sandlos, "From the Outside Looking In: Aesthetics, Politics, and Wildlife Conservation in the Canadian North," *Environmental History* 6 (January 2001): 6–31.

11 Elizabeth Vibert, "Real Men Hunt Buffalo: Masculinity, Race and Class in British Fur Traders' Narratives," in *Cultures of Empire: Colonizers in Britain and the Empire in the Nineteenth and Twentieth Centuries*, ed. Catherine Hall (New York: Routledge, 2000), 281-97; Jeffrey McNairn, "Meaning and Markets: Hunting, Economic Development and British Imperialism in Maritime Travel Narratives," *Acadiensis* 34 (2005): 1-23; David Calverley, "Who Controls the Hunt: Ontario's Game Act, the Canadian Government and the Ojibwa, 1800-1940" (PhD diss., University of Ottawa, 1999): David Calverley, "'When the Need for It No Longer Existed': Declining Wildlife and Native Hunting Rights in

Ontario, 1791-1898," in *Culture of Hunting,* ed. Manore and Miner, 104-20. See also Bill Parenteau and Richard Judd, "More Buck for the Bang: Sporting and the Ideology of Wildlife Management in New England and the Maritime Provinces, 1870–1900," in *New England and the Maritime Provinces: Comparisons and Connections,* ed. Stephen Hornsby and John Reid (Montreal and Kingston: McGill-Queen's University Press, 2006), 232-51.

12 Nancy B. Bouchier and Ken Cruikshank, "'Sportsmen and Pothunters': Environment, Conservation, and Class in the Fishery of Hamilton Harbour, 1858-1914," *Sport History Review* 28 (1997): 1-18; William Parenteau, "Care, Control, and Supervision: Native People in the Canadian Atlantic Salmon Fishery, 1867–1900," *Canadian Historical Review* 79 (March 1998): 1–35; and William Parenteau, "A 'Very Determined Opposition to the Law': Conservation, Angling Leases, and Social Conflict in the Canadian Atlantic Salmon Fishery, 1867-1914," *Environmental History* 9 (2004): 436-63; Douglas C. Harris, *Fish, Law, and Colonialism: the Legal Capture of Salmon in British Columbia* (Toronto: University of Toronto Press, 2001); J. Michael Thoms, "Ojibwa Fishing Grounds: A History of Ontario Fisheries Law, Science, and the Sportsmen's Challenge to Aboriginal Treaty Rights, 1650-1900" (PhD diss., University of British Columbia, 2004).

13 Vibert, "Real Men"; Colpitts, *Game in the Garden*; Loo, "Making a Modern Wilderness: Conserving Wildlife in Twentieth Century Canada, *Canadian Historical Review* 82, 1 (2001): 91-121; and Karen Wonders, "Hunting Narratives of the Age of Empire: A Gender Reading of Their Iconography," *Environment and History* 11 (2005): 269-91, which focuses on the areas of Alberta and British Columbia between 1875 and 1914.

14 There is a considerable relevant literature. In addition to material cited by Gillespie, perhaps begin with Joyce O. Appleby, Lynn A. Hunt, and Margaret Jacob, *Telling the Truth about History* (New York: W.W. Norton, 1994); Keith Jenkins, *Re-thinking History,* with a new preface and conversation with the author by Alun Munslow (London: Routledge, 2003); Richard J. Evans, *In Defence of History* (London: Granta, 1997); and Patrick K. O'Brien, "Book Review: An Engagement with Postmodern Foes, Literary Theorists and Friends on the Borders with History" and the response by Alan Munslow in *History in Focus* 2 (2001), http://www.history.ac.uk/ihr/Focus/Whatishistory/reviews.html.

15 The quotation is from "Cultural Studies Central," http://www.culturalstudies.net, a website that offers a catholic representation of the field. See also the *Journal of Mundane Behavior* for an explicit emphasis on the ordinary in everyday life.

16 Clifford Geertz, "Thick Description: Toward an Interpretive Theory of Culture," *The Interpretation of Cultures: Selected Essays by Clifford Geertz* (New York: Basic Books, 1973), 3-32.

17 Quotations from Geertz, "Thick Description," 5 (the "webs of significance" phrase is taken from Max Weber), 7 (the "burlesque" phrase is borrowed from Ryle), and 23.

18 For one example of historical scholarship that takes a lead from Geertz, see the work of Geertz's Princeton colleague, Robert Darnton, *The Great Cat Massacre and Other Episodes in French Cultural History* (New York: Basic Books, 1984).

19 For the term "Social Darwinism" see Geoffrey M. Hodgson, "Social Darwinism in Anglophone Journals: A Contribution to the History of the Term," *Journal of Historical Sociology* 17, 4 (2004): 428-63.

20 For one claim about the late-nineteenth-century elaboration of the hunting code see MacKenzie, *Empire of Nature,* 27. In "The Ethics of Sportsmanship," ch. 42 of William T. Hornaday, *Our Vanishing Wildlife. Its Extermination and Preservation* (New York: Charles Scribner's and Sons, 1913), the author notes, "I count it as rather strange that American and English sportsmen have hunted and shot for a century, and until 1908 formulated

practically nothing to establish and define the ethics of shooting game. Here and there, a few unwritten principles have been evolved, and have become fixed by common consent; but the total number of these is very few. Perhaps this has been for the reason that every free and independent sportsman prefers to be a law unto himself. Is it not doubly strange, however, that even down to the present year the term 'sportsmen' never has been defined by a sportsman!" The latter part of the chapter includes the following preamble: "In 1908 the Camp-Fire Club of America formally adopted, as its code of ethics, the 'Sportsman's Platform' of fifteen articles that was prepared by the writer and placed before the sportsmen of America, Great Britain and her colonial dependencies in that year." The fifteen articles of the platform follow. The sportsman's code is quoted in Gordon Hewitt, *Conservation of the Wild Life of Canada* (New York: Scribner's Sons, 1921), 298; its history in Canada is described on pp. 297-98. Izaak Walton, *The Compleat Angler or the Contemplative Man's Recreation: Being a Discourse of FISH and FISHING, Not Unworthy of the Perusal of Most Anglers* (London: T. Maxey for Rich. Marriot, 1653).

21 James Clifford, *The Predicament of Culture* (1988), and James Clifford and George Marcus, *Writing Culture: The Poetics and Politics of Ethnography* (1986) and several of the essays in Clifford Geertz, *Local Knowledge: Further Essays in Interpretive Anthropology* (New York: Basic Books, 1983).

22 Edward W. Said, *Orientalism: Western Conceptions of the Orient* (New York: Pantheon Books, 1978); David Cannadine, *Ornamentalism: How the British Saw Their Empire* (London: Penguin Books, 2001).

23 Cannadine, *Ornamentalism*, xix.

24 Mary Louise Pratt, *Imperial Eyes: Travel Writing and Transculturation* (London: Routledge, 1992); the "thereby appropriated" phrase can be found on p. 21 herein.

25 See Karen Wonders, *Habitat Dioramas: Illusions of Wilderness in Museums of Natural History* (Uppsala: ACTA Universitatis Upsaliensis, 1993).

26 Much of the recent work in this vein has focused on India. The close engagement of ideas and arguments from Gillespie and some of this literature might be very rewarding. See, for example, Ian J. Barrow, *Making History, Drawing Territory: British Mapping in India, c 1765-1905* (New Delhi: Oxford University Press, 2003); Bernard G. Cohn, *Colonialism and Its Forms of Knowledge: The British in India* (Princeton: Princeton University Press, 1996); Roland Inden, *Imagining India* (Oxford: Blackwell, 1990); Matthew H. Edney, *Mapping an Empire: The Geographical Construction of British India, 1785-1843* (Chicago: University of Chicago Press, 1997).

27 Geertz, "Thick Description," 29.

28 David Cannadine, "Making History Now (an Inaugural Lecture)," *History in Focus* 2 (2001), Institute of Historical Research, London, http://www.history.ac.uk/ihr/Focus/Whatishistory/cannadine.html.

INTRODUCTION

1 For an overview of the historical and epistemological underpinnings of the philosophy of knowledge, see the entry for "Cultural History" in Munslow, *The Routledge Companion to Historical Studies*, 64-67. For a brief review of cultural history, poststructuralism, and the need for such perspectives in the historiography of the western interior, see Gerald Friesen, "The Imagined West: Introducing Cultural History," in *From Rupert's Land to Canada*, ed.

Theodore Binnema, Gerhard J. Ens, and R.C. MacLeod (Edmonton: University of Alberta Press, 2001), 195-200.

2 Claire Elizabeth Campbell, *Shaped by the West Wind: Nature and History in Georgian Bay* (Vancouver: UBC Press, 2004); and also her dissertation entitled "Shaped by the West Wind: Nature and History in Georgian Bay," (PhD diss., University of Western Ontario, 2001).

3 R.G. Moyles and Doug Owram, *Imperial Dreams and Colonial Realities* (Toronto: University of Toronto Press, 1988), 67-68. For landscape formation contributing to a larger global British landscape in the 1700s, see John. E. Crowley, "Picturing the Caribbean in the Global British Landscape," *Studies in Eighteenth-Century Culture* 32 (2003): 323-46.

4 I.S. MacLaren provides a discussion of cultural landscape and temporality in "Cultured Wilderness in Jasper National Park," *Journal of Canadian Studies* 34, 3 (1999): 7-58.

5 An insightful discussion of landscape theory can be found in James M. Potter, "The Creation of Person, the Creation of Place: Hunting Landscapes in the American Southwest," *American Antiquity* 69, 2 (2004): 322-38.

6 Simon Ryan, *The Cartographic Eye* (Cambridge: Cambridge University Press, 1996), 6, 53; Matthew H. Edney, *Mapping an Empire: The Geographical Construction of British India, 1765-1843* (Chicago: University of Chicago Press, 1997), 53-76.

7 Andrew Edgar and Peter Sedgwick, eds., *Key Concepts in Cultural Theory* (London: Routledge, 1999), 69; the section entitled "Codes of Production" in Ryan, *Cartographic Eye*, 55-100; and Edney, *Mapping an Empire*, 57.

8 See Colin Coates, *The Metamorphoses of Landscape and Community in Early Quebec* (Montreal and Kingston: McGill-Queen's University Press, 2000); Daniel Clayton, *Islands of Truth: The Imperial Fashioning of Vancouver Island* (Vancouver: UBC Press, 2000); Elizabeth Vibert, *Traders' Tales: Narratives of Cultural Encounters in the Columbia Plateau, 1807-1846* (Norman: University of Oaklahoma Press, 1997).

9 On this point I agree with a perspective raised in a recent article in *BC Studies* that argues Canadian scholars, until recently, seem to have little desire to highlight Canada's imperial past. See Jeremy Mouat, "Situating Vancouver Island in the British World, 1846-1849," *BC Studies* 145 (Spring 2005): 5-30.

10 Emphasis on the colonized typically underscores colonial locality. Cultural geographer Cole Harris raises a note of caution on this point and suggests that scholars who emphasize culture fall short as they fail to situate their work in local knowledge, practices, and power relations. He calls for research that focuses on the colonial localities in which imperialists invoked their appropriative strategies. His perspective is an important one, but I have never viewed the examination of imperial culture and colonial locality as necessarily incongruous or believed that the study of one might lead to more or better insights than the other. The fertile ground likely rests in a negotiation of these two topics. For his insightful overview of this issue, see Cole Harris, "How did Colonialism Dispossess? Comments from the Edge of Empire," *Annals of the Association of American Geographers*, 94, 1 (2004): 165-82.

CHAPTER 1: AN IMPERIAL INTERIOR IMAGINED

1 My approach to scholarship stems from cultural history – or what historiographer Alun Munslow calls deconstructionism. For a brief overview of deconstructionist scholarship, including the sharp denial of objectivity, facts, and truth, the temporality of knowledge, and

the inescapable relationship between past and present, see Alun Munslow, *Deconstructing History* (London: Routledge, 1997), 57-98, and the entries for "Deconstructionist History" and "Relativism" in Alun Munslow, *The Routledge Companion to Historical Studies* (London: Routledge, 2000). For the positioning of Munslow's deconstructionism within sport studies, see Doug Booth, "Escaping the Past? The Linguistic Turn and Language in Sport History," *Rethinking History* 8, 1 (2004): 103-25, and most recently in Doug Booth, *The Field: Truth and Fiction in Sport History* (London: Routledge, 2005). Also see Murray Philips, ed., *Deconstructing Sport History: A Postmodern Analysis* (Albany: State University of New York Press, 2006).

2 For a brief overview of the topics and approaches in the historiography of the western interior of Canada to 1993, see the beginning of Part 1 in Irene M. Spry and Bennett McCardle, *The Records of the Department of the Interior and Research Concerning Canada's Western Frontier of Settlement* (Regina: Canadian Plains Research Center, University of Regina, 1993), 1-30.

3 Irene M. Spry, "Early Visitors to the Canadian Prairies," in Brian W. Blouet and Merlin P. Lawson, eds., *Images of the Plains: The Role of Human Nature in Settlement* (Lincoln: University of Nebraska Press, 1975), 168.

4 George Simpson, *Narrative of a Journey Round the World During the Years 1841 and 1842* (London: Henry Colburn, 1847), 1:13, 47-48.

5 This group included Lt. Colonel William Greenwood, Captains William Henry Leicester, Charles William Ridley, Robert Vansittart, and Charles Ashe Windham, Lt. William Fairholme, Ensign Henry James Warre, and Lt. General Sir Richard Downes Jackson, Commander-in-Chief of the British Forces in North America. J.E. Sunder, "British Army Officers on the Sante Fe Trail," *Bulletin of the Missouri Historical Society* 23 (1967): 147-57.

6 Spry, "Early Visitors," 169, and I.S. MacLaren, "The Influence of Eighteenth-Century British Landscape Aesthetics on Narrative and Pictorial Responses to the British North American North and West, 1769-1872," (PhD diss., University of Western Ontario, 1983), 2: 736-37.

7 Irene M. Spry, "A Visit to the Red River and the Saskatchewan, 1861 by Dr. John Rae, FRGS," *The Geographical Journal* 140 (1974): 1-17. In this article, Spry reprints the original essay, "A Brief Account of an Excursion to the Saskatchewan Prairies," submitted by Rae to the Royal Geographical Society on pages 7-17. Also see Dr. John Rae, "A Visit to Red River and the Saskatchewan," *Proceedings* of the Royal Geographical Society 8 (1861): 102-3. Spry also notes that Rae took issue with the sporting narrative of the Hon. Grantley Berkeley regarding the proper techniques of running buffalo discussed in *The English Sportsman in the Western Prairies* (London: Hurst and Blackett, 1861).

8 Although a town called Chaplin and Lake Chaplin still exist today, the Cree name of Old Wives Lake was reapplied to Lake Johnstone in 1955. For a recent account of this expedition, see John H. Hudson, "History in the Community: Dr. John Rae's 1861 Route Near Old Wives Lake and Chaplin Lake," *Saskatchewan History* 52, 1 (2000): 32-36.

9 Sunder, "British Army Officers," 147-57; Spry, "Early Visitors," 169; and Captain Henry Warre, *Sketches in North America and the Oregon Territory* (London: Dickenson, 1848), who, along with Lt. Mervin Vavasour, made a reconnaissance across the western interior in 1845-46. Warre also took part in the group of British officers who hunted buffalo in the prairies of Missouri and Kansas in 1840.

10 Spry, "Early Visitors," 169. Irene M. Spry devoted much of her attention to Palliser. See Irene M. Spry, ed., *The Papers of the Palliser Expedition, 1857-1860* (Toronto: Champlain Society, 1968); *The Palliser Expedition: An Account of John Palliser's British North American*

Expedition, 1857-1860 (Toronto: The Macmillan Company of Canada, 1963), and the second edition, *The Palliser Expedition: The Dramatic Story of Western Canadian Exploration, 1857-1860,* 2nd ed. (Saskatoon: Fifth House, 1995); "Captain John Palliser and the Exploration of Western Canada," *The Geographical Journal* 125 (1959): 149-84; as well as "The Palliser Expedition," in Richard C. Davis, ed., *Rupert's Land: A Cultural Tapestry* (Waterloo: Wilfrid Laurier University Press, 1988), 195-212. For Palliser's buffalo hunting expeditions in Canada and the United States, see John Palliser, *Papers Relative to the Exploration by Captain Palliser of that Portion of British North America* (London: Eyre and Spottiswoode, 1859), 14, and *Solitary Rambles and Adventures of a Hunter in the Prairies* (London: J. Murray, 1853), 264-88.

11 *Dictionary of Canadian Biography,* vol. 13, s.v. "Sir William Francis Butler" (Toronto: University of Toronto Press, 1994).

12 See Bouchier's discussion of the aristocratic sporting culture constructed by British half-pay officers. Nancy Bouchier, "Aristocrats and Their Noble Sport: Woodstock Officers and Cricket during the Rebellion Era," *Canadian Journal of the History of Sport* 20, 1 (1989): 16-31. For the historical association of royalty and hunting in England see Antony Taylor, "Pig-Sticking Princes: Royal Hunting, Moral Outrage, and the Republican Opposition to Animal Abuse in Nineteenth- and Early Twentieth-Century Britain," *History* 89, 293 (2004): 30-48.

13 For works that discuss the diffusion of imperial culture through sport, primarily in an American frame of reference and during the twentieth century, see Allen Guttmann, *Games and Empires: Modern Sports and Cultural Imperialism* (New York: Columbia University Press, 1994) and Gerald Gems, *The Athletic Crusade: Sport and American Cultural Imperialism* (Lincoln: University of Nebraska Press, 2004).

14 For the social value attached to the "back to nature" movement and the "simplicity" of the wilderness and rural life in the face of 1880s modernity, see Peter C. Gould, *Early Green Politics: Back to Nature, Back to the Land, and Socialism in Britain* (Sussex: The Harvester Press, 1988). George Altmeyer also touches on this anti-modern movement in "Three Ideas of Nature in Canada, 1893-1914," in *Consuming Canada: Readings in Environmental History,* ed. Chad Gaffield and Pam Gaffield (Toronto: Copp Clark, 1995), 96-118. Also see Tina Loo, *States of Nature: Conserving Canada's Wildlife in the Twentieth Century* (Vancouver: UBC Press, 2006), 32-33.

15 Little research exists specifically on the place of women, hunting, and British imperialism. Historian Andrea L. Smalley's excellent papers on women and hunting in the United States may prompt future research in this important area. See Andrea L. Smalley, "'I Just Like to Kill Things': Women, Men, and the Gender of Sport Hunting in the Hunted States, 1940-1973," *Gender and History* 17, 1 (2005): 183-209, and Andrea L. Smalley, "'Our Lady Sportsmen': Gender, Class, and Conservation in Sport Hunting Magazines, 1873-1920," *Journal of the Gilded Age and Progressive Era* 4, 4 (2005): 355-80.

16 R.G. Moyles and Doug Owram, *Imperial Dreams and Colonial Realities* (Toronto: University of Toronto Press, 1988), 68.

17 John MacKenzie, *The Empire of Nature: Hunting, Conservation, and British Imperialism* (Manchester: Manchester University Press, 1988), 125-26. MacKenzie looks at the different phases of the imperial hunt in "Chivalry, Social Darwinism, and Ritualised Killing: The Hunting Ethos in Central Africa up to 1914," in *Conservation in Africa: People, Policies, and Practice,* ed. D. Anderson and R. Grove (Cambridge: Cambridge University Press, 1987), 41-61. For a review article of big-game hunting and imperialism, see William Beinart, "Empire, Hunting, and Ecological Change in Southern and Central Africa," *Past and*

124 Notes to pages 7-9

Present 128, 1 (1990): 162-86.

18 Harriet Ritvo, *The Animal Estate: The English and Other Creatures in the Victorian Age* (Cambridge, MA: Harvard University Press, 1987), 288. Also see Harriet Ritvo, "Destroyers and Preservers: Big Game in the Victorian Empire," *History Today* 52, 1 (2002): 33-39. Ritvo discusses the place of animals in environmental historiography generally in "Animal Planet," *Environmental History* 9, 2 (2004): 204-20; Matt Cartmill, *A View to Death in the Morning: Hunting and Nature through History* (Cambridge, MA: Harvard University Press, 1993).

19 The vast nature and varied labels applied to portions of Rupert's Land have long presented a problem. See John Warkentin, *The Western Interior of Canada: A Record of Geographical Discovery* (Toronto: McClelland and Stewart, 1964).

20 The decline of the fur trade, the destruction of the plains buffalo, a change in popular perception of the West, as well as Confederation and developing Canadian expansionism led to the annexation of the territory. See the entry for "Rupert's Land" in Gerald Hallowell, ed., *The Oxford Companion to Canadian History* (Don Mills, ON: Oxford University Press, 2004), 557.

21 For the name changes in this region and the North-Western Territory specifically, see Walter Kupsch, "GSC Exploratory Wells in the West, 1873-1875," *Earth Sciences History* 12, 2 (1993): 160-79.

22 For a human geography of the western interior, see Cole Harris and John Warkentin, *Canada before Confederation: A Study in Historical Geography* (Ottawa: Carleton University Press, 1991). Irene Spry provides an overview at the beginning of her article entitled "The Great Transformation: The Disappearance of the Commons in Western Canada," in *Man and Nature on the Prairies,* ed. Richard Allen (Saskatoon: Great Plains Research Center, University of Regina, 1976), 21-45.

23 Doug Owram, *The Promise of Eden: The Canadian Expansionist Movement and the Idea of the West, 1856-1900* (Toronto: University of Toronto, 1980), 7-37; D.W. Moodie, "Early British Images of Rupert's Land," in *Man and Nature on the Prairies,* ed. Richard Allen (Saskatoon: Great Plains Research Center, University of Regina, 1976), 1-20. For an overview of the evolving images of the West, see R. Douglas Francis, "Changing Images of the West," in *The Prairie West: Historical Readings,* ed. R. Douglas Francis and Howard Palmer (Edmonton: University of Alberta Press, 1992), 717-39; "From Wasteland to Utopia: Changing Images of the Canadian West in the Nineteenth-Century," *Great Plains Quarterly* 7, 3 (1987): 178-94; and "The Ideal and the Real: The Image of Canadian West in the Settlement Period," in *Rupert's Land: A Cultural Tapestry,* ed. Richard C. Davis (Waterloo, ON: Wilfrid Laurier University Press, 1988), 253-74.

24 Owram, *The Promise of Eden,* 7-37.

25 Ibid., 16.

26 Although Palliser described the "triangle" in arid terms, boosters and Canadian expansionists preferred Hind's descriptions and enthusiasm for the "fertile belt" that stretched across the southern prairies. Palliser, *Papers Relative to the Exploration; Dictionary of Canadian Biography,* vol. 11, s.v. "John Palliser" (Toronto: University of Toronto Press, 1982); Henry Youle Hind, *Reports of Progress Together with a Preliminary and General Report, on the Assiniboine and Saskatchewan Exploring Expedition: Made under Instructions from the Provincial Secretary, Canada* (Toronto, 1859); *Narrative of the Canadian Red River Exploring Expedition of 1857 and of the Assinniboine and Saskatchewan Exploring Expedition of 1858* (London: Longman, Green, Longman, and Roberts, 1860); and *A Sketch of an Overland Route to British Columbia* (Toronto, 1862); *Dictionary of Canadian Biography,*

vol. 13, s.v. "Henry Youle Hind" (Toronto: University of Toronto Press, 1994).

    For early photography on this expedition, see R. Huyda, "Exploration Photographer: Humphrey Lloyd Hime and the Assiniboine and Saskatchewan Exploring Expedition of 1858," *Historical and Scientific Society of Manitoba Transactions Series* 3, 30 (1973): 45-59; and Edward Cavell, "Image of Transition: Photography in Rupert's Land," in *Rupert's Land: A Cultural Tapestry,* ed. Richard C. Davis (Waterloo: Wilfrid Laurier University Press, 1988), 227-52. Also see "Western Expansion," in Hallowell, *The Oxford Companion,* 660; Douglas Hill, *The Opening of the Canadian West* (Toronto: William Heinemann, 1968), 60-63; and Barry Potyondi, *In Palliser's Triangle: Living in the Grasslands, 1850-1939* (Saskatoon: Purich Publishing, 1995), 37-41.

27 For an overview of the destruction of the buffalo, see Andrew Isenberg, *The Destruction of the Bison: An Environmental History, 1750-1929* (Cambridge: Cambridge University Press, 2000); Barry Potyondi, "Loss and Substitution: The Ecology of Production in Southwestern Saskatchewan, 1860-1930," *Journal of the Canadian Historical Association* 5 (1994): 213-35; and William A. Dobak, "Killing the Canadian Buffalo, 1821-1881," *Western Historical Quarterly* 27, 1 (1996): 33-52. On the role of the United States Army in the destruction of the buffalo, see David D. Smits, "The Frontier Army and the Destruction of the Buffalo: 1865-1883," *Western Historical Quarterly* 25, 3 (1994): 312-38.

28 Edward Cavell, *Journeys to the Far West* (Toronto: James Lorimer, 1979), vi. For a brief overview of this period, see John Herd Thompson, *Forging the Prairie West: The Illustrated History of Canada* (Toronto: Oxford University Press, 1998), 23-42; Hill, *The Opening of the Canadian West,* 70-71; and Chapters 7 and 8 in Gerald Friesen, *The Canadian Prairies: A History* (Toronto: University of Toronto Press, 1984), 129-62.

29 James G. MacGregor, *Vision of an Ordered land: The Story of the Dominion Land Survey* (Saskatoon: Western Producer Prairie Books, 1981).

30 Elizabeth Vibert, *Traders' Tales: Narratives of Cultural Encounters in the Columbia Plateau, 1807-1846* (Norman, OK: University of Oklahoma Press, 1997), 84-118.

31 For CPR advertising and settler promotions, see E.J. Hart, *The Selling of Canada: The CPR and the Beginnings of Canadian Tourism* (Banff, AB: Altitude Publishing, 1983); and the revised edition entitled *Trains, Peaks, and Tourists: The Golden Age of Canadian Travel* (Banff, AB: EJH Literary Enterprises, 2000).

32 Ian MacLaren and Elizabeth Vibert also provide discussions of the editorial process. I.S. MacLaren, "From Exploration to Publication: The Evolution of a 19th-Century Arctic Narrative," *Arctic* 47, 1 (1994): 43-53; and Vibert, *Traders' Tales,* introduction.

33 For a brief overview of the genre of British travel literature, see Greg Gillespie, "Wickets in the West: Cricket, Culture, and Constructed Images of Nineteenth-Century Canada." *Journal of Sport History* 27, 1 (Spring 2000): 51-66.

34 Joanne Shattock, "Travel Writing Victorian and Modern: A Review of Recent Research," in *The Art of Travel: Essays on Travel Writing,* ed. Philip Dodd (London: Frank Cass, 1982), 154; Hilary Fraser with Daniel Brown, *English Prose of the Nineteenth Century* (New York: Addison Wesley Longman, 1996), 56. For an overview, see Patricia Jasen, *Wild Things: Nature, Culture, and Tourism in Ontario, 1790-1914* (Toronto: University of Toronto Press, 1995), 3-28.

35 See the narrative and previously published extracts identified in Edward Wyndham-Quin, *Canadian Nights* (London: Smith, Elder, 1914).

36 For a few examples of other narratives, see Frederick Selous, *A Hunter's Wanderings in Africa and Sport and Travel in the East and* West (London: Rowland Ward, 1893); Edward Wyndham-Quin, *The Great Divide: Travels in the Upper Yellowstone in the Summer of*

1874 (London: Chatto and Windus, 1876); William Frances Butler, *The Campaign of the Cataracts: A Personal Narrative of the Great Nile Expedition of 1884-1885* (London: S. Low, Marston, Searle, and Rivington, 1887); and Clive Phillipps-Wolley, *Sport in the Crimea and Caucasus* (London: R. Bentley, 1881).

37 Here I lean on the definition of James R. Ryan, *Picturing Empire: Photography and the Visualization of the British Empire* (London: Reaktion Books, 1997), 12-13; James R. Ryan, "Imperial Landscapes: Photography, Geography, and British Overseas Exploration, 1858-1872," in *Geography and Imperialism, 1820-1940*, ed. Morag Bell, Robin Butlin, and Michael Heffernan (Manchester: Manchester University Press, 1995), 53-79. Also see Greg Gillespie, "'I Was Well Pleased with Our Sport among the Buffalo': Big Game Hunting, Travel Writing, and Cultural Imperialism in the British North American West, 1847-1873," *Canadian Historical Review* 83, 4 (December 2002): 555-84; and Greg Gillespie, "The Imperial Embrace: British Sportsmen and the Appropriation of Landscape in Nineteenth-Century Canada" (PhD diss., University of Western Ontario, 2001).

38 Ryan, *Picturing Empire*, 12-13. For a traditional approach to imperialism research, see John C. Weaver, *The Great Land Rush and the Making of the Modern World, 1650-1900* (Montreal and Kingston: McGill-Queen's University Press, 2003).

39 Colin Coates, "Like the Thames towards Putney: The Appropriation of Landscape in Lower Canada," *Canadian Historical Review* 74, 3 (1993): 330.

40 David Cannadine, *Ornamentalism: How the British Saw Their Empire* (Oxford: Oxford University Press, 2001). For an engaging intellectual discussion of Ornamentalism, see Peter H. Hansen, "Ornamentalism and Orientalism: Virtual Empires and the Politics of Knowledge," *Journal of Colonialism and Colonial History* 3, 1 (2002): 1-8.

41 Historians and cultural theorists of imperialism have long informed their work through Said's concept of Orientalism. Edward Said, *Culture and Imperialism* (New York: Alfred Knopf, 1993); and *Orientalism* (New York: Pantheon Books, 1978), 202-3. For otherness, also see David Arnold, *The Problem of Nature: Environment, Culture, and European Expansion* (Oxford: Blackwell, 1996); and for imaginative geographies, see Derek Gregory, "Imaginative Geographies," *Progress in Human Geography* 19 (1995): 447-85.

42 Cannadine, *Ornamentalism*, 5.

43 Ibid., xix.

44 Mary Louise Pratt, *Imperial Eyes: Travel Writing and Transculturation* (London: Routledge, 1992), 7, 28. For me, the concept of the anti-conquest holds more insight in relation to understanding imperialist processes than does the secondary idea of contact zones.

45 Over ten years ago, John MacKenzie hinted at this point but never took the opportunity to detail the cultural contradictions within imperial hunting culture. MacKenzie, *Empire of Nature*, 43.

CHAPTER 2: THE PREFATORY PARADOX

1 For an example, see "taken on the spot" commentary in the cultural landscape work of John E. Crowley, "Taken on the Spot: The Visual Appropriation of New France for the Global British Landscape," *Canadian Historical Review* 86, 1 (2005): 1-28.

2 The fascinating aspect of the prefatory paradox is that by the first decades of the twentieth century, claims of positivism evolved and became an admission of literary overexaggeration. For a interesting parody, see E. Douglas Branch, *The Hunting of the Buffalo* (London: D.

Appleton, 1929), preface. The opening line of his preface reads, "A truthful narrative – this is one! – might well start with a whopping lie."

3 For more on the concept of narrative authority, see Simon Ryan, *The Cartographic Eye* (Cambridge: Cambridge University Press, 1996), 44, 46-47.
4 Ibid., 47.
5 Ibid., 7-9, 40.
6 Charles Alston Messiter, *Sport and Adventures among the North American Indians* (London: R.H. Porter, 1890), preface.
7 James Carnegie, *Saskatchewan and the Rocky Mountains: A Diary and Narrative of Travel, Sport, and Adventure, in 1859 and 1860* (Edinburgh: Edmonston and Douglas, 1875), preface.
8 Ryan, *Cartographic Eye*, 41.
9 Carnegie, *Saskatchewan*, preface.
10 William Francis Butler, *The Great Lone Land* (London: Sampson Low, Marston, Searle, and Rivington, 1872), preface.
11 William Fitzwilliam Milton and W.B. Cheadle, *North-West Passage by Land* (London: Cassell, Petter, Galpin, 1875), preface.
12 William Ross King, *The Sportsman and Naturalist in Canada* (London: Hurst and Blackett, 1866), preface.
13 John Palliser, *Solitary Rambles and Adventures of a Hunter in the Prairies* (London: J. Murray, 1853), preface.
14 Robert Michael Ballantyne, *The Buffalo Runners: A Tale of the Red River Plains* (London: J. Nisbet, 1891), preface; *Dictionary of Canadian Biography*, vol. 12, s.v. "Robert Michael Ballantyne" (Toronto: University of Toronto Press, 1990).
15 Milton and Cheadle, *North-West Passage*, preface.
16 George Munro Grant, *Ocean to Ocean: Sandford Fleming's Expedition through Canada in 1872* (Toronto: Belford, 1877).
17 Milton and Cheadle, *North-West Passage*, preface.
18 Ryan, *Cartographic Eye*, 40.
19 Ibid.
20 Carnegie, *Saskatchewan*, preface.
21 Ibid. Parentheses his.
22 Milton and Cheadle, *North-West Passage*, preface.
23 Mary Louise Pratt, *Imperial Eyes: Travel Writing and Transculturation* (London: Routledge, 1992), 201.
24 Ryan, *Cartographic Eye*, 23.
25 Pratt, *Imperial Eyes*, 202.
26 Ryan, *Cartographic Eye*, 23.
27 Carnegie, *Saskatchewan*, preface.
28 William Francis Butler, *The Wild North Land* (London: Low, Marston, Low, and Searle, 1873), preface.
29 Messiter, *Sport and Adventures*, preface.
30 Palliser, *Solitary Rambles*, preface.
31 Ryan, *Cartographic Eye*, 46.
32 Palliser, *Solitary Rambles*, preface.
33 Carnegie, *Saskatchewan*, preface.
34 Butler, *The Great Lone Land*, preface.
35 Butler, *The Wild North Land*, preface.

36 Messiter, *Sport and Adventures*, preface.
37 Carnegie, *Saskatchewan*, preface.
38 Ibid.
39 Ibid. Emphasis his.
40 Ryan, *Cartographic Eye*, 48-49.
41 Carnegie, *Saskatchewan*, preface.
42 Ibid.
43 Ballantyne, *Buffalo Runners*, preface.
44 Carnegie, *Saskatchewan*, preface.
45 Ibid.
46 Ryan, *Cartographic Eye*, 27-33.
47 Ibid., 30.
48 Carnegie, *Saskatchewan*, 54.
49 Milton and Cheadle, *North-West Passage*, 396.
50 Ibid., 29.
51 Ibid., 22. Also see Carnegie, *Saskatchewan*, 5.
52 Frederick Ulric Graham, *Notes of a Sporting Expedition in the Far West of Canada, 1847* (London: Private circulation, 1898), 107.
53 Ryan, *Cartographic Eye*, 42, 28.
54 Ibid., 7-9.
55 Ibid.
56 Ibid., 38. For an overview of the RGS and imperialism, see Felix Driver, *Geography Militant: Cultures of Exploration and Empire* (Oxford: Blackwell, 2001).
57 Even Pallier's RGS reports reveal his passion for big-game hunting. John Palliser, *Papers Relative to the Exploration by Captain Palliser of that Portion of British North America* (London: Eyre and Spottiswoode, 1859), 31.
58 Ryan, *Cartographic Eye*, 37.
59 Ibid., 35.
60 Selous, who hunted for British natural history institutions throughout his career, probably travelled with an agreement to obtain Canadian specimens for museums. "The entire skin of my finest caribou," wrote Selous, "I preserved and presented to the trustees of the Natural History Museum at South Kensington ... These two specimens, splendidly mounted by Rowland Ward of Piccadilly, may now be seen in the Mammalian Gallery of the Museum, and form, I think, an interesting addition to our unrivalled zoological collection." Frederick Selous, *Recent Hunting Trips in British North America* (London: Witherby and Company, 1907), preface.
61 King, *Sportsman and Naturalist*, preface.
62 Ibid.
63 Carnegie, *Saskatchewan*, preface.
64 Ryan, *Cartographic Eye*, 38.
65 Anthony Grafton, *The Footnote: A Curious History* (Cambridge, MA: Harvard University Press, 1997), 7, 15.
66 Ibid., 7-13.
67 George Catlin, *Letter and Notes on the Manners, Customs, and Condition of the North American Indians* (London: G. Catlin, 1841).
68 Carnegie, *Saskatchewan*, preface.
69 Grafton, *The Footnote*, 8-32.
70 Ibid., 9.

71 Carnegie, *Saskatchewan*, preface.
72 Ibid.
73 Ibid.
74 Ryan, *Cartographic Eye*, 8.

CHAPTER 3: CRY HAVOC?

1 J.A. Mangan, *The Games Ethic and Imperialism* (Harmondsworth: Viking, 1986), 21, 44-45, 58-69. For the issue of corporal punishment and discipline at these schools, see J.A. Mangan, "Bullies, Beatings, Battles, and Bruises: Great Days and Jolly Days at One Mid-Victorian Public School," in *Disreputable Pleasures: Less Virtuous Victorians at Play,* ed. Mike Huggins and J.A. Mangan (London: Frank Cass, 2004), 3-35.
2 Mangan, *The Games Ethic,* 21, 44-45.
3 J.A. Mangan, *Athleticism in the Victorian and Edwardian Public School: The Emergence and Consolidation of an Educational Ideology* (Cambridge: Cambridge University Press, 1981), 136.
4 Mangan, *The Games Ethic,* 18, 35-45.
5 Mangan, *Athleticism in the Victorian and Edwardian Public School,* 136-140.
6 See Roger B. Manning, *Hunters and Poachers: A Social and Cultural History of Unlawful Hunting in England, 1485-1640* (Oxford: Clarendon Press, 1993); and for class distinctions during the Middle Ages, see the entry "Hunting and Hawking" in Allen Guttmann, *Sports: The First Five Millennia* (Amherst and Boston: University of Massachusetts Press, 2004), 57-59.
7 John F. Reiger, *American Sportsmen and the Origins of Conservation* (New York: Winchester, 1975), 26; and Bill Parenteau, "Care, Control, and Supervision: Native People in the Canadian Atlantic Salmon Fishery, 1867-1900," *Canadian Historical Review* 79, 1 (1998): 28; and "Angling, Hunting, and the Development of Tourism in Late Nineteenth-Century Canada," *The Archivist: The Magazine of the National Archives of Canada* 117 (1998): 16. For more, see John Lowerson, "Izaak Walton: Father of a Dream," *History Today* 33, 12 (1983): 28-32; and Jonquil Bevan, *Izzak Walton's The Compleat Angler: The Art of Recreation* (Brighton, UK: Harvester, 1988).
8 Edward Wyndham-Quin, *Canadian Nights* (London: Smith, Elder, 1914), 27. For an excellent overview of the sporting code, see R.G. Moyles and Doug Owram, *Imperial Dreams and Colonial Realities* (Toronto: University of Toronto Press, 1988), 63. For the hunting ethos, as well as the importance of viewing big-game hunting as a fraternal practice, see Callum McKenzie, "The British Big-Game Hunting Tradition, Masculinity, and Fraternalism with Particular Reference to the Shikar Club," *The Sports Historian* 20, 1 (2000): 70-96.
9 Nancy Bouchier and Ken Cruikshank, "Sportsmen and Pothunters: Environment, Conservation, and Class in the Fishery of Hamilton Harbour, 1858-1914," *Sport History Review* 28, 1 (1997): 1-18; for more on the sporting code and the term "pothunter," see Chapter 1, "Game, Landscape, and the Law," in Nicolas W. Proctor, *Bathed in Blood: Hunting and Mastery in the Old South* (Charlottesville, VA: University of Virginia Press, 2002), 5-36. For spear-fishing, see Victor Lytwyn, "Torchlight Prey: Night Hunting and Fishing by Aboriginal People in the Great Lakes Region," *Papers of the Algonquian Conference* 23 (2001): 304-17. For the fly-fishing debate and the development of the sport fishery in British Columbia, see J. Michael Thoms, "A Place Called Pennask: Fly-Fishing and Colonialism at a British Columbia Lake," *BC Studies* 133, Spring (2002): 69-98; and on fly-fishing generally, see Adrian Bantjes, "Introduction: Bourdieu on the Bighorn? Or, towards

a Cultural History of Fly-Fishing in Wyoming and the Rocky Mountain West," *Annals of Wyoming: The Wyoming History Journal* 76, 2 (2004): 2-5; as well as "Nature, Culture, and the Fly-Fishing of Wyoming and the Rocky Mountain West," *Annals of Wyoming* 76, 2 (2004): 41-53.

10 John Sandlos, "From the Outside Looking In: Aesthetics, Politics, and Wildlife Conservation in the Canadian North," *Environmental History* 6, 1 (2001): 6-31.

11 James Carnegie, *Saskatchewan and the Rocky Mountains: A Diary and Narrative of Travel, Sport, and Adventure, in 1859 and 1860* (Edinburgh: Edmonston and Douglas, 1875), 216-17; J.A. Mangan, "Social Darwinism and Upper Class Education in Late Victorian and Edwardian England," in *Manliness and Morality: Middle-Class Masculinity in Britain and America, 1800-1940*, ed. J.A. Mangan and James Walvin (Manchester: Manchester University Press, 1987), 135-59.

12 John MacKenzie, *The Empire of Nature: Hunting, Conservation, and British Imperialism* (Manchester: Manchester University Press, 1988), 27. For an overview of colonial hunting, see Chapter 2 in William Beinart and Peter Coates, *Environment and History: The Taming of Nature in the USA and South Africa* (London: Routledge, 1995), 17-33.

13 Harriet Ritvo, *The Animal Estate: The English and Other Creatures in the Victorian Age* (Cambridge, MA: Harvard University Press, 1987), 281.

14 Colin Howell, *Blood, Sweat, and Cheers: Sport in the Making of Modern Canada* (Toronto: Toronto University Press, 2001), 14-17. For an outline of the sportsman's code, see Tina Loo, "Of Moose and Men: Hunting for Masculinities in British Columbia, 1880-1939," *Western Historical Quarterly* 32, 3 (2001): 296-319; Thomas Altherr, "The American Hunter-Naturalist and the Development of the Code of Sportsmanship," *Journal of Sport History* 5, 1 (1978): 7-22; Thomas R. Dunlap, *Saving America's Wildlife* (Princeton, NJ: Princeton University Press, 1988), 8-17; Jeffery L. McNairn, "Meaning and Markets: Hunting, Economic Development, and British Imperialism in Maritime Travel Narratives to 1870," *Acadiensis* 34, 2 (2005): 1-23.

15 Howell, *Blood, Sweat, and Cheers*, 14-16. For a specific discussion of big-game hunting and masculinity during a later period, see Loo, "Of Moose and Men," 296-319.

16 Frederick Ulric Graham, *Notes of a Sporting Expedition in the Far West of Canada, 1847* (London: Private circulation, 1898), 72.

17 Frederick Selous, *Recent Hunting Trips in British North America* (London: Witherby, 1907). For examples of such techniques in relation to caribou hunting, see Darrin McGrath, "Salted Caribou and Sportsmen-Tourists: Conflicts over Wildlife Resources in Newfoundland at the Turn of the Twentieth-Century," *Newfoundland Studies* 10, 2 (1994): 208-25.

18 Selous, *Recent Hunting Trips*, 69.

19 John MacKenzie, "The Imperial Pioneer and Hunter and the British Masculine Stereotype in Late Victorian and Edwardian Times," in *Manliness and Morality: Middle-Class Masculinity in Britain and America, 1800-1940*, ed. J.A. Mangan and James Walvin (Manchester: Manchester University Press, 1987), 176-98.

20 For a brief overview of hunting among the British elite, and the social distinctions invoked by the terms "hunter" and "poacher," see Nancy Struna, *People of Prowess: Sport, Leisure, and Labor in Early Anglo-America* (Urbana: University of Illinois Press, 1996), 20-23.

21 Ritvo, *Animal Estate*, 263.

22 For the codification of the elite hunting code into early game laws in nineteenth-century Canada generally, see Greg Gillespie and Kevin Wamsley, "Clandestine Means: The Aristocratic Hunting Code and Early Game Legislation in Nineteenth-Century Canada," *Sporting Traditions* 22, 1 (2005): 99-120. For the implementation of the code and game laws

among sporting clubs, see Bill Parenteau and Richard W. Judd, "More Buck for the Bang: Sporting and the Ideology of Fish and Game Management in Northern New England and the Maritime Provinces, 1870-1930," in *New England and the Maritime Provinces: Connections and Comparisons,* ed. Stephen J. Hornsby and John G. Reid (Montreal and Kingston: McGill-Queen's University Press, 2005), 232-51.

23 See Graham, *Notes of a Sporting Expedition,* 90.

24 James Carnegie, *Saskatchewan,* 216.

25 The changes in, and adherence to, the hunting code, reveal the evolving priorities of British imperialism over the nineteenth century. Hunting characterized as unconstrained slaughter took place typically during the initial exploration phase of the imperial advance. Hunters employed the code during this early stage in a process of wildlife destruction, collection, collation, and classification. After the stages of exploitation and colonization, unconstrained hunting changed towards an emphasis on protection, and finally, conservation. Although the hunting code changed and evolved over the course of the nineteenth century, its priorities, such as class exclusion, sportsmanship, marksmanship, natural history, and conservation, all existed to varying degrees in the early nineteenth century. Rather than focusing on big game as an impediment to colonization and progress, with time the British began to view colonial game as an exploitable resource. Colonial game became imperial property that required their watchful protection and husbandry. For more on this process in relation to game laws, see Kevin Wamsley, "Good Clean Sport and a Deer Apiece: Game Legislation and State Formation in 19th Century Canada," *Canadian Journal of the History of Sport* 25, 2 (1994): 1-20; and "Leisure and Legislation in Nineteenth-Century Canada," (PhD diss., University of Alberta, 1992).

26 Ritvo, *Animal Estate,* 270-78.

27 Carnegie, *Saskatchewan,* 126.

28 Cyndy Hendershot, *The Animal within Man: Masculinity and the Gothic* (Ann Arbor: University of Michigan Press, 1998). James Turner also discusses this point in *Reckoning with the Beast: Animals, Pain, and Humanity in the Victorian Mind* (Baltimore: Johns Hopkins University Press, 1980), 67.

29 Mackenzie, *Empire of Nature,* 45-46.

30 For discussions of sport and gentrified masculinities, see Greg Gillespie, "Sport and Masculinities in Early Nineteenth-Century Ontario: The British Travellers' Image," *Ontario History* 92, 2 (2000): 113-26; and Kevin Wamsley, "The Public Importance of Men and the Importance of Public Men: Sport and Masculinities in 19th Century Canada," in *Sport and Gender in Canada,* ed. Philip White and Kevin White (New York: Oxford University Press, 1999), 24-39.

31 Moyles and Owram, *Imperial Dreams,* 68. Karen Wonders also provides a discussion of natural history and hunting culture in *Habitat Dioramas: Illusions of Wilderness in Museums of Natural History* (Uppsala, Sweden: ACTA Universitatis Upsaliensis, 1993).

32 The connection between sport hunting, angling, and natural history probably stemmed from the example set by the aforementioned Walton and his *Compleat Angler.* Fascinated by natural history, Walton cited texts on geography and biology published in the early 1600s. P.G. Stanwood, *Izaak Walton* (New York: Twayne, 1998), 62.

33 Mackenzie, *Empire of Nature,* 39.

34 Ibid., 51.

35 James R. Ryan, *Picturing Empire: Photography and the Visualization of the British Empire* (Chicago: University of Chicago Press, 1997), 115.

36 Ibid., 115-16.

37 Ritvo, *Animal Estate*, 253.
38 Ryan, *Picturing Empire*, 115.
39 For a discussion of the quantifiable aspects of trophies, see Ritvo, *Animal Estate*, 271-75.
40 Carnegie, *Saskatchewan*, 216.
41 Selous, *Recent Hunting Trips*, 349.
42 Carnegie, *Saskatchewan*, 216-17.
43 Selous, *Recent Hunting Trips*, 350.
44 Graham, *Notes of a Sporting Expedition*, 79.
45 Ritvo, *Animal Estate*, 248.
46 Loo, "Of Moose and Men," 7.
47 Carnegie, *Saskatchewan*, 210.
48 Ibid., 215.
49 Ibid., 126.
50 William Fitzwilliam Milton and W.B. Cheadle, *North-West Passage by Land* (London: Cassell, Petter, Galpin, 1875), 98; *Dictionary of Canadian Biography*, vol. 10, s.v. "William Fitzwilliam Milton," (Toronto: University of Toronto Press, 1972).
51 Even author and angler Walton in his *Compleat Angler* referred to fish as gallant and noble. See Stanwood, *Izaak Walton*, 59-77. For examples of "noble" buffalo, see Carnegie, *Saskatchewan*, 93, 94.
52 Thomas Dunlap, "Remaking the Land: The Acclimatization Movement and Anglo Ideas of Nature," *Journal of World History* 8, 2 (1997): 309-10. Also see Richard Ormond, Joseph Rishel, and Robin Hamlyn, *Sir Edwin Landseer* (New York: Rizzoli, 1981), 174.
53 Dunlap, "Remaking the Land," 310. For a broader discussion of deer stalking among the British elite on Scottish sporting estates, see Hayden Lorimer, "Guns, Game, and the Grandee: The Cultural Politics of Deerstalking in the Scottish Highlands," *Ecumene: A Journal of Environment, Culture, and Meaning* 7, 4 (2000): 403-31, and Andy Wightman, Peter Higgins, Grant Jarvie, and Robbie Nicol, "The Cultural Politics of Hunting: Sporting Estates and Recreational Land Use in the Highlands and Islands of Scotland," *Culture, Sport, Society* 5, 1 (2002): 53-70.
54 The buffalo became known as the Monarch of the Prairie. For more on the moose in the eastern provinces, see Campbell Hardy, *Sporting Adventures in the New World; or, Days and Nights of Moose-Hunting in the Pine Forests of Acadia* (London: Hurst and Blackett, 1855), 1:193.
55 "Calling the moose" was the primary method for hunting moose during the rut. The practice entailed the Native guide climbing a tree during the autumn evening and bellowing to the moose through a birchbark megaphone. The stag would then approach within gunshot, thinking a female initiated a mating call.
56 For the aristocratic construction of the tiger in India see Joseph Sramek, "Face Him Like a Briton: Tiger Hunting, Imperialism, and British Masculinity in Colonial India, 1800-1875," *Victorian Studies* 48, 4 (2006): 659-680.
57 Carol Adams, *The Sexual Politics of Meat* (New York: Continuum, 1990), 40. For an overview on meat and sport hunting in the late nineteenth century, see George Colpitts, *Game in the Garden: A Human History of Wildlife in Western Canada to 1940* (Vancouver: UBC Press, 2002).
58 Adams, *Politics of Meat*, 33.
59 Loo, "Of Moose and Men," 7.
60 Elizabeth Vibert, *Traders' Tales: Narratives of Cultural Encounters in the Columbia Plateau, 1807-1846* (Norman, OK: University of Oklahoma Press, 1997).

61 See David Cannadine, *The Pleasures of the Past* (New York: W.W. Norton, 1989), 230-36.

62 Graham, *Notes of a Sporting Expedition*, 43.

63 Mackenzie, *Empire of Nature*, 305.

64 Adams, *Politics of Meat*, 33.

65 After his death, Selous' widow donated his collection to the British Museum of Natural History in 1919. His personal collection included approximately five hundred trophies, including nineteen lions, twenty-nine antelopes, and ten rhinos. Young boys in British public schools idolized Selous for his prowess and accomplishments. Ritvo, *Animal Estate*, 249; Mackenzie, *Empire of Nature*, 30; Ryan, *Picturing Empire*, 107. For a biography of Selous and his exploits, see Stephen Taylor, *The Mighty Nimrod: A Life of Frederick Courteney Selous, African Hunter and Adventurer 1851-1917* (London: Collins, 1989).

66 For an overview of masculinity and imperialism, see J.A. Mangan, "Social Darwinism," 135-59. Also see J.A. Mangan and Callum McKenzie, "Radical Conservatives: Middle Class Masculinity, the Shikar Club, and Big Game Hunting," *European Sport History Review* 4 (March 2002): 185-209.

67 MacKenzie, "The Imperial Pioneer and Hunter," 176-98.

68 William K. Stoery, "Big Cats and Imperialism: Lion and Tiger Hunting in Kenya and Northern India, 1898-1930," *Journal of World History* 2, 2 (1991): 135-73.

69 Ritvo, *Animal Estate*, 251.

70 Ryan, *Picturing Empire*, 116.

71 Ritvo, *Animal Estate*, 264.

72 Mackenzie, *Empire of Nature*, 98-99.

73 Ryan, *Picturing Empire*, 107.

74 For example, fur trader Alexander Ross wrote, "there is not an animal that roams in this, or in the wilds of any other country, more fierce and formidable, than the buffalo bull during the rutting season: neither the Polar bear, nor the Bengal tiger, surpass that animal in ferocity. When not mortally wounded, buffalo turn upon man or horse; but when mortally wounded, they stand fiercely eyeing their assailant, until life ebbs away." Alexander Ross, *The Fur Hunters of the Far West: A Narrative of Adventures in the Oregon and Rocky Mountains* (London: Smith, Elder, 1855), 125. Fur trader John McLean wrote, "the buffalo hunt affords much of the excitement, and some of the dangers, of the battlefield. The horses are often gored by the infuriated bulls, to the great peril – sometimes to the loss – of the rider's life." John McLean, *Notes of a Twenty-Five Years' Service in the Hudson's Bay Territory* (London: R. Bentley, 1849), 301; *Dictionary of Canadian Biography*, vol. 11, s.v. "John McLean" (Toronto: University of Toronto Press, 1982).

Artist and traveller Paul Kane observed, "the scene now became one of intense excitement; the huge bulls thundering over the plain in headlong confusion, whilst the fearless hunters rode recklessly in their midst, keeping up an incessant fire at but a few yards' distance from their victims." Paul Kane, *Wanderings of an Artist among the Indians of North America: From Canada to Vancouver's Island and Oregon through the Hudson's Bay Company's Territory and Back Again* (London: Longman, Brown, Green, Longmans, and Roberts, 1859), 86; for more on Kane, see I.S. MacLaren, "Paul Kane and the Authorship of *Wanderings of an Artist*," in *From Rupert's Land to Canada*, ed. Theodore Binnema, Gerhard J. Ens, and R.C. MacLeod (Edmonton: University of Alberta Press, 2001), 225-48; Ann Davis and Robert Thacker, "Pictures and Prose: Romantic Sensibility and the Great Plains in Catlin, Kane, and Miller," *Great Plains Quarterly* 6, 1 (1986): 3-20. See also Diane Eaton and Sheila Urbanek, *Paul Kane's Great Nor-West* (Vancouver: UBC Press, 1995), 42, 140; and *Dictionary of Canadian Biography*, vol. 10, s.v. "Paul Kane" (Toronto: University of Toronto Press, 1972).

75 Quotations in this paragraph are from Graham, *Notes of a Sporting Expedition*, 63-82.
76 Ibid., 52.
77 Carnegie, *Saskatchewan*, 126.
78 Graham, *Notes of a Sporting Expedition*, 62.
79 Ibid., 83.
80 Milton and Cheadle, *North-West Passage*, 63. Exhilarating descriptions of the buffalo and buffalo hunting can also be found throughout Henry Youle Hind, *Narrative of the Canadian Red River Exploring Expedition of 1857 and of the Assinniboine and Saskatchewan Exploring Expedition of 1858* (London: Longman, Green, Longman, and Roberts, 1860).
81 Carnegie, *Saskatchewan*, 5.
82 Ritvo, *Animal Estate*, 262. For a broader discussion of the Métis and the buffalo hunt, see John E. Foster, "The Métis and the End of the Plains Buffalo in Alberta," in *Buffalo*, ed. John E. Foster, Dick Harrison, and I.S. MacLaren (Edmonton: University of Alberta Press, 1992), 61-77; and Barry Potyondi, *In Palliser's Triangle: Living in the Grasslands, 1850-1939* (Saskatoon: Purich Publishing, 1995), 27-37.
83 Parenteau, "Care, Control, and Supervision," 25. For an extension of his work dealing with social conflict, see his "A Very Determined Opposition to the Law: Conservation, Angling Leases, and Social Conflict in the Canadian Atlantic Salmon Fishery, 1867-1914," *Environmental History* 9, 3 (2004): 436-63.
84 Parenteau, "Care, Control, and Supervision," 23-25.
85 For an excellent discussion of this point, see Ritvo, *Animal Estate*, 267-68.
86 Milton and Cheadle, *North-West Passage*, 290.
87 Ibid., 293. H. Somers Somerset, in a slightly later period, also resorted to eating his horses, as recounted in *The Land of the Muskeg* (London: William Heinemann, 1895), 179.
88 Parenteau, "Care, Control, and Supervision," 25.
89 Ritvo, *Animal Estate*, 261-62.
90 For examples, see Wyndham-Quin, *Canadian Nights*, 103-4, 118-19; Charles Alston Messiter, *Sport and Adventures among the North American Indians* (London: R.H. Porter, 1890), 46; Parenteau, "Care, Control, and Supervision," 31.
91 Parenteau, "Care, Control, and Supervision," 32. For a brief discussion of the Métis buffalo hunt from Red River, see Gerhard J. Ens, *Homeland to Hinterland: The Changing Worlds of the Red River Métis in the Nineteenth Century* (Toronto: University of Toronto Press, 1996), 40-42.
92 William Francis Butler, *The Wild North Land* (London: Low, Marston, Low, and Searle, 1873), 45.
93 Ibid., 125-26.
94 Carnegie, *Saskatchewan*, 39, 59, 64, 258, 261. Even as late as the 1880s and 1890s, explorer and hunter David Hanbury took height measurements of Inuit and attempted to transcribe the Native language. David Hanbury, *Sport and Travel in the Northlands of Canada* (London: Edward Arnold, 1904), 292; *Dictionary of Canadian Biography*, vol. 13, s.v. "David Theophilus Hanbury" (Toronto: University of Toronto Press, 1994).

CHAPTER 4: THE SCIENCE OF THE HUNT

1 Simon Ryan, *The Cartographic Eye* (Cambridge: Cambridge University Press, 1996), 104 and "Inscribing the Emptiness: Cartography, Exploration, and the Construction of Australia," in *De-Scribing Empire: Postcolonialism and Textuality*, ed. Chris Tiffin and Alan

Lawson (London: Routledge, 1994), 115-30.

2 J.B. Harley, "Maps, Knowledge, and Power," in *The Iconography of Landscape: Essays on the Symbolic Representation, Design, and Use of Past Environments,* ed. Denis Cosgrove and Stephen Daniels (Cambridge: Cambridge University Press, 1988), 277-312.

3 Daniel Clayton, "Circumscribing Vancouver Island," *BC Studies* 122, Summer (1999): 19; and *Islands of Truth: The Imperial Fashioning of Vancouver Island* (Vancouver: UBC Press, 2000), 165-204.

4 Harley, "Maps, Knowledge, and Power," 282.

5 Graham Burnett, *Masters of All They Surveyed: Exploration, Geography, and a British El Dorado* (Chicago: University of Chicago Press, 2000), 170; Ryan, *Cartographic Eye*, 105.

6 James R. Ryan, "Imperial Landscapes: Photography, Geography, and British Overseas Exploration, 1858-1872," in *Geography and Imperialism, 1820-1940,* Morag Bell, Robin Butlin, and Michael Heffernan (Manchester: Manchester University Press, 1995), 74; and Tina Loo, "Making a Modern Wilderness: Conserving Wildlife in Twentieth-Century Canada," *Canadian Historical Review* 82, 1 (2001): 104-5.

7 Ryan, *Cartographic Eye*, 6-8, 102.

8 Richards, *Imperial Archive*, 6-7.

9 Harley, "Maps, Knowledge, and Power," 282.

10 Ryan, *Cartographic Eye*, 105; G.N.G. Clarke, "Taking Possession: The Cartouche as Cultural Text in Eighteenth-Century American Maps," *Word and Image* 4, 2 (1988): 455.

11 Daniel Clayton, "The Creation of Imperial Space in the Pacific Northwest," *Journal of Historical Geography* 26, 3 (2000): 327-50.

12 Ryan, *Cartographic Eye*, 103.

13 Ibid., 101, 7, 6.

14 Burnett, *Masters of All They Surveyed*, 129.

15 Ryan, *Cartographic Eye*, 102.

16 Ibid., 4-5.

17 For the reference to "geographical reconnaissance," see Dan Clayton, "On Not Going on a Field Trip: Absence, Memory and Geography," *BC Studies* 132, Winter (2001/2002): 65-79.

18 Burnett, *Masters of All They Surveyed*, 6, 2.

19 For the cartographic foundation of Rupert's Land constructed by fur traders prior to its purchase by the Dominion of Canada, see Richard Ruggles, "Mapping the Interior Plains of Rupert's Land by the Hudson's Bay Company to 1870," in *Mapping the North American Plains: Essays in the History of Cartography,* ed. Frederick C. Luebke, Frances W. Kaye, and Gary E. Moulton (Norman, OK: University of Oklahoma Press, 1987), 145-60. Also see James M. Richtik, "Mapping the Quality of Land for Agriculture in Western Canada," in *Mapping the North American Plains: Essays in the History of Cartography,* ed. Frederick C. Luebke, Frances W. Kaye, and Gary E. Moulton (Norman, OK: University of Oklahoma Press, 1987), 161-72.

20 Ryan, *Cartographic Eye*, 123. For primary sources, see the map entitled "The Western Portion of British North America Showing the Route Followed by Lord Milton and Dr. Cheadle from the Saskatchewan to British Columbia 1863-1864," in William Fitzwilliam Milton and W.B. Cheadle, *North-West Passage by Land* (London: Cassell, Petter, Galpin, 1875), frontispiece. For an example from a slightly later period, see Henry Somers Somerset, *The Land of the Muskeg* (London: William Heinemann, 1895), 14.

21 William Francis Butler, *The Great Lone Land* (London: Sampson Low, Marston, Searle, and Rivington, 1872). See the frontispiece map entitled "Map of British America from Lake Superior to the Rocky Mountains."

22 James Carnegie, *Saskatchewan and the Rocky Mountains: A Diary and Narrative of Travel, Sport, and Adventure, in 1859 and 1860* (Edinburgh: Edmonston and Douglas, 1875), 234.

23 This practice continued well into the late nineteenth century with hunters who travelled to unmapped sections of the arctic coastline in the North-West Territory. David Hanbury, *Sport and Travel in the Northlands of Canada* (London: Edward Arnold, 1904).

24 William Francis Butler, *The Wild North Land* (London: Low, Marston, Low, & Searle, 1873), frontispiece; and Butler, *The Great Lone Land*, frontispiece. For Butler's official report see *Report by Lieutenant Butler (69th Regiment) of His Journey from Fort Garry to Rocky Mountain House and Back: Under Instructions from the Lieut.-Governor of Manitoba During the Winter of 1870-71* (Ottawa: The Times, 1871).

25 See "Map of Lord Southesk's Route from Crow-wing to the Ricky Mountains" on the endpapers of Carnegie, *Saskatchewan*, and "Sketch Map of Part of the Rocky Mountains Showing Lord Southesk's Route," 234; Butler, *The Wild North Land*, frontispiece; Somerset, *Muskeg*, "Dunvegan to Fort McLeod," 56.

26 Butler, *The Wild North Land*, frontispiece; and *The Great Lone Land*, frontispiece.

27 Butler, *The Great Lone Land*, frontispiece. Along a similar pattern, H. Somers Somerset combined, overwrote, or included Native and British colonial history such as "Old Fort Assiniboine (Abandoned)" or "Ft. Chipewyan." He also included both Native and English place names, such as the "Ka-ska pa-te-si-pi-sis or Sweat House River." Somerset, *Land of the Muskeg*, 14.

28 Butler, *The Great Lone Land*, frontispiece; and *The Wild North Land*, frontispiece.

29 Butler, *The Wild North Land*, frontispiece; and Milton and Cheadle, *North-West Passage*, frontispiece.

30 For examples of place naming in other areas of the country, such as Newfoundland, see John Guille Millais, *Newfoundland and Its Untrodden Ways* (London: Longmans, Green, 1907), 50, 230, 276, 206, 212, 282.

31 Carnegie, *Saskatchewan*, 200-2, 196. See pp. 193, 222, and "Sketch Map of the Rocky Mountains Showing Lord Southesk's Route," 234. For more on the discourse surrounding symbolic geographical conquest, see Peter H. Hansen, "Confetti of Empire: The Conquest of Everest in Nepal, India, Britain, and New Zealand," *Comparative Studies in Society and History* 42, 2 (2000): 307-22; and "Vertical Boundaries, National Identities: British Mountaineering on the Frontiers of Europe and the Empire, 1868-1914," *Journal of Imperial and Commonwealth History* 24, 1 (1996): 48-71. Also relevant to this discussion, Andrea Kunard presents an insightful analysis of the interplay of text and image in the construction and appropriation of space in "Relationships of Photography and Text in the Colonization of the Canadian West: The 1858 Assiniboine and Saskatchewan Exploring Expedition," *International Journal of Canadian Studies* 26 (Fall 2002): 77-100.

32 Milton and Cheadle, *North-West Passage*, 246, 269.

33 Ibid., 249, 285, 288, 297, 307.

34 David Cannadine, *Ornamentalism: How the British Saw Their Empire* (Oxford: Oxford University Press, 2001), 102.

35 Extending beyond the period covered by this book, British hunter-explorers like H. Somers Somerset and David Hanbury continued the naming tradition into the final years of the nineteenth and early twentieth centuries. Hanbury claimed that he preferred to use Aboriginal place names: "Whenever I have been in unexplored regions I have invariably made it a strict rule to ascertain and adhere to local and native names ... it is of the greatest service to the travellers who finds himself in the country for the first time. If he has a map in his possession, and on this map finds the native name for every place, he will have no

difficulty in making the natives understand the route he wishes to follow."

Hanbury's main route took him along the length of the Ark-i-linik River northeast of Great Slave Lake. Hanbury explored the region and recorded meteorological observations, as well as collecting botanical, geological, and entomological specimens. He took photographs and body measurements of the local Inuit peoples. Due to the successful nature of his expedition, as relayed through his narrative, *Sport and Travel in the Northland of Canada*, the Canadian Geographical Board renamed the Ark-i-linik the Hanbury River, which still bears his name today. Nevertheless, Hanbury himself named several geographical landmarks after friends. He stated that after he failed to "ascertain the native name" of a small body of water northeast of Great Slave Lake he decided to name the lake after his friend Dr. W.L. Abbott. Hanbury named other features based on a geographically functional approach, such as Portage Inlet, Limestone Island, Sandy Creek, and Long Lake. Hanbury, *Sport and Travel*, 11, 18, 36, 56, 70, 223, 229; and *Dictionary of Canadian Biography*, vol. 13, s.v. "David Theophilus Hanbury" (Toronto: University of Toronto Press, 1994). For the Ark-i-linik River, see the *Atlas of Canada* (Canada: Reader's Digest Association, 1981), plate 45. Also see Somerset, *Land of the Muskeg*, 56, for the use of place names and landmarks from the narratives of the hunters and explorers under examination in this book.

Like Hanbury, John Guille Millais applied new place names in Newfoundland during the same period. Millais gave his own name to Millais' Lake, which he identified on the map that accompanied his travel narrative. Millais christened two other bodies of water Lake McGraw and Lake Prowse after his hunting companion and a local magistrate respectively. He named other topographical features Northern Diver Lake, Mount Frances, and Shoe Hill Lake as he crossed central Newfoundland. Millais, *Newfoundland*, 50, 230, 276, 206, 212, 282, 228.

36 Lawrence D. Berg and Robin A. Kearns, "Naming as Norming: Race, Gender, and the Identity Politics of Naming Places in Aotearoa/New Zealand," *Society and Space* 14, 1 (1996): 99-122.

37 Paul Carter, *The Road to Botany Bay: An Essay in Spatial History* (London: Faber and Faber, 1987), xxiv.

38 For an excellent analysis dealing with the role and use of landmarks, see Burnett, *Masters of All They Surveyed*, 110-17.

39 Ibid., 110, 168, 171.

40 Ibid., 15-16, 129-30.

41 Ibid., 111-12, 167-69, 190, 161, 212.

42 Butler, *The Wild North Land*, 31.

43 Carnegie, *Saskatchewan*, 200-2.

44 Burnett, *Masters of All They Surveyed*, 183.

45 Ibid., 189.

46 Genesis 2:19-20, King James version.

47 Colin M. Coates, "Like the Thames towards Putney: The Appropriation of Landscape in Lower Canada," *Canadian Historical Review* 74, 3 (1993): 330; and *The Metamorphoses of Landscape and Community in Early Quebec* (Montreal and Kingston: McGill-Queen's University Press, 2000), 151-52. For the scientific gaze, see Mary Louise Pratt, *Imperial Eyes: Travel Writing and Transculturation* (London: Routledge, 1992), 26-36; Matthew H. Edney, *Mapping an Empire: The Geographical Construction of British India, 1765-1843* (Chicago: University of Chicago Press, 1997), 49-50, 54-55; Ryan, *Cartographic Eye*, 57.

48 Edney, *Mapping an Empire*, 54.

49 For an overview, see Victoria Dickenson, *Drawn from Life: Science and Art in the Portrayal*

of the New World (Toronto: University of Toronto Press, 1998), 169-88; and Pratt, *Imperial Eyes*, 25. For a reconsideration of Pratt, travel literature, and the Linnaean system, see William Beinart, "Men, Science, Travel and Nature in the Eighteenth and Nineteenth-Century Cape," *Journal of Southern African Studies* 24, 4 (1998): 775-99.

50 Pratt, *Imperial Eyes*, 25. Also see Lisbet Koerner, "Purposes of Linnean Travel," in *Visions of Empire: Voyages, Botany, and Representations of Empire,* ed. David Miller and Peter Reill (Cambridge: Cambridge University Press, 1996), 117-52.

51 Pratt, *Imperial Eyes*, 31-32.

52 Ibid., 25.

53 Ibid. For an example of geology and cultural imperialism, see Robert Stafford, "Geological Surveys, Mineral Discoveries, and British Expansion, 1835-1871," *Journal of Imperialism and Commonwealth History* 12, 3 (1984): 5-32.

54 Pratt, *Imperial Eyes*, 25.

55 For examples of British science and appropriation in other colonial territories, see Pratt, *Imperial Eyes*, 26-36; Edney, *Mapping an Empire*, 49-50, 54-55; and Ryan, *Cartographic Eye*, 57.

56 Carnegie, *Saskatchewan*, 91, 113, 243; William Ross King, *The Sportsman and Naturalist in Canada* (London: Hurst and Blackett, 1866), 145, 85-85, 73.

57 Pratt, *Imperial Eyes*, 30. For an early application of Pratt's systematization of nature, see Bruce McLeod, *The Geography of Empire in English Literature 1580-1745* (Cambridge: Cambridge University Press, 1999), 11, 30, 37, 218.

58 Pratt, *Imperial Eyes*, 7, 28.

59 Ibid., 31. For an excellent example from a later period, see the natural history specimen sketches of Arctic butterflies caught and arranged by Hanbury, *Sport and Travel*, 274.

60 Pratt, *Imperial Eyes*, 38.

61 Historian Suzanne Zeller argues that Canadian nation builders used the Linnaean system and other scientific modes of representation to help create the idea of a transcontinental nation in the post-Confederation period. Suzanne Zeller, *Inventing Canada: Early Victorian Science and the Idea of a Transcontinental Nation* (Toronto: University of Toronto Press, 1987), 4-6, 269-70. More recently, she discusses the classical foundations of appropriative imperial culture in "Classical Codes: Biogeographical Assessments of Environment in Victorian Canada," *Journal of Historical Geography* 24, 1 (1998): 20-35. Also see Carl Berger, *Science, God, and Nature in Victorian Canada* (Toronto: University of Toronto Press, 1983), preface and 3-30. For a general overview of science, exploration, and imperialism in British North America, see Robert Stafford, *Scientist of Empire: Sir Roderick Murchison, Scientific Exploration, and Victorian Imperialism* (Cambridge: Cambridge University Press, 1989), 64-81.

 For the role played by key inventory scientists George Mercer Dawson and John Macoun, see Suzanne Zeller's and Gale Avrith-Wakeam's entry, *Dictionary of Canadian Biography,* vol. 13, s.v. "George Mercer Dawson" (Toronto: University of Toronto Press, 1994). Also see William Chalmers, *George Mercer Dawson: Geologist, Scientist, Explorer* (Montreal: XYZ Publishing, 2000); Douglas Cole and Bradley Lockner, eds., *The Journals of George M. Dawson: British Columbia, 1875-1878* (Vancouver: UBC Press, 1989); as well as Dawson's own work in the *Report on the Geology and Resources of the Region in the Vicinity of the Forty-Ninth Parallel: From the Lake of the Woods to the Rocky Mountains, with Lists of Plants and Animals Collected and Notes on the Fossils* (Montreal: Dawson, 1875); and *Sketches of the Past and Present Condition of the Indians of Canada* (1877). Dawson served as the naturalist and geologist for the Joint British-American International Boundary Survey to demarcate the forty-ninth parallel from the Lake of the Woods to the Rocky Mountains. Dawson also contributed three hundred natural history specimens to the collection of the British Museum and added to the maps previously created by the expeditions of Palliser and Hind. He also spent two years with the Geological Survey of Canada (GSC) in the region of British Columbia. For John Macoun, natural history, and "inventory science" with the GSC in the northwest, see W.A. Waiser, *The Field Naturalist: John Macoun, the Geological Survey, and Natural Science* (Toronto: University of Toronto Press, 1989). Waiser also contributed notes in the second edition of John Macoun, *Autobiography of John Macoun: Canadian Explorer and Naturalist, 1831-1920*, 2nd ed. (Ottawa: Ottawa Field-Naturalists' Club, 1979). Waiser additionally wrote the entry, *Dictionary of Canadian Biography*, vol. 14, s.v. "John Macoun" (Toronto: University of Toronto Press, 1998).

62 Edney, *Mapping an Empire*, 55. For similar two-plane constructions of plants from a slightly earlier period, see Charlotte Klonck, *Science and the Perception of Nature: British Landscape Art in the Late Eighteenth and Early Nineteenth Centuries* (New Haven, CT: Yale University Press, 1996), 49.

63 I use "associationism" here to emphasize the importance of comparison in the systematizing of game as a strategy in the overall imperial fashioning of the land. Also see G. Malcolm Lewis, "Rhetoric of the Western Interior: Modes of Environmental Description in American Promotional Literature of the Nineteenth-Century," in *The Iconography of Landscape: Essays on the Symbolic Representation, Design, and Use of Past Environments*, ed. Denis Cosgrove and Stephen Daniels (Cambridge: Cambridge University Press, 1988), 179-93.

64 Pratt, *Imperial Eyes*, 27-28.

65 In his work on landscape, MacLaren refers only to landscape associationism. However, British big-game hunters, eager to inventory the fauna of the land, compared and contrasted British North American game with that of Great Britain. I refer to this process as "game associationism." For landscape associationism, see I.S. MacLaren, "Aesthetic Mappings of the West by the Palliser and Hind Survey Expeditions, 1857-1859," *Studies in Canadian Literature* 10, 1 (1985): 30.

66 Pratt, *Imperial Eyes*, 60.

67 Carnegie, *Saskatchewan*, 210.

68 Milton and Cheadle, *North-West Passage*, 204.

69 King, *Sportsman and Naturalist*, 85-86.

70 R.G. Moyles and Doug Owram, *Imperial Dreams and Colonial Realities* (Toronto: University of Toronto Press, 1988), 66.

71 Thomas Dunlap, "Remaking the Land: The Acclimatisation Movement and Anglo Ideas of Nature," *Journal of World History* 8, 2 (1997): 303-19; and Michael A. Osborne, "Acclimatizing the World: A History of the Paradigmatic Colonial Science," *Osiris* 15 (2000): 135-51. For more on the British Acclimatisation Society, see Harriet Ritvo, *The Animal Estate: The English and Other Creatures in the Victorian Age* (Cambridge, MA: Harvard University Press, 1987), 239-42. For an example of acclimatization of the black grouse and the capercaillie in Newfoundland, see Millais, *Newfoundland*, 264, 335.

72 For ecological imperialism, see Richard H. Grove, *Green Imperialism: Colonial Expansion, Tropical Island Edens, and the Origins of Environmentalism, 1600-1860* (Cambridge: Cambridge University Press, 1995); Alfred W. Crosby, *Ecological Imperialism* (Cambridge: Cambridge University Press, 1986); and "Ecological Imperialism: The Overseas Migration of Western Europeans as a Biological Phenomenon," in *The Ends of the Earth: Perspectives on Modern Environmental History*, ed. Donald Worster (Cambridge: Cambridge University Press, 1988), 103-17. For English weeds on the Canadian Prairies, see Clinton L. Evans, *The War on Weeds in the Prairie West: An Environmental History* (Calgary: University of

Calgary Press, 2002). For an overview of the history of the British Acclimatisation Society and acclimatized animals in Great Britain, see Christopher Lever, *The Naturalised Animals of the British Isles* (London: Hutchinson, 1977). Lever outlines economic, ornamental, and sport reasons for the acclimatization of animals in England.

73 John MacKenzie, *The Empire of Nature: Hunting, Conservation, and British Imperialism* (Manchester: Manchester University Press, 1988), 296-97.

74 Dunlap, "Remaking the Land," 303-19.

75 Society for the Acclimatisation ..., *First Annual Report of the Society for the Acclimatisation of Animals, Birds, Fishes, Insects and Vegetables within the United Kingdom* (London: The Society, 1861), 5-6.

76 Linden Gillbank, "The Origins of the Acclimatisation Society of Victoria: Practical Science in the Wake of the Gold Rush," *Historical Records of Australian Science* 6, 3 (1986): 360-61. European powers such as the French, Dutch, and Portuguese conducted similar experiments as early as 1600.

77 Lever, *Naturalised Animals*, 22.

78 Gillbank, "Origins," 363.

79 Ritvo, *Animal Estate*, 240.

80 Many of the members of the Acclimatisation Society of Great Britain were avid sportsmen. Game birds and sport fish factored prominently into the short-term and long-term plans of the society. Their annual report of 1861 reminded members that, in addition to sporting interests, they must also seek the public good. "The cultivation of birds of game may be a very pleasant diversion in its own way ... but if the Society is to command the general respect and support of the public it must be by importations calculated to increase and agreeably vary the natural products of the country, and above all the food of the people." Although the sportsmen among the acclimatizers desired the introduction of new species purely for their exclusive hunting and fishing pleasure, the society recognized the importance of expanding beyond the self-serving interests of its elite members. Certainly the landed and sporting elite in England gained most from the acclimatization of colonial game.

Those Englishmen living abroad complained that they found little sport with indigenous animals, especially in Australia. The landed elite living in the colonies acclimatized both for ornamental reasons, to hear the familiar sounds of English songbirds, and to accommodate the hunt of the landed elite. Moreover, members of the Acclimatisation Society, in Australia, for example, undertook a policy of protectionism and preservationism to ensure that future access to the elite hunt remained restricted.

The socially elite members used their society to codify and institutionalize the language of appropriation and exploitation of colonial wildlife. The objectives of the Acclimatisation Society reveal the Ornamentalist discourse and the importance of the foreign and the familiar in the cultural appropriation of colonial territories. The objectives of the society consisted of the following: "First, the society sought the introduction, acclimatisation, and domestication of all innoxious animals, birds, fishes, insects, and vegetables, whether useful or ornamental. Second, the perfection, propagation, and hybridization of races newly introduced or already domesticated. Third, the spread of indigenous animals, &c from parts of the United Kingdom where they are already known, to other localities where they are not known. Fourth, the procuration, whether by purchase, gift, or exchange, of animals &c, from British Colonies and foreign countries. Fifth, the transmission of animals, &c from England to her colonies and foreign parts in exchange for others thence to the Society. Sixth, the holding of periodical meetings, and the publication of reports and transactions for the purpose of spreading knowledge of acclimatisation, and inquiry into the causes of success or failure." Society for the Acclimatisation ..., *First Annual Report,* 2.

In their first year, they boasted the acclimatization of quail from the provinces of British North America, Chinese yams, beans and peas from Africa, and a pair of miniature sheep from Brittany. They planned to procure other animals and plant an acre of land with the aforementioned yams. At the society's expense, they sent an agent to Prussia to obtain and import a species of pond fish. They offered a premium to anyone who could obtain a specimen of the Murray cod – a freshwater fish from Australia. The society listed their initial successes, which included the acclimatization of English sheep, alpaca, angora goat, camel, red deer, fallow deer, spotted axis, pea fowl, common pheasant, partridge, swan, carp, goldfish, thrush, blackbird, starling, linnet, goldfinch, java sparrow, squirrel, and glow-worm in Australia. Gillbank, "Origins," 359-74. For more on the transfers of seeds and plants across the British empire, see Lucile H. Brockway, *Science and Colonial Expansion: The Role of the British Royal Botanic Gardens* (New York: Academic Press Inc., 1979), 45-56.

81 Gillbank, "Origins," 360. For an interesting discussion of the place and role of natural history museums in the context of imperialism, see Susan Sheets-Pyenson, "How to 'Grow' a Natural History Museum: The Building of Colonial Collections, 1850-1900," *Archives of Natural History* 15, 2 (1988): 121-47; and Beth Fowkes Tobin, *Picturing Imperial Power: Colonial Subjects in Eighteenth-Century British Painting* (Durham: Duke University Press, 1999), 174-201.

82 Ibid. Also see vols. 1 and 2 of Campbell Hardy, *Sporting Adventures in the New World; or, Days and Nights of Moose-Hunting in the Pine Forests of Acadia* (London: Hurst and Blackett, 1855).

The British Acclimatisation Society spawned a sister society in Australia; the Acclimatisation Society of Victoria (Australia) formed in 1861, a year after the society in London. The like-minded members of the Victoria society actively promoted the modification of the alien-looking Australian landscape. Their stated objectives followed those of the parent body almost to the letter. They sought the introduction, naturalization, and domestication of all animal and plant life they deemed innocuous for either practical use or ornamental purposes. Like the British society, the Australians sought, through selective breeding and hybridization, to perfect specific species. The Victoria society further exported many animals and plants native to the Australian continent for introduction across the world, and they sought deer, partridge, hare, and the sparrow from Great Britain. Through importation, the Acclimatisation Society of Victoria waged an environmental war in an effort to remake the landscape into something that resembled Great Britain. To acclimatizers living abroad, English songbirds and their ornamental value were just as important as the introduction of familiar plants and familiar game for sport.

The Acclimatisation Society of Victoria produced dramatic changes in the Australian landscape. An estimated 365 non-indigenous plant species existed in the area around Victoria by 1900. Instead of introducing new species in a careful and considered manner, the Victoria society sought to "supplant" indigenous species rather than "supplement" them. The members of both societies viewed their actions as legitimate and decidedly imperial activities. Acclimatizers believed the diversification of Australian flora and fauna promoted a healthy environment. Although the Victoria society experienced some success, they also caused widespread devastation to the landscape. The seeds of the blackberry bush (*Rubus Fruticosus*) that spread during the early 1860s developed into an agricultural nuisance. Through the enabling features of a warmer climate, the natural adaptive capabilities of the plant, and the absence of natural constraints, the blackberry spread as a weed across the landscape. A similar problem existed for the hawthorn (used to grow English hedgerows), which proliferated to the point of destroying indigenous plants. See Gillbank, "Origins," 359-74; and for consumption of colonial animals, see Lever, *Naturalized Animals*, 31-33.

83 King, *Sportsman and Naturalist*, 153.
84 Ibid., 161-64.
85 Ibid., 294, 317-18, 321.

CHAPTER 5: HUNTING FOR LANDSCAPE

1 Graham Burnett, *Masters of All They Surveyed: Exploration, Geography, and a British El Dorado* (Chicago: University of Chicago Press, 2000), 147-48, 194, 196.
2 Some might suggest that by the early to mid-1800s, these landscape principles no longer held the meanings invested in them during the late eighteenth century. In my view, this perspective fails to address the nuanced and considered application of the picturesque and the sublime in all genres of British travel literature into the early 1870s. Simply put, why did the British continue to employ the picturesque and the sublime, literally around the globe, if they were devoid of meaning? There are several possible explanations. On one hand, many obscure parts of the empire, not yet appropriated aesthetically into the empire, still called to British explorers and travellers. Once in these yet-to-be-appropriated venues, they relied on the cultural principles used in other colonies in the late eighteenth and early nineteenth centuries. The picturesque and the sublime, in my view, still held important residual meanings – the social and cultural ties between the landed elite and the land ran deep. British travellers of all kinds, including big-game hunters, modified the application of these malleable landscape principles during the mid-nineteenth century, specifically in frontier colonial localities that looked nothing like England. One cannot simply dismiss the amount of literary time, space, and effort British big-game hunters devoted to landscape descriptions in their narratives. From this perspective, my approach parallels that of Burnett in *Masters of All They Surveyed*, 146, 131-35.
3 Colin M. Coates, "Like the Thames towards Putney: The Appropriation of Landscape in Lower Canada," *Canadian Historical Review* 74, 3 (1993): 320-22. Also see Colin Coates, *The Metamorphoses of Landscape and Community in Early Quebec* (Montreal and Kingston: McGill-Queen's University Press, 2000), 144-61.
4 Simon Ryan, *The Cartographic Eye* (Cambridge: Cambridge University Press, 1996), 62.
5 William Gilpin, *Three Essays: On Picturesque Beauty; On Picturesque Travel; and On the Art of Sketching Landscape* (London: R. Blamire, 1792), 36, emphasis his.
6 Gilpin, *Three Essays*, 26, emphasis his.
7 The work of Ian MacLaren bridges the development of the picturesque in England with its application in the British North American West. MacLaren focuses on the application of the picturesque in the travel narratives of late eighteenth- and nineteenth-century British explorers and fur traders. He scrutinizes the narratives of such prominent British figures as George Vancouver, Archibald Menzies, George Back, John Franklin, George Simpson, Alexander Mackenzie, John Palliser, and Henry Hind. Examination of MacLaren's work reveals that the transportation and application of the picturesque to British North America required its modification – particularly in the West and Northwest.

For an overview of the picturesque and the sublime in the Pacific Northwest, see Maria Tippett and Douglas Cole, *From Desolation to Splendour: Changing Perceptions of the British Columbia Landscape* (Toronto: Clarke, Irwin, 1977). For specific references to the aspects of the picturesque outlined in this paragraph, see I.S. MacLaren, "Retaining Captaincy of the Soul: Responses to Nature in the First Franklin Expedition," *Essays on Canadian Writing* 28 (Spring 1984): 64; I.S. MacLaren, "The Aesthetic Map of the North, 1845-1859," *Arctic* 38, 2 (1985): 89-103; I.S. MacLaren, "The Grandest Tour: The Aesthetics of Landscape in Sir George Back's Explorations of the Eastern Arctic, 1833-1837," *English Studies in Canada* 10, 4 (1984): 440; I.S. MacLaren, "The Aesthetic Mapping of Nature in the Second Franklin Expedition," *Journal of Canadian Studies* 20, 1 (1985): 46; I.S. MacLaren, "Alexander Mackenzie and the Landscapes of Commerce," *Studies in Canadian Literature* 7, 2 (1982): 149; I.S. MacLaren, "The Limits of the Picturesque in British North America," *Journal of Garden History*," 5, 1 (1985): 97-111; I.S. MacLaren, "The Influence of Eighteenth-Century British Landscape Aesthetics on Narrative and Pictorial Responses to the British North American North and West, 1769-1872," (PhD diss., University of Western Ontario, 1983), 1:68.

8   Humphry Repton, *Landscape Gardening and Landscape Architecture* (London: Longman, 1840), 222.

9   Matthew H. Edney, *Mapping an Empire: The Geographical Construction of British India, 1765-1843* (Chicago: University of Chicago Press, 1997), 62.

10 Patricia Jasen, *Wild Things: Nature, Culture, and Tourism in Ontario, 1790-1914* (Toronto: University of Toronto Press, 1995), 20.

11 For the connection between landscape and the agrarian revolution in England see Ann Bermingham, *Landscape and Ideology: The English Rustic Tradition, 1740-1860* (Berkley: University of California Press, 1986); and John Barrel, *The Dark Side of Landscape: The Rural Poor in English Painting 1730-1840* (Cambridge: Cambridge University Press, 1980).

12 Ryan, *Cartographic Eye*, 72.

13 Bermingham, *Landscape and Ideology*, 75.

14 Ryan, *Cartographic Eye*, 71; and Simon Ryan, "Exploring Aesthetics: The Picturesque Appropriation of Land in Journals of Australian Exploration," *Australian Literary Studies* 15, 4 (1992): 287.

15 MacLaren, "Aesthetic Mapping of Nature," 30.

16 James Carnegie, *Saskatchewan and the Rocky Mountains: A Diary and Narrative of Travel, Sport, and Adventure, in 1859 and 1860* (Edinburgh: Edmonston and Douglas, 1875), 170.

17 Ibid., 252-53.

18 Frederick Ulric Graham, *Notes of a Sporting Expedition in the Far West of Canada, 1847* (London: Private circulation, 1898), 85.

19 Ibid., 50.

20 I.S. MacLaren, "Aesthetic Mappings of the West, by the Palliser and Hind Survey Expeditions, 1857-59," *Studies in Canadian Literature* 10, 1 (1985): 30.

21 Ryan, *Cartographic Eye*, 75.

22 For John Franklin, see MacLaren, "Retaining Captaincy of the Soul," 69; For John Palliser, see MacLaren, "Aesthetic Mappings of the West," 32; and Archibald Menzies in MacLaren, "Limits of the Picturesque," 99. The idea of rich, park-like lands corresponds with a broader change in perspective on the West and Northwest. Also see Chapter 3, "Landscaping the Wilds" in Elizabeth Vibert, *Traders' Tales: Narratives of Cultural Encounters in the Columbia Plateau* (Norman, OK: University of Oklahoma Press, 1997).

23 Graham, *Notes of a Sporting Expedition*, 73, 47, 77-78.

24 William Fitzwilliam Milton and W.B. Cheadle, *North-West Passage by Land* (London: Cassell, Petter, Galpin, 1875), 224.

25 William Francis Butler, *The Wild North Land* (London: Low, Marston, Low, and Searle, 1873), 235.
26 Milton and Cheadle, *North-West Passage*, 54-55, 71-72.
27 Carnegie, *Saskatchewan*, 147.
28 Ibid.
29 Milton and Cheadle, *North-West Passage*, 175.
30 For scholars who consider the interconnectedness of the sublime with British imperialism, see Coates, *The Metamorphoses of Landscape;* and Coates, "Like the Thames towards Putney," 317-43; Ryan, *Cartographic Eye*, 83-85; and Ryan, "Exploring Aesthetics," 282-93. See also MacLaren, "Influence of Eighteenth-Century British Landscape Aesthetics," vols. 1 and 2; "Limits of the Picturesque," 97-111; and "Aesthetic Map of the North," 89-103; Edney, *Mapping an Empire*.
31 Jasen, *Wild Things*, 8.
32 Burke's analysis of the relationship between emotion, beauty, and art is recognized as not only an important and influential work of aesthetic theory but also one of the first major works in European literature on the sublime, a subject that has fascinated thinkers from various disciplines from its publication to today. Edmund Burke, *A Philosophical Enquiry into the Origin of Our Ideas of the Sublime and Beautiful* (1757), edited with an introduction by Adam Philips (Oxford: Oxford University Press, 1990).
33 Jasen, *Wild Things*, 8.
34 MacLaren, "Influence of Eighteenth-Century British Landscape Aesthetics," 31; and Burnett, *Masters of All They Surveyed*, 144.
35 Burke, *Philosophical Enquiry*, 36, emphasis his.
36 MacLaren, "Retaining Captaincy of the Soul," 58.
37 Jasen, *Wild Things*, 9.
38 Ibid. Also see Patricia Jasen, "Romanticism, Modernity, and the Evolution of Tourism on the Niagara Frontier, 1790-1850," *Canadian Historical Review* 72, 3 (1991): 283-318.
39 Burke, *Philosophical Enquiry*, 7-10.
40 Jasen, *Wild Things*, 8.
41 MacLaren, "Retaining Captaincy of the Soul," 63.
42 MacLaren, "Aesthetic Map of the North," 92-93.
43 MacLaren, "Retaining Captaincy of the Soul," 58-59.
44 Ibid., 64-65.
45 MacLaren, "Influence of Eighteenth-Century British Landscape Aesthetics," 31.
46 Ibid., 23.
47 Ryan, *Cartographic Eye*, 85-86.
48 Burke, *Philosophical Enquiry*, 53.
49 Ibid.
50 Carnegie, *Saskatchewan*, 178.
51 Butler, *The Wild North Land*, 58, 243-46.
52 Burke, *Philosophical Enquiry*, 53.
53 MacLaren, "Aesthetic Mapping of Nature," 43; and "Limits of the Picturesque," 101.
54 MacLaren, "Aesthetic Mapping of Nature," 43.
55 MacLaren, "Aesthetic Map of the North," 100-1; and "Aesthetic Mappings of the West," 26.
56 William Ross King, *The Sportsman and Naturalist in Canada* (London: Hurst and Blackett, 1866), 147-48.
57 Ibid.

58 Butler, *The Wild North Land*, 44, 49-50.
59 For a similar gateway-style landscape construction in British Guiana, see Burnett, *Masters of All They Surveyed*, 179.
60 MacLaren, "Influence of Eighteenth-Century British Landscape Aesthetics," 776.
61 Butler, *The Wild North Land*, 30-31.
62 Burnett, *Masters of All They Surveyed*, 183.
63 Butler, *The Wild North Land*, 30-31.
64 Ibid.
65 Ibid., 68-69, emphasis his.
66 Ibid., 58.
67 Milton and Cheadle, *North-West Passage*, 281.
68 Burke, *Philosophical Enquiry*, 54.
69 Ibid., 66.
70 Butler, *The Wild North Land*, 271.
71 Ibid., 280-81.
72 Ibid.
73 Jasen, *Wild Things*, 82.
74 Burke, *Philosophical Enquiry*, 54.
75 Edward Wyndham-Quin, *Canadian Nights* (London: Smith, Elder, 1914), 260.
76 Ibid., 290.
77 Jasen, *Wild Things*, 83.
78 King, *The Sportsman and Naturalist*, 112.
79 Milton and Cheadle, *North-West Passage*, 281-82. The construction of sublime primeval forests and themes of decay continued in big-game hunting narratives through the 1890s. During his travel through present-day Alberta during the 1890s, H. Somers Somerset commented, "The trees bent one against the other in melancholy decay, covered with long grey lichen and huge fungus. Overhead the matted branches seemed to rot upon the trunks, grey with mould. Huge dead logs strewed the ground, crumbling at the touch of a foot. The place was most melancholy and weird." He again used the motif of decay near the Peace River (Alberta) when he wrote, "It was a wild spot. Sombre cliffs rose abruptly from the water on the northern shore. On our side lay the dense forest, matted and decaying, and fraught with all the melancholy of the North. The sky was dull, and cast a sombre hue over the lake. No scene could have been more cheerless." Somerset's depiction of the forest near the Peace River sets the landscape firmly within the aesthetic of the sublime. The feeling of melancholy, the motif of decay, overgrown vegetation, and the sense of weirdness all contribute to the British aesthetic construction of the foreign. Henry Somers Somerset, *The Land of the Muskeg* (London: William Heinemann, 1895), 148, 183.
80 Burke, *Philosophical Enquiry*, 75.
81 Ibid., 77.
82 Ibid., 40.
83 Butler, *The Wild North Land*, 182-83, emphasis his.
84 Ibid., 266-67.
85 Burke, *Philosophical Enquiry*, 63-64.
86 Jasen, *Wild Things*, 32.
87 Carnegie, *Saskatchewan*, 27.
88 Milton and Cheadle, *North-West Passage*, 252-53.
89 Butler, *The Wild North Land*, 243-46.

90 Ibid.
91 Wyndham-Quin, *Canadian Nights*, 290.
92 Butler, *The Wild North Land*, 182-83.
93 Ibid.

CHAPTER 6: FROM COLONIAL TO CORPORATE LANDSCAPES

1 Canadian Pacific Railway, *Fishing and Shooting along the Line of the Canadian Pacific Railway, in the Provinces of Ontario, Quebec, British Columbia, the Maritime Provinces, and the Prairies and Mountains of Western Canada, Issued by the General Passenger Department, Canadian Pacific Railway,* brochure (Montreal: CPR, 1893), 61.

2 Historian Michael Dawson also touches on the connection between the sublime and anti-modernism in the first years of the 1900s in his excellent discussion of tourism in British Columbia. See Michael Dawson, *Selling British Columbia: Tourism and Consumer Culture, 1890-1970* (Vancouver: UBC Press, 2004).

3 For the popularity of the rugged and primeval in CPR wilderness landscape photography during and after this period, see Margery Tanner Hadley, "Photography, Tourism, and the CPR: Western Canada, 1884-1914" in *Essays on the Historical Geography of the Canadian West: Regional Perspectives on the Settlement Process,* ed. L.A. Rosenvall and S.M. Evans (Calgary: University of Calgary, 1987), 48-69.

4 Canadian Pacific Railway, *Fishing Resorts along the Canadian Pacific Railway: Where to Go for Trout, Bass and Maskinoge, and What It Costs to Get There,* brochure (Montreal: CPR, 1887), 7.

5 Railfare Enterprises, *The Canadian Pacific, the New Highway to the East across the Mountains, Prairies, & Rivers of Canada,* brochure (Montreal: Railfare Enterprises, 1887), 1-2.

6 Fred Mason, "Advertising Eden: Sport and the Cultural Landscapes of the Canadian Pacific Railway, 1885-1920" (paper presented at the North American Society for Sport History Conference, University of Western Ontario, London, 2001), 1-26.

7 For a sampling of the references to paradise and Eden, see William Fitzwilliam Milton and W.B. Cheadle, *North-West Passage by Land* (London: Cassell, Petter, Galpin, 1875), 383-84; William Francis Butler, *The Wild North Land* (London: Low, Marston, Low, and Searle, 1873), 30-31, 230-31, 264-65, 121-23. Clive Phillipps-Wolley, *A Sportsman's Eden* (London: R. Bentley, 1888), 87; David Hanbury, *Sport and Travel in the Northlands of Canada* (London: Edward Arnold, 1904), 226. For the construct of the Empire's Eden, see Greg Gillespie, "The Imperial Embrace: British Sportsmen and the Appropriation of Landscape in Nineteenth-Century Canada" (PhD diss., University of Western Ontario, 2001). Also see R. Douglas Francis, *Images of the West: Responses to the Canadian Prairies* (Saskatoon: Western Producer Prairie Books, 1989); Karen Wonders, "A Sportsman's Eden: Part 1," *Beaver* 79, 5 (1999): 26-32, and "A Sportsman's Eden: Part 2," *Beaver* 79, 6 (1999): 30-37. For the exclusionary discourse behind the construction of the "Sportsman's Paradise" motif see Lynda Jessup, "Landscapes of Sport, Landscapes of Exclusion: The "Sportsman's Paradise" in Late-Nineteenth-Century Canadian Painting," *Journal of Canadian Studies* 40, 1 (2006): 71-123.

8 For examples of the Eden/paradise motif across British North America and nineteenth-century Canada, see Beriah Watson, *The Sportsman's Paradise* (London: J. Bumpus,

1889); William Robert Kennedy, *Sport, Travel, and Adventure in Newfoundland* (London: Blackwood, 1885), 253; John Rowan, *The Emigrant and Sportsman in Canada* (London: E. Stanford, 1876), 324-25; John Guille Millais, *Newfoundland and Its Untrodden Ways* (London: Longmans, Green, 1907), 100, 103, 138. For images of Eden and wildlife overabundance in the twentieth century, see Tina Loo, "Making a Modern Wilderness: Conserving Wildlife in Twentieth-Century Canada," *Canadian Historical Review* 82, 1 (2001): 92-121; and Gerald L. Pocius, "Tourists, Health Seekers, and Sportsmen: Luring Americans to Newfoundland in the Early Twentieth Century," in *Twentieth-Century Newfoundland: Explorations,* ed. James Hiller and Peter Neary (St. John's: Breakwater, 1994), 47-78; Greg Gillespie, "The Empire's Eden: British Hunters, Travel Writing, and Imperialism in Nineteenth-Century Canada," in *The Culture of Hunting in Canada*, ed. Jean Manore and Dale G. Miner (Vancouver: UBC Press, 2007), 42-55.

9 See George Colpitts, *Game in the Garden: A Human History of Wildlife in Western Canada to 1940* (Vancouver: UBC Press, 2002), 103-24; George Colpitts, "Wildlife Promotions, Western Canada Boosterism, and the Conservation Movement, 1890-1914," *The American Review of Canadian Studies* 28, 1-2 (1998): 103-30.

10 Mason, "Advertising Eden," 1-26. Also see Chris Williams, "That Boundless Ocean of Mountains: British Alpinists and the Appeal of the Canadian Rockies, 1885-1920," *International Journal of the History of Sport* 22, 1 (2005): 70-87. For the CPR's advertising of the "Canadian Alps," see Zac Robinson, "Storming the Heights: Canadian Frontier Nationalism and the Making of Manhood in the Conquest of Mount Robson, 1906-1913," *International Journal of the History of Sport* 22, 3 (2005): 415-33; Zac Robinson, "The Golden Years of Canadian Mountaineering: Asserted Ethics, Form, and Style, 1886-1925," *Sport History Review* 35, 1 (2004): 1-19; and Douglas A. Brown, "Fleshing-Out Field Notes: Prosaic, Poetic, and Picturesque Representations of Canadian Mountaineering, 1906-1940," *Journal of Sport History* 30, 3 (2003): 347-71. Also see Zac Robinson and PearlAnn Reichwein, "Canada's Everest? Rethinking the First Ascent of Mount Logan and the Politics of Nationhood, 1925," *Sport History Review* 35, 2 (2004): 95-121. For the concept of the landscape of consumption, see an excellent study of skiing by Annie Gilbert Coleman, *Ski Style: Sport and Culture in the Rockies* (Lawrence: University Press of Kansas, 2004), 219.

The CPR knew how to target British sportsmen effectively, and the sporting images and landscapes directed toward these men varied from those presented to other groups. The images constructed and marketed to settlers, for example, varied significantly from those for British big-game hunters. Settlement landscapes possessed little association to the untamed wilderness. The CPR filled their landscapes with long open prairies rather than impenetrable mountains filled with ferocious grizzly bears. To potential colonists, the CPR spoke to issues of land and soil quality – the Canadian West would be an agricultural country. One settlement brochure extolled these virtues: "Canada's greatest wealth is its soil; and it is as an agricultural country that it principally appeals to immigrants. For them, if they are willing and capable, it offers a competence in its fertile and easily acquired lands. While all the provinces contain arable land, open for settlement, the distinctively agricultural section is that known as "Western Canada." The CPR's settlement landscapes focused on order, control, and future potential. The sublimity of nature, a virtually meaningless construct to lower-class settler communities, did not intrude in the CPR's construction of the agrarian idyll. George Colpitts, *Game in the Garden*, 117. For an overview of tourism and the CPR, see John A. Eagle, *The Canadian Pacific Railway and the Development of Western Canada, 1896-1914* (Montreal and Kingston: McGill-Queen's University Press, 1989), 148-72; E.J. Hart, *The Selling of Canada: The CPR and the Beginnings of Canadian Tourism* (Banff, AB: Altitude Publishing, 1983); Canadian Pacific Railway, *Western Canada: Manitoba, Alberta, Saskatchewan and New Ontario: How to Reach It, How to Obtain Lands, How to Make a Home* (Montreal: CPR, 1908), 6.

11 For early big-game hunting among British fur traders, see Elizabeth Vibert, *Traders' Tales: Narratives of Cultural Encounters in the Columbia Plateau, 1807-1846* (Norman, OK: University of Oklahoma Press, 1997); and Elizabeth Vibert, "Real Men Hunt Buffalo: Masculinity, Race, and Class in British Fur Traders' Narratives," in *Cultures of Empire: Colonizers in Britain and the Empire in the Nineteenth and Twentieth Centuries*, ed. Catherine Hall (New York: Routledge, 2000), 281-97.

12 This general preference in scholarship has been noted by historians of sport, imperialism, and environmental history for decades. For specific examples, see John MacKenzie, *The Empire of Nature: Hunting, Conservation, and British Imperialism* (Manchester: Manchester University Press, 1988), 7; and Thomas L. Altherr, and John F. Reiger, "Academic Historians and Hunting: A Call for More and Better Scholarship," *Environmental History Review* 19, 3 (1995): 39-56.

13 For the term "geographical reconnaissance" in reference to "travel writing, landscape description, surveying, map-making, and the compilation of resource inventories," see Dan Clayton, "On Not Going on a Field Trip: Absence, Memory and Geography," *BC Studies* 132 (2001-2): 65-79.

Bibliography

PRIMARY SOURCES

Ballantyne, Robert Michael. *The Buffalo Runners: A Tale of the Red River Plains*. London: J. Nisbet, 1891.

Berkeley, Grantley Fitzhardinge. *The English Sportsman in the Western Prairies*. London: Hurst and Blackett, 1861.

Branch, E. Douglas. *The Hunting of the Buffalo*. London: D. Appleton, 1929.

Burke, Edmund. *A Philosophical Enquiry into the Origin of Our Ideas of the Sublime and Beautiful*. Edited with an introduction by Adam Philips. 1757. Oxford: Oxford University Press, 1990.

Butler, William Frances. *The Campaign of the Cataracts: A Personal Narrative of the Great Nile Expedition of 1884-1885*. London: S. Low, Marston, Searle, and Rivington, 1887.

—. *The Great Lone Land*. London: Sampson Low, Marston, Searle, and Rivington, 1872.

—. *The Wild North Land*. London: Low, Marston, Low, and Searle, 1873.

—. *Report by Lieutenant Butler (69th Regiment) of His Journey from Fort Garry to Rocky Mountain House and Back: Under Instructions from the Lieut.-Governor of Manitoba during the Winter of 1870-71*. Ottawa: The Times, 1871.

Canadian Pacific Railway. *Fishing and Shooting along the Line of the Canadian Pacific Railway, in the Provinces of Ontario, Quebec, British Columbia, the Maritime Provinces, and the Prairies and Mountains of Western Canada, Issued by the General Passenger Department, Canadian Pacific Railway*. Brochure. Montreal: CPR, 1893.

—. *Fishing Resorts along the Canadian Pacific Railway: Where to Go for Trout, Bass and Maskinonge, and What It Costs to Get There*. Brochure. Montreal: Passenger Department, CPR, 1887.

—. *Western Canada: Manitoba, Alberta, Saskatchewan and New Ontario: How to Reach It, How to Obtain Lands, How to Make a Home*. Brochure. Montreal: CPR, 1908.

Carnegie, James. *Saskatchewan and the Rocky Mountains: A Diary and Narrative of Travel, Sport, and Adventure, in 1859 and 1860*. Edinburgh: Edmonston and Douglas, 1875.

Catlin, George. *Letter and Notes on the Manners, Customs, and Condition of the North American Indians*. London: G. Catlin, 1841.

Dawson, George M. *Report on the Geology and Resources of the Region in the Vicinity of the Forty-Ninth Parallel: From the Lake of the Woods to the Rocky Mountains, with Lists of Plants and Animals Collected and Notes on the Fossils.* Montreal: Dawson, 1875.

—. *Sketches of the Past and Present Condition of the Indians of Canada.* N.p., 1877.

Gilpin, William. *Three Essays: On Picturesque Beauty; On Picturesque Travel; and On the Art of Sketching Landscape.* London: R. Blamire, 1792.

Graham, Frederick Ulric. *Notes of a Sporting Expedition in the Far West of Canada, 1847.* London: Private circulation, 1898.

Grant, George Munro. *Ocean to Ocean: Sandford Fleming's Expedition through Canada in 1872.* Toronto: Belford, 1877.

Hanbury, David. *Sport and Travel in the Northlands of Canada.* London: Edward Arnold, 1904.

Hardy, Campbell. *Sporting Adventures in the New World; or, Days and Nights of Moose-Hunting in the Pine Forests of Acadia.* 2 vols. London: Hurst and Blackett, 1855.

Hind, Henry Youle. *Narrative of the Canadian Red River Exploring Expedition of 1857 and of the Assinniboine and Saskatchewan Exploring Expedition of 1858.* London: Longman, Green, Longman, and Roberts, 1860.

—. *Reports of Progress Together with a Preliminary and General Report, on the Assiniboine and Saskatchewan Exploring Expedition: Made under Instructions from the Provincial Secretary, Canada.* Toronto, 1859.

—. *A Sketch of an Overland Route to British Columbia.* Toronto, 1862.

Kane, Paul. *Wanderings of an Artist among the Indians of North America: From Canada to Vancouver's Island and Oregon through the Hudson's Bay Company's Territory and Back Again.* London: Longman, Brown, Green, Longmans and Roberts, 1859.

Kennedy, William Robert. *Sport, Travel, and Adventure in Newfoundland.* London: Blackwood, 1885.

King, William Ross. *The Sportsman and Naturalist in Canada.* London: Hurst and Blackett, 1866.

McLean, John. *Notes of a Twenty-Five Years' Service in the Hudson's Bay Territory.* London: R. Bentley, 1849.

Messiter, Charles Alston. *Sport and Adventures Among the North American Indians.* London: R.H. Porter, 1890.

Millais, John Guille. *Newfoundland and Its Untrodden Ways.* London: Longmans, Green, 1907.

Milton, William Fitzwilliam, and W.B. Cheadle. *The North-West Passage by Land*, 6th ed. Reprint. Toronto: Coles Publishing, 1970.

—. *The North-West Passage by Land*, 8th ed. London: Cassell, Peter, Galpin, 1875.

Palliser, John. *Papers Relative to the Exploration by Captain Palliser of that Portion of British North America.* London: Eyre and Spottiswoode, 1859.

—. *Solitary Rambles and Adventures of a Hunter in the Prairies.* London: J. Murray, 1853.

Phillipps-Wolley, Clive. *Sport in the Crimea and Caucasus.* London: R. Bentley, 1881.

—. *A Sportsman's Eden.* London: R. Bentley, 1888.

Rae, Dr. John. "A Brief Account of an Excursion to the Saskatchewan Prairies." Report reprinted in Irene M. Spry, "A Visit to the Red River and the Saskatchewan, 1861, by Dr. John Rae, FRGS." *The Geographical Journal* 140 (1974): 7-17.

—. "A Visit to Red River and the Saskatchewan." *Proceedings of the Royal Geographical Society* 8 (1861): 102-3.

Railfare Enterprises. *The Canadian Pacific, the New Highway to the East across the Mountains,*

Prairies, & Rivers of Canada. Brochure. Montreal: Railfare Enterprises, 1887.

Repton, Humphry. *Landscape Gardening and Landscape Architecture*. London: Longman, 1840.

Ross, Alexander. *The Fur Hunters of the Far West: A Narrative of Adventures in the Oregon and Rocky Mountains*. London: Smith, Elder, 1855.

Rowan, John. *The Emigrant and Sportsman in Canada*. London: E. Stanford, 1876.

Selous, Frederick. *A Hunter's Wanderings in Africa and Sport and Travel in the East and West*. London: Rowland Ward, 1893.

—. *Recent Hunting Trips in British North America*. London: Witherby, 1907.

Simpson, George. *Narrative of a Journey Round the World during the Years 1841 and 1842*. 2 vols. London: Henry Colburn, 1847.

Society for the Acclimatisation of Animals, Birds, Fishes, Insects and Vegetables within the United Kingdom. *First Annual Report*. London, 1861.

Somerset, Henry Somers. *The Land of the Muskeg*. London: William Heinemann, 1895.

Warre, Henry. *Sketches in North America and the Oregon Territory*. London: Dickenson, 1848.

Watson, Beriah. *The Sportsman's Paradise*. London: J. Bumpus, 1889.

Wyndham-Quin, Edward. *Canadian Nights*. London: Smith, Elder, 1914.

—. *The Great Divide: Travels in the Upper Yellowstone in the Summer of 1874*. London: Chatto and Windus, 1876.

SECONDARY SOURCES

Atlas of Canada. Canada: Reader's Digest Association, 1981.

Adams, Carol. *The Sexual Politics of Meat*. New York: Continuum, 1990.

Altherr, Thomas. "The American Hunter-Naturalist and the Development of the Code of Sportsmanship." *Journal of Sport History* 5, 1 (1978): 7-22.

Altherr, Thomas L. and John F. Reiger. "Academic Historians and Hunting: A Call for More and Better Scholarship." *Environmental History Review* 19, 3 (1995): 39-56.

Altmeyer, George. "Three Ideas of Nature in Canada, 1893-1914." In *Consuming Canada: Readings in Environmental History*, ed. Chad Gaffield and Pam Gaffield, 96-118. Toronto: Copp Clark, 1995.

Arnold, David. *The Problem of Nature: Environment, Culture, and European Expansion*. Oxford: Blackwell, 1996.

Bantjes, Adrian. "Introduction: Bourdieu on the Bighorn? Or, Towards a Cultural History of Fly-Fishing in Wyoming and the Rocky Mountain West." *Annals of Wyoming: The Wyoming History Journal* 76, 2 (2004): 2-5.

—. "Nature, Culture, and the Fly-Fishing of Wyoming and the Rocky Mountain West." *Annals of Wyoming: The Wyoming History Journal* 76, 2 (2004): 41-53.

Barrel, John. *The Dark Side of Landscape: The Rural Poor in English Painting 1730-1840*. Cambridge: Cambridge University Press, 1980.

Beinart, William. "Empire, Hunting, and Ecological Change in Southern and Central Africa." *Past and Present* 128, 1 (1990): 162-86.

—. "Men, Science, Travel and Nature in the Eighteenth and Nineteenth-Century Cape." *Journal of Southern African Studies* 24, 4 (1998): 775-99.

Beinart, William, and Peter Coates. *Environment and History: The Taming of Nature in the*

USA and South Africa. London: Routledge, 1995.

Berg, Lawrence D., and Robin A. Kearns. "Naming as Norming: Race, Gender, and the Identity Politics of Naming Places in Aotearoa/New Zealand." *Society and Space* 14, 1 (1996): 99-122.

Berger, Carl. *Science, God, and Nature in Victorian Canada*. Toronto: University of Toronto Press, 1983.

Bermingham, Ann. *Landscape and Ideology: The English Rustic Tradition, 1740-1860*. Berkeley: University of California Press, 1986.

Bevan, Jonquil. *Izzak Walton's The Compleat Angler: The Art of Recreation*. Brighton, UK: Harvester, 1988.

Booth, Doug. "Escaping the Past? The Linguistic Turn and Language in Sport History." *Rethinking History* 8, 1 (2004): 103-25.

—. *The Field: Truth and Fiction in Sport History*. London: Routledge, 2005.

Bouchier, Nancy. "Aristocrats and Their Noble Sport: Woodstock Officers and Cricket during the Rebellion Era." *Canadian Journal of the History of Sport* 20, 1 (1989): 16-31.

—. *For the Love of the Game: Amateur Sport in Small-Town Ontario, 1838-1895*. Montreal and Kingston: McGill-Queen's University Press, 2003.

Bouchier, Nancy, and Ken Cruikshank. "Sportsmen and Pothunters: Environment, Conservation, and Class in the Fishery of Hamilton Harbour, 1858-1914." *Sport History Review* 28, 1 (1997): 1-18.

Breen, David. *The Canadian Prairie West and the Ranching Frontier, 1874-1924*. Toronto: University of Toronto Press, 1983.

Brockway, Lucile H. *Science and Colonial Expansion: The Role of the British Royal Botanic Gardens*. New York: Academic Press, 1979.

Brown, Douglas A. "Fleshing-Out Field Notes: Prosaic, Poetic, and Picturesque Representations of Canadian Mountaineering, 1906-1940." *Journal of Sport History* 30, 3 (2003): 347-71.

Burnett, Graham. *Masters of All They Surveyed: Exploration, Geography, and a British El Dorado*. Chicago: University of Chicago Press, 2000.

Campbell, Claire Elizabeth. "Shaped by the West Wind: Nature and History in Georgian Bay." PhD diss., University of Western Ontario, 2001.

—. *Shaped by the West Wind: Nature and History in Georgian Bay*. Vancouver: UBC Press, 2004.

Cannadine, David. *Ornamentalism: How the British Saw Their Empire*. Oxford: Oxford University Press, 2001.

—. *The Pleasures of the Past*. New York: W.W. Norton, 1989.

Carter, Paul. *The Road to Botany Bay: An Essay in Spatial History*. London: Faber and Faber, 1987.

Cartmill, Matt. *A View to Death in the Morning: Hunting and Nature through History*. Cambridge, MA: Harvard University Press, 1993.

Cavell, Edward. "Image of Transition: Photography in Rupert's Land." In *Rupert's Land: A Cultural Tapestry*, ed. Richard C. Davis, 227-52. Waterloo: Wilfrid Laurier University Press, 1988.

—. *Journeys to the Far West*. Toronto: James Lorimer, 1979.

Chalmers, William. *George Mercer Dawson: Geologist, Scientist, Explorer*. Montreal, XYZ Publishing, 2000.

Clarke, G.N.G. "Taking Possession: The Cartouche as Cultural Text in Eighteenth-Century American Maps." *Word and Image* 4, 2 (1988): 455-75.

Clayton, Daniel. "Circumscribing Vancouver Island." *BC Studies* 122 (Summer 1999): 7-22.

—. "The Creation of Imperial Space in the Pacific Northwest." *Journal of Historical Geography* 26, 3 (2000): 327-50.

—. *Islands of Truth: The Imperial Fashioning of Vancouver Island.* Vancouver: UBC Press, 2000.

—. "On Not Going on a Field Trip: Absence, Memory and Geography." *BC Studies* 132 (Winter 2001-2): 65-79.

Coates, Colin. "Like the Thames towards Putney: The Appropriation of Landscape in Lower Canada." *Canadian Historical Review* 74, 3 (1993): 317-43.

—. *The Metamorphoses of Landscape and Community in Early Quebec.* Montreal and Kingston: McGill-Queen's University Press, 2000.

Cole, Douglas, and Bradley Lockner, eds. *The Journals of George M. Dawson: British Columbia, 1875-1878.* Vancouver: UBC Press, 1989.

Coleman, Annie Gilbert. *Ski Style: Sport and Culture in the Rockies.* Lawrence: University Press of Kansas, 2004.

Colpitts, George. *Game in the Garden: A Human History of Wildlife in Western Canada to 1940.* Vancouver: UBC Press, 2002.

—. "Wildlife Promotions, Western Canada Boosterism, and the Conservation Movement, 1890-1914." *The American Review of Canadian Studies* 28, 1-2 (1998): 103-30.

Crosby, Alfred W. *Ecological Imperialism.* Cambridge: Cambridge University Press, 1986.

—. "Ecological Imperialism: The Overseas Migration of Western Europeans as a Biological Phenomenon." In *The Ends of the Earth: Perspectives on Modern Environmental History,* ed. Donald Worster, 103-17. Cambridge: Cambridge University Press, 1988.

Crowley, John. E. "Picturing the Caribbean in the Global British Landscape." *Studies in Eighteenth-Century Culture* 32 (2003): 323-46.

—. "Taken on the Spot: The Visual Appropriation of New France for the Global British Landscape." *Canadian Historical Review* 86, 1 (2005): 1-28.

Davis, Ann, and Robert Thacker. "Pictures and Prose: Romantic Sensibility and the Great Plains in Catlin, Kane, and Miller." *Great Plains Quarterly* 6, 1 (1986): 3-20.

Dawson, Michael. *Selling British Columbia: Tourism and Consumer Culture, 1890-1970.* Vancouver: UBC Press, 2004.

Dickenson, Victoria. *Drawn from Life: Science and Art in the Portrayal of the New World.* Toronto: University of Toronto Press, 1998.

Dictionary of Canadian Biography. Vols. 10-14. Toronto: University of Toronto Press, 1972, 1982, 1990, 1994, 1998.

Dobak, William A. "Killing the Canadian Buffalo, 1821-1881." *Western Historical Quarterly* 27, 1 (1996): 33-52.

Driver, Felix. *Geography Militant: Cultures of Exploration and Empire.* Oxford: Blackwell, 2001.

Dunlap, Thomas. "Remaking the Land: The Acclimatization Movement and Anglo Ideas of Nature." *Journal of World History* 8, 2 (1997): 303-19.

—. *Saving America's Wildlife.* Princeton, NJ: Princeton University Press, 1988.

Eagle, John A. *The Canadian Pacific Railway and the Development of Western Canada, 1896-1914.* Montreal and Kingston: McGill-Queen's University Press, 1989.

Eaton, Diane, and Sheila Urbanek. *Paul Kane's Great Nor-West.* Vancouver: UBC Press, 1995.

Edgar, Andrew, and Peter Sedgwick, eds. *Key Concepts in Cultural Theory.* London: Routledge, 1999.

Edney, Matthew H. *Mapping an Empire: The Geographical Construction of British India, 1765-1843*. Chicago: University of Chicago Press, 1997.

Ens, Gerhard J. *Homeland to Hinterland: The Changing Worlds of the Red River Métis in the Nineteenth Century*. Toronto: University of Toronto Press, 1996.

Evans, Clinton L. *The War on Weeds in the Prairie West: An Environmental History*. Calgary: University of Calgary Press, 2002.

Foster, John E. "The Métis and the End of the Plains Buffalo in Alberta." In *Buffalo,* ed. John E. Foster, Dick Harrison, and I.S. MacLaren, 61-77. Edmonton: University of Alberta Press, 1992.

Francis, R. Douglas. "Changing Images of the West." In *The Prairie West: Historical Readings,* ed. R. Douglas Francis and Howard Palmer, 717-39. Edmonton: University of Alberta Press, 1992.

—. "From Wasteland to Utopia: Changing Images of the Canadian West in the Nineteenth Century." *Great Plains Quarterly* 7, 3 (1987): 178-94.

—. "The Ideal and the Real: The Image of Canadian West in the Settlement Period." In *Rupert's Land: A Cultural Tapestry,* ed. Richard C. Davis, 253-74. Waterloo: Wilfrid Laurier University Press, 1988.

—. *Images of the West: Responses to the Canadian Prairies*. Saskatoon: Western Producer Prairie Books, 1989.

Fraser, Hilary with Daniel Brown. *English Prose of the Nineteenth Century*. New York: Addison Wesley Longman, 1996.

Friesen, Gerald. *The Canadian Prairies: A History*. Toronto: University of Toronto Press, 1984.

—. "The Imagined West: Introducing Cultural History." In *From Rupert's Land to Canada,* ed. Theodore Binnema, Gerhard J. Ens, and R.C. MacLeod, 195-200. Edmonton: University of Alberta Press, 2001.

Gems, Gerald. *The Athletic Crusade: Sport and American Cultural Imperialism*. Lincoln: University of Nebraska Press, 2004.

Gillbank, Linden. "The Origins of the Acclimatisation Society of Victoria: Practical Science in the Wake of the Gold Rush." *Historical Records of Australian Science* 6, 3 (1986): 359-74.

Gillespie, Greg. "'I Was Well Pleased with Our Sport among the Buffalo': Big Game Hunting, Travel Writing, and Cultural Imperialism in the British North American West 1847-1873." *Canadian Historical Review* 83, 4 (2002): 555-84.

—. "The Empire's Eden: British Hunters, Travel Writing, and Imperialism in Nineteenth-Century Canada." In *The Culture of Hunting in Canada,* ed. Jean Manore and Dale G. Miner, 42-55. Vancouver: UBC Press, 2007.

—. "The Imperial Embrace: British Sportsmen and the Appropriation of Landscape in Nineteenth-Century Canada." PhD diss., University of Western Ontario, 2001.

—. "Sport and Masculinities in Early Nineteenth-Century Ontario: The British Travellers' Image." *Ontario History* 92, 2 (2000): 113-26.

—. "Wickets in the West: Cricket, Culture, and Constructed Images of Nineteenth-Century Canada." *Journal of Sport History* 27, 1 (Spring 2000): 51-66.

Gillespie, Greg, and Kevin Wamsley. "Clandestine Means: The Aristocratic Hunting Code and Early Game Legislation in Nineteenth-Century Canada." *Sporting Traditions* 22, 1 (2005): 99-120.

Gould, Peter C. *Early Green Politics: Back to Nature, Back to the Land, and Socialism in Britain*. Sussex: The Harvester Press, 1988.

Grafton, Anthony. *The Footnote: A Curious History*. Cambridge, MA: Harvard University Press, 1997.

Gregory, Derek. "Imaginative Geographies." *Progress in Human Geography 19* (1995): 447-85.

Grove, Richard H. *Green Imperialism: Colonial Expansion, Tropical Island Edens, and the Origins of Environmentalism, 1600-1860*. Cambridge: Cambridge University Press, 1995.

Guttmann, Allen. *Games and Empires: Modern Sports and Cultural Imperialism*. New York: Columbia University Press, 1994.

—. *Sports: The First Five Millennia*. Amherst and Boston: University of Massachusetts Press, 2004.

Hadley, Margery Tanner. "Photography, Tourism, and the CPR: Western Canada, 1884-1914." In *Essays on the Historical Geography of the Canadian West: Regional Perspectives on the Settlement Process,* ed. L.A. Rosenvall and S.M. Evans, 48-69. Calgary: University of Calgary, 1987.

Hallowell, Gerald, ed. *The Oxford Companion to Canadian History*. Don Mills, ON: Oxford University Press, 2004.

Hansen, Peter H. "Confetti of Empire: The Conquest of Everest in Nepal, India, Britain, and New Zealand." *Comparative Studies in Society and History* 42, 2 (2000): 307-22.

—. "Ornamentalism and Orientalism: Virtual Empires and the Politics of Knowledge." *Journal of Colonialism and Colonial History* 3, 1 (2002): 1-8.

—. "Vertical Boundaries, National Identities: British Mountaineering on the Frontiers of Europe and the Empire, 1868-1914." *Journal of Imperial and Commonwealth History* 24, 1 (1996): 48-71.

Harley, J.B. "Maps, Knowledge, and Power." In *The Iconography of Landscape: Essays on the Symbolic Representation, Design, and Use of Past Environments,* ed. Denis Cosgrove and Stephen Daniels, 277-312. Cambridge: Cambridge University Press, 1988.

Harris, Cole. "How Did Colonialism Dispossess? Comments from the Edge of Empire." *Annals of the Association of American Geographers* 94, 1 (2004): 165-82.

Harris, Cole, and John Warkentin. *Canada before Confederation: A Study in Historical Geography*. Ottawa: Carleton University Press, 1991.

Hart, E.J. *The Selling of Canada: The CPR and the Beginnings of Canadian Tourism*. Banff, AB: Altitude Publishing, 1983.

—. *Trains, Peaks, and Tourists: The Golden Age of Canadian Travel*. Banff, AB: EJH Literary Enterprises, 2000.

Hendershot, Cyndy. *The Animal within Man: Masculinity and the Gothic*. Ann Arbor: University of Michigan Press, 1998.

Hill, Douglas. *The Opening of the Canadian West*. Toronto: William Heinemann, 1968.

Howell, Colin. *Blood, Sweat, and Cheers: Sport in the Making of Modern Canada*. Toronto: University of Toronto Press, 2001.

Hudson, John H. "History in the Community: Dr. John Rae's 1861 Route Near Old Wives Lake and Chaplin Lake." *Saskatchewan History* 52, 1 (2000): 32-36.

Huyda, R. "Exploration Photographer: Humphrey Lloyd Hime and the Assiniboine and Saskatchewan Exploring Expedition of 1858." *Historical and Scientific Society of Manitoba Transactions Series* 3, 30 (1973): 45-59.

Isenberg, Andrew. *The Destruction of the Bison: An Environmental History, 1750-1929*. Cambridge: Cambridge University Press, 2000.

Jasen, Patricia. "Romanticism, Modernity, and the Evolution of Tourism on the Niagara Frontier, 1790-1850." *Canadian Historical Review* 72, 3 (1991): 283-318.

—. *Wild Things: Nature, Culture, and Tourism in Ontario, 1790-1914*. Toronto: University of Toronto Press, 1995.

Jessup, Lynda. "Landscapes of Sport, Landscapes of Exclusion: The 'Sportsman's Paradise' in Late-Nineteenth-Century Canadian Painting," *Journal of Canadian Studies* 40, 1 (2006): 71-123.

Klonck, Charlotte. *Science and the Perception of Nature: British Landscape Art in the Late Eighteenth and Early Nineteenth Centuries.* New Haven, CT: Yale University Press, 1996.

Koerner, Lisbet. "Purposes of Linnean Travel." In *Visions of Empire: Voyages, Botany, and Representations of Empire,* ed. David Miller and Peter Reill, 117-52. Cambridge: Cambridge University Press, 1996.

Kunard, Andrea. "Relationships of Photography and Text in the Colonization of the Canadian West: The 1858 Assiniboine and Saskatchewan Exploring Expedition." *International Journal of Canadian Studies* 26 (Fall 2002): 77-100.

Kupsch, Walter. "GSC Exploratory Wells in the West, 1873-1875." *Earth Sciences History* 12, 2 (1993): 160-79.

Lever, Christopher. *The Naturalised Animals of the British Isles.* Foreword by Peter Scott. London: Hutchinson, 1977.

Lewis, G. Malcolm. "Rhetoric of the Western Interior: Modes of Environmental Description in American Promotional Literature of the Nineteenth Century." In *The Iconography of Landscape: Essays on the Symbolic Representation, Design, and Use of Past Environments,* ed. Denis Cosgrove and Stephen Daniels, 179-93. Cambridge: Cambridge University Press, 1988.

Loo, Tina. *States of Nature: Conserving Canada's Wildlife in the Twentieth Century.* Vancouver: UBC Press, 2006.

—. "Of Moose and Men: Hunting for Masculinities in British Columbia, 1880-1939." *Western Historical Quarterly* 32, 3 (2001): 296-319.

—. "Making a Modern Wilderness: Conserving Wildlife in Twentieth-Century Canada." *Canadian Historical Review* 82, 1 (2001): 92-121.

Lorimer, Hayden. "Guns, Game, and the Grandee: The Cultural Politics of Deerstalking in the Scottish Highlands." *Ecumene: A Journal of Environment, Culture, and Meaning* 7, 4 (2000): 403-31.

Lowerson, John. "Izaak Walton: Father of a Dream." *History Today* 33, 12 (1983): 28-32.

Lytwyn, Victor. "Torchlight Prey: Night Hunting and Fishing by Aboriginal People in the Great Lakes Region." *Papers of the Algonquian Conference* 23 (2001): 304-17.

MacGregor, James G. *Vision of an Ordered Land: The Story of the Dominion Land Survey.* Saskatoon: Western Producer Prairie Books, 1981.

MacKenzie, John. "Chivalry, Social Darwinism, and Ritualised Killing: The Hunting Ethos in Central Africa up to 1914." In *Conservation in Africa: People, Policies, and Practice,* ed. D. Anderson and R. Grove, 41-61. Cambridge: Cambridge University Press, 1987.

—. *The Empire of Nature: Hunting, Conservation, and British Imperialism.* Manchester: Manchester University Press, 1988.

—. "The Imperial Pioneer and Hunter and the British Masculine Stereotype in Late Victorian and Edwardian Times." In *Manliness and Morality: Middle-Class Masculinity in Britain and America, 1800-1940,* ed. J.A. Mangan and James Walvin, 176-98. Manchester: Manchester University Press, 1987.

MacLaren, I.S. "The Aesthetic Map of the North, 1845-1859." *Arctic* 38, 2 (1985): 89-122.

—. "The Aesthetic Mapping of Nature in the Second Franklin Expedition." *Journal of Canadian Studies* 20, 1 (1985): 39-57.

—. "Aesthetic Mappings of the West by the Palliser and Hind Survey Expeditions, 1857-

1859." *Studies in Canadian Literature* 10, 1 (1985): 24-52.

—. "Alexander Mackenzie and the Landscapes of Commerce." *Studies in Canadian Literature* 7, 2 (1982): 141-50.

—. "Cultured Wilderness in Jasper National Park." *Journal of Canadian Studies* 34, 3 (1999): 7-58.

—. "From Exploration to Publication: The Evolution of a 19th-Century Arctic Narrative." *Arctic* 47, 1 (1994): 43-53.

—. "The Grandest Tour: The Aesthetics of Landscape in Sir George Back's Explorations of the Eastern Arctic, 1833-1837." *English Studies in Canada* 10, 4 (1984): 436-56.

—. "The Influence of Eighteenth-Century British Landscape Aesthetics on Narrative and Pictorial Responses to the British North American North and West, 1769-1872." 2 vols. PhD diss., University of Western Ontario, 1983.

—. "The Limits of the Picturesque in British North America." *Journal of Garden History* 5, 1 (1985): 97-111.

—. "Paul Kane and the Authorship of *Wanderings of an Artist*." In *From Rupert's Land to Canada,* ed. Theodore Binnema, Gerhard J. Ens, and R.C. MacLeod, 225-47. Edmonton: University of Alberta Press, 2001.

—. "Retaining Captaincy of the Soul: Responses to Nature in the First Franklin Expedition." *Essays on Canadian Writing* 28 (Spring 1984): 57-92.

Macoun, John. *Autobiography of John Macoun: Canadian Explorer and Naturalist, 1831-1920.* 2nd ed. Ottawa: Ottawa Field-Naturalists' Club, 1979.

Mangan, J.A. *Athleticism in the Victorian and Edwardian Public School: The Emergence and Consolidation of an Educational Ideology.* Cambridge: Cambridge University Press, 1981.

—. "Bullies, Beatings, Battles, and Bruises: Great Days and Jolly Days at One Mid-Victorian Public School." In *Disreputable Pleasures: Less Virtuous Victorians at Play,* ed. Mike Huggins and J.A. Mangan, 3-35. London: Frank Cass, 2004.

—. *The Games Ethic and Imperialism.* Harmondsworth: Viking, 1986.

—. "Social Darwinism and Upper Class Education in Late Victorian and Edwardian England." In *Manliness and Morality: Middle-Class Masculinity in Britain and America, 1800-1940,* ed. J.A. Mangan and James Walvin, 135-59. Manchester: Manchester University Press, 1987.

Mangan, J.A., and Callum McKenzie. "Radical Conservatives: Middle-Class Masculinity, the Shikar Club, and Big-Game Hunting." *European Sport History Review* 4 (March 2002): 185-209.

Manning, Roger B. *Hunters and Poachers: A Social and Cultural History of Unlawful Hunting in England, 1485-1640.* Oxford: Clarendon Press, 1993.

Mason, Fred. "Advertising Eden: Sport and the Cultural Landscapes of the Canadian Pacific Railway, 1885-1920." Paper presented at the North American Society for Sport History Conference, University of Western Ontario, London, Ontario, Canada, 2001.

McGrath, Darrin. "Salted Caribou and Sportsmen-Tourists: Conflicts over Wildlife Resources in Newfoundland at the Turn of the Twentieth Century." *Newfoundland Studies* 10, 2 (1994): 208-25.

McKenzie, Callum. "The British Big-Game Hunting Tradition, Masculinity, and Fraternalism with Particular Reference to the Shikar Club." *The Sports Historian* 20, 1 (2000): 70-96.

McLeod, Bruce. *The Geography of Empire in English Literature 1580-1745.* Cambridge: Cambridge University Press, 1999.

McNairn, Jeffery L. "Meaning and Markets: Hunting, Economic Development, and British Imperialism in Maritime Travel Narratives to 1870." *Acadiensis* 34, 2 (2005): 1-23.

Moodie, D.W. "Early British Images of Rupert's Land." In *Man and Nature on the Prairies,* ed. Richard Allen, 1-20. Saskatoon: Great Plains Research Center, University of Regina, 1976.

Morrow, Don, and Kevin Wamsley. *Sport in Canada: A History.* Don Mills, ON: Oxford University Press, 2005.

Mouat, Jeremy. "Situating Vancouver Island in the British World, 1846-1849." *BC Studies* 145 (Spring 2005): 5-30.

Moyles, R.G., and Doug Owram. *Imperial Dreams and Colonial Realities.* Toronto: University of Toronto Press, 1988.

Munslow, Alun. *Deconstructing History.* London: Routledge, 1997.

—. *The Routledge Companion to Historical Studies.* London: Routledge, 2000.

Ormond, Richard. *Sir Edwin Landseer.* With contributions by Joseph Rishel and Robin Hamlyn. New York: Rizzoli, 1981.

Osborne, Michael A. "Acclimatizing the World: A History of the Paradigmatic Colonial Science." *Osiris* 15 (2000): 135-51.

Owram, Doug. *The Promise of Eden: The Canadian Expansionist Movement and the Idea of the West, 1856-1900.* Toronto: University of Toronto, 1980.

Parenteau, Bill. "Angling, Hunting, and the Development of Tourism in Late Nineteenth-Century Canada." *The Archivist: The Magazine of the National Archives of Canada* 117 (1998): 10-19.

—. "Care, Control, and Supervision: Native People in the Canadian Atlantic Salmon Fishery, 1867-1900." *Canadian Historical Review* 79, 1 (1998): 1-35.

—. "A Very Determined Opposition to the Law: Conservation, Angling Leases, and Social Conflict in the Canadian Atlantic Salmon Fishery, 1867-1914." *Environmental History* 9, 3 (2004): 436-63.

Parenteau, Bill, and Richard W. Judd. "More Buck for the Bang: Sporting and the Ideology of Fish and Game Management in Northern New England and the Maritime Provinces, 1870-1930." In *New England and the Maritime Provinces: Connections and Comparisons,* ed. Stephen J. Hornsby and John G. Reid, 232-51. Montreal and Kingston: McGill-Queen's University Press, 2005.

Philips, Murray, ed. *Deconstructing Sport History: A Postmodern Analysis.* Albany: State University of New York Press, 2006.

Pocius, Gerald L. "Tourists, Health Seekers, and Sportsmen: Luring Americans to Newfoundland in the Early Twentieth Century." In *Twentieth-Century Newfoundland: Explorations,* ed. James Hiller and Peter Neary, 47-78. St. John's: Breakwater, 1994.

Potter, James M. "The Creation of Person, the Creation of Place: Hunting Landscapes in the American Southwest." *American Antiquity* 69, 2 (2004): 322-38.

Potyondi, Barry. *In Palliser's Triangle: Living in the Grasslands, 1850-1930.* Saskatoon: Purich Publishing, 1995.

—. "Loss and Substitution: The Ecology of Production in Southwestern Saskatchewan, 1860-1930." *Journal of the Canadian Historical Association* 5 (1994): 213-35.

Pratt, Mary Louise. *Imperial Eyes: Travel Writing and Transculturation.* London: Routledge, 1992.

Proctor, Nicolas W. *Bathed in Blood: Hunting and Mastery in the Old South.* Charlottesville, VA: University of Virginia Press, 2002.

Reiger, John F. *American Sportsmen and the Origins of Conservation.* New York: Winchester, 1975.

Richards, Thomas. *The Imperial Archive: Knowledge and the Fantasy of Empire.* London: Verso, 1993.

Richtik, James M. "Mapping the Quality of Land for Agriculture in Western Canada." In *Mapping the North American Plains: Essays in the History of Cartography,* ed. Frederick C. Luebke, Frances W. Kaye, and Gary E. Moulton, 161-72. Norman: University of Oklahoma Press, 1987.

Ritvo, Harriet. *The Animal Estate: The English and Other Creatures in the Victorian Age.* Cambridge, MA: Harvard University Press, 1987.

—. "Animal Planet." *Environmental History* 9, 2 (2004): 204-20.

—. "Destroyers and Preservers: Big Game in the Victorian Empire." *History Today* 52, 1 (2002): 33-39.

Robinson, Zac. "The Golden Years of Canadian Mountaineering: Asserted Ethics, Form, and Style, 1886-1925." *Sport History Review* 35, 1 (2004): 1-19.

—. "Storming the Heights: Canadian Frontier Nationalism and the Making of Manhood in the Conquest of Mount Robson, 1906-1913." *International Journal of the History of Sport* 22, 3 (2005): 415-33.

Robinson, Zac, and PearlAnn Reichwein. "Canada's Everest? Rethinking the First Ascent of Mount Logan and the Politics of Nationhood, 1925." *Sport History Review* 35, 2 (2004): 95-121.

Ruggles, Richard. "Mapping the Interior Plains of Rupert's Land by the Hudson's Bay Company to 1870." In *Mapping the North American Plains: Essays in the History of Cartography,* ed. Frederick C. Luebke, Frances W. Kaye, and Gary E. Moulton, 145-60. Norman, OK: University of Oklahoma Press, 1987.

Ryan, James R. "Imperial Landscapes: Photography, Geography, and British Overseas Exploration, 1858-1872." In *Geography and Imperialism, 1820-1940,* ed. Morag Bell, Robin Butlin, and Michael Heffernan, 53-79. Manchester: Manchester University Press, 1995.

—. *Picturing Empire: Photography and the Visualization of the British Empire.* London: Reaktion Books, 1997.

Ryan, Simon. *The Cartographic Eye.* Cambridge: Cambridge University Press, 1996.

—. "Exploring Aesthetics: The Picturesque Appropriation of Land in Journals of Australian Exploration." *Australian Literary Studies* 15, 4 (1992): 282-93.

—. "Inscribing the Emptiness: Cartography, Exploration, and the Construction of Australia." In *De-Scribing Empire: Postcolonialism and Textuality,* ed. Chris Tiffin and Alan Lawson, 115-30. London: Routledge, 1994.

Said, Edward W. *Culture and Imperialism.* New York: Alfred Knopf, 1993.

—. *Orientalism.* New York: Pantheon Books, 1978.

Sandlos, John. "From the Outside Looking In: Aesthetics, Politics, and Wildlife Conservation in the Canadian North." *Environmental History* 6, 1 (2001): 6-31.

Shattock, Joanne. "Travel Writing Victorian and Modern: A Review of Recent Research." In *The Art of Travel: Essays on Travel Writing,* ed. Philip Dodd, 151-64. London: Frank Cass, 1982.

Sheets-Pyenson, Susan. "How to 'Grow' a Natural History Museum: The Building of Colonial Collections, 1850-1900." *Archives of Natural History* 15, 2 (1988): 121-47.

Smalley, Andrea L. "I Just Like to Kill Things: Women, Men, and the Gender of Sport Hunting in the United States, 1940-1973." *Gender and History* 17, 1 (2005): 183-209.

—. "Our Lady Sportsmen: Gender, Class, and Conservation in Sport Hunting Magazines, 1873-1920." *Journal of the Gilded Age and Progressive Era* 4, 4 (2005): 355-80.

Smits, David D. "The Frontier Army and the Destruction of the Buffalo: 1865-1883." *Western Historical Quarterly* 25, 3 (1994): 312-38.

Spry, Irene M. "Captain John Palliser and the Exploration of Western Canada." *The Geographical Journal* 125 (1959): 149-84.

—. "Early Visitors to the Canadian Prairies." In *Images of the Plains: The Role of Human Nature in Settlement,* ed. Brian W. Blouet and Merlin P. Lawson, 165-80. Lincoln: University of Nebraska Press, 1975.

—. "The Great Transformation: The Disappearance of the Commons in Western Canada." In *Man and Nature on the Prairies,* ed. Richard Allen, 21-45. Saskatoon: Great Plains Research Center, University of Regina, 1976.

—. "The Palliser Expedition." In *Rupert's Land: A Cultural Tapestry,* ed. Richard C. Davis, 195-212. Waterloo: Wilfrid Laurier University Press, 1988.

—. *The Palliser Expedition: An Account of John Palliser's British North American Expedition, 1857-1860.* Toronto: Macmillan, 1963.

—. *The Palliser Expedition: The Dramatic Story of Western Canadian Exploration, 1857-1860.* 2nd ed. Saskatoon: Fifth House, 1995.

—. "A Visit to the Red River and the Saskatchewan, 1861 by Dr. John Rae, FRGS." *The Geographical Journal* 140 (1974): 1-17.

Spry, Irene M., ed. *The Papers of the Palliser Expedition, 1857-1860.* Toronto: Champlain Society, 1968.

Spry, Irene M., and Bennett McCardle. *The Records of the Department of the Interior and Research Concerning Canada's Western Frontier of Settlement.* Regina: Canadian Plains Research Center, University of Regina, 1993.

Stafford, Robert. "Geological Surveys, Mineral Discoveries, and British Expansion, 1835-1871." *Journal of Imperialism and Commonwealth History* 12, 3 (1984): 5-32.

—. *Scientist of Empire: Sir Roderick Murchison, Scientific Exploration, and Victorian Imperialism.* Cambridge: Cambridge University Press, 1989.

Stanwood, P.G. *Izaak Walton.* New York: Twayne, 1998.

Stevenson, Catherine Barnes. *Victorian Women Travel Writers in Africa.* Boston: Twayne, 1982.

Stoery, William K. "Big Cats and Imperialism: Lion and Tiger Hunting in Kenya and Northern India, 1898-1930." *Journal of World History* 2, 2 (1991): 135-73.

Struna, Nancy. *People of Prowess: Sport, Leisure, and Labor in Early Anglo-America.* Urbana: University of Illinois Press, 1996.

Sramek, Joseph. "Face Him Like a Briton: Tiger Hunting, Imperialism, and British Masculinity in Colonial India, 1800-1875," *Victorian Studies* 48, 4 (2006): 659-80.

Sunder, J.E. "British Army Officers on the Sante Fe Trail." *Bulletin of the Missouri Historical Society* 23 (1967): 147-57.

Taylor, Antony. "Pig-Sticking Princes: Royal Hunting, Moral Outrage, and the Republican Opposition to Animal Abuse in Nineteenth- and Early Twentieth-Century Britain," *History,* 89, 293 (2004): 30-48.

Taylor, Stephen. *The Mighty Nimrod: A Life of Frederick Courteney Selous, African Hunter and Adventurer 1851-1917.* London: Collins, 1989.

Thompson, John Herd. *Forging the Prairie West: The Illustrated History of Canada.* Toronto: Oxford University Press, 1998.

Thoms, J. Michael. "A Place Called Pennask: Fly-Fishing and Colonialism at a British Columbia Lake." *BC Studies* 133 (Spring 2002): 69-98.

Tippett, Maria, and Douglas Cole. *From Desolation to Splendour: Changing Perceptions of the British Columbia Landscape.* Toronto: Clarke, Irwin, 1977.

Tobin, Beth Fowkes. *Picturing Imperial Power: Colonial Subjects in Eighteenth-Century*

British Painting. Durham: Duke University Press, 1999.

Turner, James. *Reckoning with the Beast: Animals, Pain, and Humanity in the Victorian Mind.* Baltimore: Johns Hopkins University Press, 1980.

Vibert, Elizabeth. "Real Men Hunt Buffalo: Masculinity, Race, and Class in British Fur Traders' Narratives." In *Cultures of Empire: Colonizers in Britain and the Empire in the Nineteenth and Twentieth Centuries,* ed. Catherine Hall, 281-97. New York: Routledge, 2000.

—. *Traders' Tales: Narratives of Cultural Encounters in the Columbia Plateau, 1807-1846.* Norman, OK: University of Oklahoma Press, 1997.

Waiser, W.A. *The Field Naturalist: John Macoun, the Geological Survey, and Natural Science.* Toronto: University of Toronto Press, 1989.

Wamsley, Kevin. "Good Clean Sport and a Deer Apiece: Game Legislation and State Formation in 19th Century Canada." *Canadian Journal of the History of Sport* 25, 2 (1994): 1-20.

—. "Leisure and Legislation in Nineteenth-Century Canada." PhD diss., University of Alberta, 1992.

—. "The Public Importance of Men and the Importance of Public Men: Sport and Masculinities in 19th Century Canada." In *Sport and Gender in Canada,* ed. Philip White and Kevin White, 24-39. New York: Oxford University Press, 1999.

Warkentin, John. *The Western Interior of Canada: A Record of Geographical Discovery.* Toronto: McClelland and Stewart, 1964.

Weaver, John C. *The Great Land Rush and the Making of the Modern World, 1650-1900.* Montreal and Kingston: McGill-Queen's University Press, 2003.

Wightman, Andy, Peter Higgins, Grant Jarvie, and Robbie Nicol. "The Cultural Politics of Hunting: Sporting Estates and Recreational Land Use in the Highlands and Islands of Scotland." *Culture, Sport, Society* 5, 1 (2002): 53-70.

Williams, Chris. "That Boundless Ocean of Mountains: British Alpinists and the Appeal of the Canadian Rockies, 1885-1920." *International Journal of the History of Sport* 22, 1 (2005): 70-87.

Wonders, Karen. *Habitat Dioramas: Illusions of Wilderness in Museums of Natural History.* Uppsala, Sweden: ACTA Universitatis Upsaliensis, 1993.

—. "A Sportsman's Eden: Part 1." *Beaver* 79, 5 (1999): 26-32.

—. "A Sportsman's Eden: Part 2." *Beaver* 79, 6 (1999): 30-37.

Zeller, Suzanne. "Classical Codes: Biogeographical Assessments of Environment in Victorian Canada." *Journal of Historical Geography* 24, 1 (1998): 20-35.

—. *Inventing Canada: Early Victorian Science and the Idea of a Transcontinental Nation.* Toronto: University of Toronto Press, 1987.

Index

authors
  disassociation from texts, 20-21, 22, 34
  as narrators, 17, 21, 26, 29, 34
  as protagonists, 17, 21, 26, 29, 34

Baird, Spencer Fullerton, 29
  Mammals of North America, 32
Ballantyne, Robert Michael, 20, 25
  Hudson's Bay, 31
Battle River, 84
Berkeley, Grantley Fitzhardinge, 7f, 122n7
big-game hunting. *See* hunting
Blackwood's Magazine, 11
British Acclimatisation Society, 29, 76-77,
  140n80, 141n82
British Columbia, 8
Brown, Lancelot Capability, 81, 85
buffalo, 73
  destruction of, 9
  hunting of, 2, 3, 4, 8, 40, 41, 46, 55, 96,
    111
Burke, Edmund, 103, 105-6, 144n32
  *Philosophical Enquiry into the Origin
    of Our Ideas of the Sublime and
    Beautiful,* 88-89, 91-92
Butler, William Francis, 5, 6f
  "Alone in the Wilderness," 99, 100f
  and anticipatory geography, 112-13
  "Cutting Up the Moose," 98f, 99, 102
  establishment of own authority by, 26
  on extinction of Native peoples, 58
  The Great Lone Land, 31, 86
  and horizontal sublime, 102-3
  on isolation in wilderness, 105
  "The Look-Out Mountain," 102f, 103
  maps, 64
  on mystery of nature, 107
  on ocean-like landscape, 93, 95-96,
    102-3
  on park-like land, 86
  prefatory remarks, 20, 22, 23
  on presence of God, 106
  "The Rocky Mountains at the Sources
    of the Saskatchewan," 86f
  self-deprecatory remarks, 22, 23
  and Spathanaw Watchi, 68, 69, 94f,
    94-95
  speechlessness of, 91, 96

"Sunset Scene, with Buffalo," 96, 97f
"Tent in the Great Prairie," 95f, 95-96,
  97f
on truthfulness of narratives, 20
"View from the Spathanaw Watchi,"
  94f
The Wild North Land, 86, 93-96

Caledon, Earl of, 2-3
Canadian Pacific Railway (CPR), 9, 10,
  110-12
Canadian Red River Exploring Expedition
  (Hind), 31
Cannadine, David, xviii, 12-13
Carnegie, James, Earl of Southesk, 4, 5, 29
  associationism of, 83-84
  on buffalo hunting, 40, 41, 46-47, 55
  citations used by, 30-31
  and colonial class relations, 112
  on editorial methods, 23-25
  entourage of, 56
  errata included by, 33
  on evidence in narratives, 33
  "Head of a Buffalo Bull," 73
  "Head of a Rocky Mountain Ram," 73,
    74f
  "Head of a Cabree," 47f
  identification of animals, 71-72
  illustrations, 20, 33
  journals of, 19, 25
  maps, 63-64, 65
  "Mount Dalhousie, North River
    Valley," 65f
  naming of mountains, 65
  objectification of game, 73, 74f
  on prairie landscape, 106
  prefatory remarks, 19, 22, 25-26, 31
  relations with labourers, 27
  on richness of land for use, 87
  and Rocky Mountain ram, 74f, 75
  self-deprecation by, 22
  "Southesk's Cairn," 65
  speechlessness of, 91
  on success in hunting, 49
  trophies collected by, 48
  on truthfulness of narrative, 19-20,
    25-26
  "Valleys for the First Time Explored"